I0831468

HOMER'S TURK

Homer's Turk

How Classics Shaped Ideas of the East

Jerry Toner

HARVARD UNIVERSITY PRESS
Cambridge, Massachusetts, and London, England
2013

Library of Congress Cataloging-in-Publication Data

Toner, J. P.
Homer's Turk : how classics shaped ideas of the East / Jerry Toner.
p. cm.
Includes bibliographical references and index.
ISBN 978-0-674-07314-2 (hardcover : alk. paper)
1. Orientalism—Great Britain—History. 2. Orient—Historiography—Great Britain—History. 3. Orient—Description and travel—Early works to 1800. 4. Classical literature—Influence. 5. Travel writing—Great Britain—History. 6. Historiography—Great Britain—History. I. Title.
DS61.85.T66 2013
950.072'041—dc23 2012031914

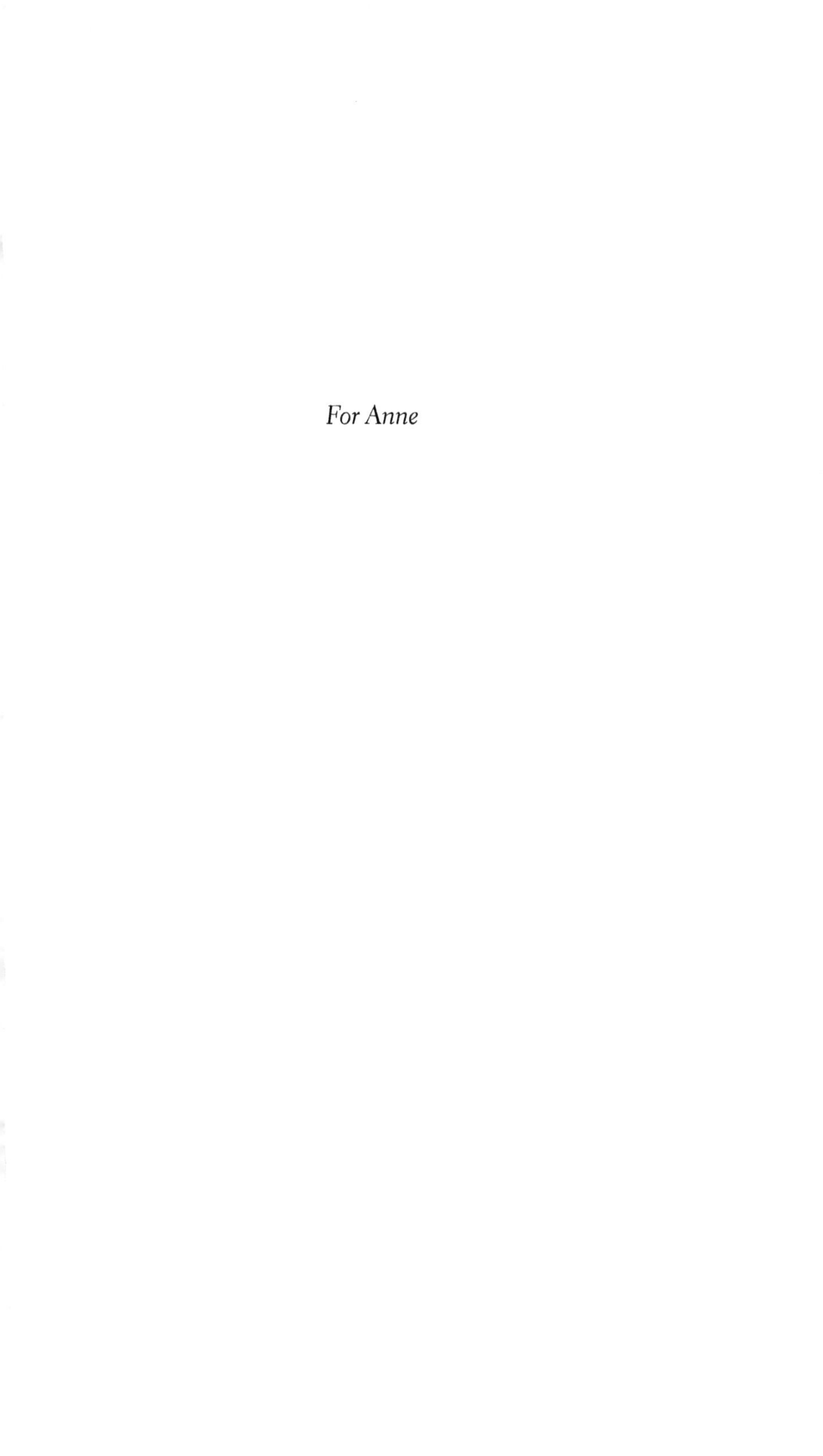

For Anne

Contents

Preface

This book is about how English historians and travelers have often seen the East through the medium of the ancient past. It explores how they have turned to classical Greek and Roman sources to help them understand and construct images of Islam and what used to be called "the Orient." It also tries to contextualize these views historically, socially, and politically to reveal how such circumstances defined the "oriental other" and attitudes toward it. Classics has played such a pivotal role in Western culture that it has had an extraordinary influence on how writers have seen other cultures. When faced with new worlds, it has often been to the old world that they have turned to help them understand such novelty. This is a vast topic. I have chosen to focus on the effect that classics had on English views of the East. The first reason for this is that trade and later imperial interests meant that for long periods England was at the forefront of dealing with the East. The second is that classics and elite English education were so intertwined that it seemed natural for writers to turn to antiquity in justifying their endeavors. Even then, I have had to be selective and I have tried to give important exemplars from the main periods in the rise and fall of English power: the early modern, the Augustan, the imperial, the end of empire, and the postmodern. This is clearly not a subject that is of relevance only to classicists. Anyone who reads the works of English travelers and historians will be aware of the classical influences at work. Anyone who has opinions on today's rising Eastern powers may be less familiar with the historical influence that classics has had on the development of those views. I have, therefore, tried to keep the book as readable and accessible as possible, while keeping sufficient detail and reference material to make the book academically useful. Producing such an account, however selective it has necessarily been, has left me in great debt to a number of people, and it is a pleasure to have the opportunity to thank them, above all Pierre Caquet, Peter Garnsey, and Justin Meggitt, as well as Melanie Wright, who so sadly died last year. I am grateful to the President and Fellows of Hughes Hall, Cambridge, for their generous award of a Research Fellowship, which allowed me to complete the work in such a pleasant and stimulating environment. It would have been impossible to carry out the research without the help of the dedicated staff of the Cambridge University Library and Classics Faculty. Sharmila Sen and Harvard University Press have done an excellent job in producing the book. Their anonymous readers were also particularly helpful in providing many astute comments and helpful criticisms. The book is dedicated to my wife, Anne, who married me during and despite of the writing of it, and to whose wonderfulness no amount of classical comparisons can do justice.

HOMER'S TURK

PART I

Contexts

1

Classicizing Orientalisms

When the thirty-two-year-old George Sandys set out on his travels to the Eastern Mediterranean in 1610, he was keen to satisfy a growing hunger in the English reading public for knowledge about the distant lands where fortunes could be made in the burgeoning spice and luxury-goods trade. The problem he faced was one that confronts all those who write about other cultures, whether historians or travel writers: how to represent the sometimes strangely disturbing features of foreign life in ways that are understandable to an audience back home. Having studied at Oxford, though without taking a degree, and the son of an archbishop of York, Sandys had, like most educated men of his day, a profound knowledge of what we would now call classics—the surviving literature of Greece and Rome. Later in his life he was to publish a translation of part of Ovid's *Metamorphoses* and he worked on another of Virgil's *Aeneid*. To a man of such erudition, it was only natural that he should turn to these ancient works for resources to help him convey to his readership the kind of customs and beliefs that he had encountered in his travels in the East. His account, published in four books in 1615 as *The Relation of a Journey begun an. Dom. 1610*, became a standard work of reference for the area of the Eastern Mediterranean that was then under the control of the Ottoman Empire. Its carefully crafted prose is replete with classical references, mythology, and historical precedent. It was through the ancients that Sandys understood this new world, it was through the ancients that he brought it into the collective consciousness, and it was through the ancients that he delivered to his empire-envious English audience an understanding of the greatest European power of the day. All of which was done in a manner that was appropriately urbane and sophisticated for a nation with social aspirations. So when, for example, he described the procession of the crack troops of the Ottoman Empire, the Janissaries, it was not sufficient to note how they had "models of Elephants, boots, swords of wood, and the like borne before them for their ensignes: and the royall standard is no other then a horse taile tied to the end of a staffe." Sandys felt compelled to bring in a classical comparison to explain fully to his readers the pomp, and even pomposity, of these terrifying Asians: "which though seeming rude, and answerable to their originall, doth retaine, perhaps something of Antiquity. For Homer sticketh the like in the gallantly armed (though not so spirited) Paris."[1] For Sandys, therefore, the Turk could be fully comprehended, and indeed made fully comprehensible, only as part of a landscape that stretched back to the mythological past. To read and know classical sources was necessary to know and understand the total history and tradition of the place, a place in which the Turk had merely taken up a relatively recent residence. The Turk, therefore, was in a real sense Homer's Turk.

Yet the effect of comparing the terrible Janissaries with the foppish Paris was also to undercut their dreadfulness. Paris was a man who, as Sandys quotes in his own translation, was overdressed to kill:

"Then puts he on a helme well wrought, and brave; Plum'd with horse haires that horribly did wave." Just how terrifying could a warrior be who paid so much attention to his appearance? Classics therefore also provided the writer with a vocabulary with which to communicate more subtle and critical readings of the Turk. Moreover, Sandys's use of the Homeric image raised all kinds of questions about the cultural identity of Paris's effeminacy. The conflict between the Greeks and the Trojans had itself brought out important issues about the Greekness of the Greeks and the Easternness of the Trojans. To what extent therefore could Paris simply be equated with the later Turks? To what extent were the powerful Turks comparable to the Trojans, who could only keep the Greeks at bay before finally crumbling? Was there any real prospect of this happening at the time Sandys was writing? Moreover, if the use of classical imagery was in some sense an attempt to lay claim to the classical past, to what extent did Paris's softness actually reflect badly on those who like Sandys were staking a claim to have inherited such a tradition? By deploying a Homeric comparison, therefore, the effect of Sandys's text was not simply to praise or denigrate the Turks, but to highlight the complexity of the traveling Englishman's relationship with both the Ottoman Empire and the classical learning he took as his companion.

This book is not just about Homer and the Turks. It is about how English historians and travelers have used a range of classical Greek and Roman authors in formulating images of Islam and the East. It brings together much classical material relevant to the formation of English "orientalism," in the sense of imagery and discourse concerning the East, and examines it in different historical contexts. Classicists have not examined this material in any depth, and I believe this is an important omission because of the fundamental role classics has played in the image-making of English historiography and travel literature. The topic has much modern relevance, given the importance of Islamic-Western relations at the current time, the rise to superpower status of India and China, and the West's need to come to terms with that. Although there has been some excellent work done on the ways in which the Orient has been represented in the West, particularly in the imperial period, very little has been done on the centrality of classics to this process.[2] This is an oversight, given the fact that many British travelers and historians who had contact with the East were well versed in the classics. The classics were considered a natural part of a proper education, and so it was equally natural for these writers to turn to these sources for inspiration, authority, and explanation. It is sometimes hard for us in the twenty-first century to realize just how potent a force the study of classics used to be among the educated, primarily the wealthy, classes. Classical authors were copied, read, and cited with ease in the original tongue. Quotes from the works of the ancients combined common currency with prestige. Nor did knowledge of classics serve only to mark off an elite. Antiquity, for many, represented the pinnacle of what human civilization could achieve, and its great writers provided much-loved ideals of thought and art. This shared treasure trove of knowledge brought with it certain collective expectations and influences, with the result that many writers shaped what they saw and chose to narrate according to an assumed facility of classical knowledge among their readers. As David Holton says, "It was inevitable that travelers to classical lands should relate their contemporary observations to their knowledge of the civilizations that had formerly flourished on the same territory."[3] Classics helped express views, provided models and exemplars, it provided a repertoire of rhetorical styles, imagery, comparisons, tropes, and representative figures. Classics acted as a prism through which writers saw the object of their study, one that refracted the images they saw.

The Importance of Classics

Classics was able to act in so pivotal a way because it sat at the heart of English education. Classics rivaled even the Bible as a widespread, flexible vehicle of Western thought.[4] Of course, when we talk of English education, we mean primarily the education of English elites. Classics was instrumental in the teaching of the wealthy and, indeed, for centuries "provided one of the main sources of their social distinction."[5] In fact, classical education was always an exclusive practice used to define membership of an elite.[6] This class element to the term *classics* was evident from its first usage. The second-century writer Aulus Gellius ascribed to the Latin writer Fronto the use of *classicus*; he says he heard Fronto tell "some learned and eminent poet," in a discussion about correct linguistic usage, to "investigate whether any orator or poet, provided he belongs to that older group—that is, some first-class [classicus], first-rate [literally 'landowning'] writer, not one of the lowest class—has ever said 'four-horse chariot' in the singular and 'sand' in the plural."[7] From the outset, therefore, classic writing has been about high socioeconomic status, perceived quality, notions of proper usage, and, conversely, the kind of high-class writing that the poor could not manage to do.

By 1711 the plural term *classics* was used in English to designate the corpus of Greek and Latin literature.[8] The lack of a term before that reflected the fact that for most educated people, classical literature *was* literature. For upper-class Englishmen in the late medieval and especially early modern period, classical education was the only kind of humanistic higher education available. Even then, the range of classical authors studied was constrained to a far narrower range of authors and texts than was to become available later. To some extent, then, the use of classical motifs as a means to understand the Orient was not really a matter of choice. If some early English travelers, for example, thought that the Turks were Trojans, this was not an attempt to understand the Turks, but, as far as these authors were concerned, a simple matter of historical fact. Viewing them in these classical terms was a predominating frame of reference they had to understand all reality, not only the "oriental other." It is certainly true that their classical education colored all of their perceptions, not just those concerning the Orient. Nevertheless, some degree of choice will always exist: a privileging of a classical analogy above one from the Bible, say. Limited though this choice might seem by comparison with later periods, when the opportunities for historical and literary comparison had expanded dramatically, within the context of the period classics did not represent the complete palette available. And even if it were not accepted that this represented much in the way of genuine choice, the use of comparative material did offer writers a wide variety of ways to express themselves. Such imagery in early English writers, and the specific analogies or allusions they employed, represented positive selections on these authors' part. It was how they thought they could best say what they wanted to say and get their message across to their readership.

The late seventeenth and eighteenth centuries were the high-water mark of classicism in England. But this was also a period when classics was starting to lose its significance. Ancient texts were no longer so necessary for practical matters such as law, medicine, philosophy, mathematics, and agriculture. England was at the forefront of the scientific revolution that was rendering many of these old authorities obsolete, and against such a background classical knowledge became "an accomplishment, not a necessity—except for social purposes."[9] The end of the eighteenth century, however, saw a revival of interest in Greek and Roman culture, which was fostered in part by the Romantic enthusiasm for the Greek revolt against the Turks, by the discovery of the ruins of Pompeii, and above all by the growing importance of the public schools.[10] As Suzanne Marchand has observed in her study of German orientalism in the age of empire, the growth of interest in the study of classics was also part of a cultural renewal, over and against the landed aristocracy, baroque culture, and orthodox clergy of the previous era.[11] In fact, a close, formative relationship existed between the study of oriental languages and the study of classical antiquity. Both relied on the same well-educated, liberal, and middle-class social group for their health, even if the growth in the academic study of oriental literature also helped to destroy a narrow Christian and classical canon of works.[12]

But if classics benefited during this period from liberalism, its survival at the core of English liberal education in the nineteenth century was a function of political conservatism. Classics came to be associated with the virtues of the aristocracy, as opposed to the disquieting middle-class desire for progress and meritocracy. In response to this middle-class challenge, elite institutions such as the public schools, Oxford and Cambridge Universities, and British governmental offices all tried to raise their collective drawbridge and maintain upper-class status by making it academically harder to get in. This they achieved by placing greater emphasis on knowledge of Greek and Latin.[13] With the acquisition of empire, Britain's public schools were to place even more emphasis on the seemingly timeless advice on ruling that ancient texts were thought to offer. Not only were Greek and Latin believed to help train the mind and make good citizens, but a profound knowledge of the history of the Roman Empire was held to be indispensable for the administrators of British overseas possessions.

The study of Greek and Roman cultures was used to validate British imperialism. Latin and Greek became steadily more important in the second half of the nineteenth century as Britain sought to increase the number of "gentlemen imperialists" leaving Oxford and

Cambridge. Between 1892 and 1914, 49 percent of recruits to the Indian Civil Service came from Oxford and 30 percent from Cambridge. Most of those from Cambridge had read mathematics, and most of those from Oxford had studied classics. Although the ICS entrance examinations were in theory open to anyone within the British Empire, the heavy emphasis on the learning of Latin and Greek by a young age made it extremely difficult for any Indians to succeed. The period 1904–1913 saw 501 Europeans pass the examinations and only 27 Indians.[14] As Phiroze Vasunia has noted, the British operated their empire on a "racialized notion of civility," with British civil servants conceptualized as gentlemen who knew Latin and Greek.[15] The desire for colonial administrators to be highly skilled in such arcane arts as Greek verse composition reflected the British self-image of themselves as being both the inheritors of the classical tradition and its surpassers.

Classics was deeply engrained in political life in the nineteenth century. Studying classical orators such as Cicero was part of rhetorical training, and quoting from classical authors was a recognized stylistic engine in the House of Commons, as members "watched a piece of oratory moving from point to point, to culminate in the *expected* passage from Virgil or Horace."[16] Classically trained members of Parliament knew what passages were likely to come up and must have enjoyed the sense of class superiority and solidarity that this expectation provided. But classics in the Victorian period was not only the preserve of the political elite. Knowledge of antiquity also helped form and identify an important segment of the burgeoning middle class. In Victorian Britain the class structure was marked to a large extent by knowledge of Greek and Latin in elites, Latin among gentlemen, and English among the masses. The important point to note is that classics never only belonged to one simple and definable class. The mushrooming of public schools in the late nineteenth century saw many of the middle class exposed to the supposed benefits of classical education.[17] W. D. Rubinstein has calculated that as many as 25 percent of the young British population would have been incorporated into the value system of the elite by means of ordinary secondary schools aping the distinctive features of public schools: houses, uniforms, games, and the teaching of classics.[18] Even if this figure is the maximum possible for the candidate group for elite recruitment and the reality was much lower, it shows how the British imperial elite did not draw simply from the aristocratic class. Nor was classics wholly unavailable to the working classes, nor were they indifferent to it, as cheap translations became increasingly available through the public library network.[19]

The Reception of Classics

What will be abundantly clear by now is that as English needs changed, classics itself was adapted to meet them. Writers used classics to help them reflect their own contemporary agendas. It is striking that Elizabethan travelers, Gibbon, and Indian civil servants all had in common their education in, and often love of, the classics. But seeing the East with classical eyes did not mean picturing the peoples and cultures of the East in the same way. No simple continuity existed in views of the East from antiquity down to the modern era. As the complexity of English relations with the East increased, classics also had to shift to reflect the changes in cultural and intellectual life in England caused by those changes in that relationship. Classics was not, therefore, a fixed pole of comparison. Rather, what people understood by classics and what they thought the ancient world represented was under constant reformulation. The relationship between classics and the East was never stable, and indeed, it was this very instability that made classics such a useful resource for writers seeking to portray the Orient to their audiences back home.

I have focused on examining the reception of classical ideas in England. Such reception looks at the ways in which Greek and Roman material has been "transmitted, translated, excepted, interpreted, rewritten, reimagined and represented."[20] Meaning is seen as being realized at the point of reception, when the reader interprets the classical text; or the postclassical writer employs a classical reference, which is itself reinterpreted when encountered by the reader.[21] Reception therefore concentrates on the historical contexts in which classics has been used and emphasizes the impact of such reception in shaping contemporary perceptions of the world. It insists on the historical contingency of the interpreter's position. The worlds of ancient writers and later readers are marked by different institutions, social relations, concepts, beliefs, and experiences, all of which combine to generate completely different interpretations. Classics is no longer seen in such an approach as a tradition with fixed meaning to be handed down passively from generation to generation. Rather it is an active, two-way process that seeks to appreciate the historical depth of interpretations of the classical past.[22] Reception privileges the role of the reader in finding his or her own meanings to allusions, not simply trying to recreate the intention of the original author, even if that were itself possible. Classics has been molded and shaped by each generation of readers and writers, and the continuing power of classics stems not from its relation to the past but from its relation to the current social, political, and moral values that it helps sustain.[23] The use of classics, therefore, in later postclassical writing cannot be seen in an unideological way. Using classics was a way to build new ideologies around the persistent ideals of the ancient past.[24] Simon Goldhill sees "reception" as too passive a term for this process, for what he calls the "dynamics of resistance and appropriation, recognition and self-aggrandisement that make up this drama of cultural identity."[25]

This book, then, is not about what the ancients thought about the East. Nor does it try to trace how stock images of the Orient were handed down through the ages into the modern world. It tries to show how the image of the East has been historically received in England and has been adapted to suit the political and social needs of the time by means of the classics. Historical events have consistently and repeatedly changed the English image of Islam and the East, and each new development has called on the ancients to help account for and make sense of such change. But it is worth remembering that for nearly all of the writers we shall encounter, and indeed their readers, classics *was* very much a tradition, one that they believed to be unchanging and true. To see all meaning as being determined solely at the point of reception by the reader is no doubt literally true, but readers themselves are, at least in part, created by their historical contexts. Their readings are themselves the product of a complex dialogue between the producer and the receiver, one that has been refracted through a long line of historical interpreters. English views, therefore, did not suddenly shift from one generation to another. They evolved steadily in line with the pace of English history. It is also worth remembering that, as Marchand has shown, orientalist and classical discourse were inextricably intertwined. The result is that, as Donald Reid says, "sometimes one cannot tell whether the classics framed and distorted European views of modern Egypt or the other way around."[26] We are looking at texts acting as mirrors within mirrors, reflecting and refracting the many different images within them. The influence of classics on images of the East was not only one-way. Changing attitudes to the Orient and the study of oriental languages and cultures themselves contributed to developments in the treatment of classical texts and ideas about what antiquity itself represented.

Orientalism?

In his radical and important work on the subject, Said argued that in the West's discourse on the East there were certain long-standing characteristics that did not reflect any attempt to describe the East, but rather relied on preexisting stereotypes that drew on Western dreams and fantasies for their power. He claimed that "the Orient was almost a European invention" and that, since antiquity, the Orient has been for Western writers a place of romance, exotic beings, haunting memories and landscapes, and remarkable experiences.[27] In this view, orientalism was not simply a way of thinking or an idea; its construction was closely linked to the inequality of power relations that existed between the East and the West, especially in the imperial period. It acted as a system of ideas used to express and reinforce the position of strength of the Western nations and to keep the poor Easterner downtrodden. Orientalism placed the Westerner in a superior relationship with the East and then helped manage that relationship by ensuring that the image of the Orient remained characterized by weakness and ineffectiveness. In effect, Said argued, the West produced the Orient in order to justify and help in its own subjugation.

Said's paradigmatic work was reacting to the dominant political discourse of the time, and, as many scholars have subsequently shown, the West has historically created a far more wide-ranging and subtle set of images than the stereotypical version found in Said's orientalism, even in the imperial period.[28] Marchand has pointed out that colonial encounters were only one form of encounter between the East and the West, albeit an important one. Even then, not all orientalist knowledge "inevitably contributed to the building of empires." Moreover, the Saidian view creates a simple binary opposition between Europe and the Orient that binds all classes, genders, and social groups. Categories such as "European" and "oriental" were not all-encompassing or even always that important. Above all, it underplays the richness and complexity of Europeans' relations with the Orient.[29] As Vasunia has noted, the widespread notion of orientalism needs to be understood in the light of profound cross-cultural interaction between the two groups that took place in areas such as literature, material goods, and social custom.[30] The relationship between East and West, therefore, was always a complex dialectical phenomenon, whereby various traditions engaged with each other, that cannot be reduced to a single, global view. This is also apparent in the various images created in the classicizing, orientalist texts in this study. Many early English travelers, such as Sandys, could not help but be impressed by the power, wealth, and sophistication of the Ottoman Empire.

The ancients themselves also in reality possessed a more nuanced approach than Said gave them credit for. They held many diverse and often incoherent views about the East. Said saw Aeschylus's *Persae* as the first step in the process of orientalization. It represented, in Edith Hall's words, the "first unmistakable file in the archive of Orientalism, the discourse by which the European imagination has dominated Asia ever since by conceptualizing its inhabitants as defeated, luxurious, emotional, cruel, and always as dangerous."[31] But this harshly xenophobic view was the product of a specific moment in history: the Persian invasions in the early fifth century BCE. The united military effort to repel these outsiders created a highly concentrated idea of exactly what attributes made the Greek different from the barbarian. But no such simple dichotomy ever characterized all Greek discourse concerning the East. In fact, the Greeks seem to have held a wide range of ideas concerning barbarians rather than simply seeing them as their polar opposites. Xenophon, for example, was never only hostile to the Persians; he also portrayed them as often reasonable, moderate, and, in the case of Cyrus, model rulers.[32] In his *Oeconomicon*, Xenophon praises the Persian king for his administrative skills, and commends the Persian system of punishment and reward over the Greek system of punishment alone. To be sure, some writers went along with the extreme characterization of the barbarian as the ultimate in slavish, cowardly, and effeminate behavior; one such was Isocrates, who often called for the Greeks to unite and take the fight to the Persian barbarian.[33] But Isocrates's view was marginal and his calls were certainly never heeded. Nor did barbarians have a monopoly on deceit: Greeks were also often portrayed as untrustworthy and guileful. Greek rulers, like Alexander the Great, showed respect for Persian culture and their kings, even if it was driven by the political need for an accommodation. And as Miller has argued, the Athenians did not in fact hate Persia: there was a richly complex response to various levels of interaction between the two cultures.[34] Many Greeks were familiar with many aspects of Persian culture, meaning that they were not simply the scary monsters of some far off, unknown land. A variety of views concerning barbarians therefore circulated in Greek society, from the fiercely derogatory to the flatteringly complimentary.[35]

Of course, no simple equivalence should be drawn between the Greeks and later Westerners. "The Greeks were no Europeans," as Strohmaier puts it.[36] And as Martin Bernal argued in *Black Athena*, we must also be careful not to create a simple line of inheritance from the Western world back to the Greeks that acts to exclude the influence of the East.[37] What we can say is that Said's view of a monolithic discourse of orientalism dominating Western views of the Orient conceals the fact that a range of Western attitudes toward the East has always existed. English attitudes changed in line with English needs and were moved by a variable nexus of economic, political, and cultural forces.[38] If, therefore, there ever was such a discourse as orientalism, it was not a single developmental tradition but was "profoundly heterogeneous."[39] In fact, the very heterogeneity of the Orient constantly undercut the possibility of any orientalist project. No single totalizing framework could ever adequately account for the wide range of concerns the various Eastern cultures have generated in the West. There can be no doubt that, as Hall argues, the derogatory type of discourse concerning barbarians found in the *Persae* was to be of "lasting influence on western views of foreign cultures, especially the portrait of Asiatic peoples as effeminate, despotic, and cruel."[40] But this was only one type of image of the East. In fact, it soon becomes apparent when studying such things as English travel accounts of journeys to the East that most travelers did not see the oriental as barbarian. Often, if anything, it was the Turk who looked down on and sneered at the backward English. Indeed, from the seventh century until the battle of Lepanto in 1571, Islam dominated and threatened Christianity.

Choices

I am not an orientalist but a classicist. This has inevitably colored my approach to the subject. I came to it by reading Said, sharing the concerns about his generalizing view that many have had, but recognizing also that classics had played an important role in the creation of images of the East. I decided to focus on travel writers and historians for two principal reasons. The first was that these writers tried explicitly to describe and analyze Eastern cultures to their audiences back home. To help them in this they turned to imaginative resources that they knew they shared with their reading public. I decided to leave alone more overtly literary texts concerned with the Orient. Although works such as Byron's *Childe Harold's Pilgrimage* and Beckford's *Vathek* were certainly important in creating and disseminating classically influenced images of the Orient among English audiences, the purpose of such works is not always, if ever, primarily aimed at informing the reader about the East. Such literary classicism has also often been commented on. The second reason is that history and travel writing were things the English excelled at. The growing interest in the Orient that accompanied and fed the desire for overseas possessions meant that there was strong demand in England for books that dealt with the East. Whether through trade or colonial administration, the East offered the ambitious English tremendous opportunities for personal advancement. As Robert Clive famously said when questioned in Parliament about the vast wealth he had appropriated in India, "By God . . . I stand astonished at my own moderation." Many of these books tell us something important, therefore, about how the English set out to conquer the world intellectually. They describe and analyze places where the English imagination could run riot in anticipation of the great riches and power that were attainable there. These were texts where domestic fantasies coincided with the realities of increasing English influence in the East.

It would be a lie to say that the particular texts and periods on which I have chosen to focus do not reflect personal preferences. I could not have left Gibbon out even though so much has been written about him already. When I set out on this project I was keen to avoid focusing purely on "great men" but in reality found that so little was written about the ways in which English writers classicized the Orient that I felt that I should start with the writers who would be best known to my readership but might appear less familiar from this angle. The case studies that make up Part II of this book are, however, consciously designed to represent a cross-section of the principal different periods in the rise and fall of English power: the early modern, the Augustan, the imperial, the end of empire, and the postmodern. The selections of both periods and authors cannot make any claim to be comprehensive. Instead, the aim is to chart some of the main points of the mental map of the Orient that English historians and travel writers sought to create. I have also focused on those writers for whom antiquity was especially influential, thereby revealing the huge range of uses to which classics was put in the English imaginative foray into the East. In doing so I have tried to bring to the fore the main themes that concerned the English and were articulated through the medium of classical reference. I have, in other words, used English historiography and travel writing as means to examine the nature of the oriental image they created, while, conversely, using the image of the Orient as a tool to analyze English historiography and travel writing.

This book is certainly not an attempt to describe what Islam or the East were actually like. It is about visions of the Orient created in England. It is about how writers endowed distant lands with imagined attitudes. The fact that this is a book about English images also means that the voice of the Easterner is largely absent. There has been too little attention paid to the ways in which the peoples colonized by the English themselves used classics.[41] For the most part, the difficulty of studying classics for the subordinate members of the British Empire meant that this was an avenue of communication that was simply not open to them. Only those who had the resources to access the limited routes to social mobility occasioned by such institutions as the Indian Civil Service could play the classical game in their writings. Independence was to see some attempts by Eastern nations to use classics to assert their new freedoms. Egypt, for example, had no state school teaching Latin in 1902, but when the new Egyptian University opened in 1925 it contained its very own Department of Classics.

It is also worth emphasizing that I am certainly not arguing that classics was the only prism through which English perceptions of the East were refracted. Christianity and the Bible were probably more influential overall, an influence that has already been well studied.[42] Nor did all writers use classical references. But many did assume in their readers a universal intimacy and empathy with the writers of antiquity. It is fair to say that there are fewer classical references in lower-class texts, but that is hardly surprising—before translations became freely available, one needed an expensive education to appreciate the classics. This has had the consequence that the classics tend to appear most liberally in the texts of the wealthy and the powerful. In itself this is not a weakness if the aim is to try to see how the dominant discourse of the day reacted to Islam and the East. This is perhaps where the use of classical reference is most revealing of the attitudes of the English elite toward the Orient. More accessible referents such as the Bible or popular culture were implicitly and often explicitly rejected by elite authors precisely because of this accessibility. In many ways, classics represented a private language with which the elite could communicate with each other and express opinions that were, in their eyes, unsullied by the demands of pubic opinion.

Some terms need to be briefly discussed. By "classics" I mean the texts, traditions, and mythology that survived from Greece and Rome from roughly the fifth century BCE to the fifth century CE. I have tried to stick to referring to the English, but use English and British interchangeably during the imperial period. It is worth noting that prior to the sixteenth century the terms *Islam* and *Muslim* were not generally used; instead the commonly used terms were ethnic, such as *Arab*, *Moor*, *Turk*, and *Saracen*. Until the seventeenth century, for the most part, Islam was considered the Orient. It was not until trade routes opened up more widely that knowledge of the further Eastern regions became more widespread. The "East" and the now outdated term *Orient* were, therefore, plastic concepts but broadly covered the

Maghreb, the Levant, the Middle East, India, China, Japan, and other countries of the Far East. This conceptual confusion between the Turkish, the oriental, and the Islamic underlines how vague and condescending many English ideas about the East often were. Because this is a book about the contribution classics made to these very confusions, I have made little attempt to impose greater accuracy on the original texts and use the terms *East* and *Orient* interchangeably. I use the term *Islam*, though, more exactly to mean the religion articulated by the religious text, the Quran, as revealed to the Prophet Muhammad. I refer to Muslims as the adherents of the religion Islam. I use spellings as written here, but when quoting primary and secondary sources I keep to the original usage. Islam itself is, of course, a vast generalization, covering, to name but the main ones, Arab, Ottoman, North African, Spanish, Indian, and Far Eastern forms, but I must reemphasize that this is not a book about actual Islam or the East, but the use to which ancient texts were put to create images of these regions and their cultures for Western consumption.

The Structure of This Book

This book has three parts. It has begun in this chapter by looking at the importance of classical texts in English oriental image-making, and by discussing the issues of classical reception and orientalism. Chapter 2 examines the huge range of applications and purposes to which classical reference has been applied in English texts. It tries to establish a typology of classical allusion within the context of historiography and travel writing. It also tries to set out the key themes and messages that such allusions were designed as vehicles to carry. Of course, classical sources had already influenced many writers before the English became interested in the East. Chapter 3 looks at the historical background to the emergence of specifically English views concerning the Orient by providing an overview of the classical influence on medieval images of Islam. The Islamic invasions of what had been the eastern provinces of the Roman Empire had had the effect of shoving the center of Christian civilization northward, away from the Mediterranean. This itself created a need for a new conception of Europe and its ideals. In this way Islam has always played a special role within Europe as the defining other. In Edward Said's words, Islam was "the very epitome of an outsider against which the whole of European civilization from the Middle Ages on was founded."[43] Suffering from what Richard Southern called the "ignorance of a confined space,"[44] European writers relied on rumors for their information and also often fell back on preconceived classical ideas to give shape to their fears. Early authors often sought to locate Islam within the tradition of early Christian heretics in the Roman Empire. As Norman Daniel says, "The West inherited from its own past the notion that Islam was a sexually corrupt tyranny based on false teaching."[45] The Crusades played an important part in disseminating more widely such hostile views of Islam and the East. Chroniclers of the Crusades, such as William of Tyre and Guibert of Nogent, relied heavily on classical precedent and reference to build up their images of Islam and the Saracen enemy. Guibert's hostility to the Saracens was informed by his unshakable Christian faith and his belief that their purpose was purely to act as a spur to the morally weak Christians. William of Tyre, by contrast, who lived in the Levantine kingdom, used classical texts to help him portray a far more subtle and positive image of the Saracen foe. If anyone falls short by comparison with antiquity, it is the Christian kings, whereas the Saracens are often seen as brave and worthy opponents.

Part II contains a series of case studies of English writers from different stages of English history. These case studies show how the uses of classics have operated and developed in a representative sample of English historiographical and travel texts from different periods. The organization of these studies is chronological, which has the benefit of simplicity and also of showing how various ideas, tropes, and interpretations have gone in and out of fashion throughout the history of England's engagement with the East. Chapter 4 examines the relationship between England and Islam during the seventeenth century when English travelers and merchants sought much closer links with the Ottoman Empire. This was a period when trade as much as war characterized the relationship between Christianity and Islam.[46] By the early modern period the broadly negative image of the Muslim had become well established and spread by accounts and tales of the Crusades. The arrival of a terrifying new form of oriental, Islamic enemy in the form of the Turk only exacerbated this feeling of hostility. However, in the face of the overwhelming and obvious military and cultural superiority of the Ottoman Empire, it was impossible for early travelers who had direct contact with that empire to be anything other than impressed, if not actually positively disposed. Some writers saw the Turks as the successors to the Trojans as a way of explaining their great military skill. Others, such as George Sandys, undertook a detailed description of the empire in terms of its classical past in order to give a three-dimensional historical sense of the lands though which he was traveling. Many Elizabethan travelers commented on the cleanliness of the Turks and their civility toward strangers; writers such as Richard Knolles exalted them for their unity, toughness, and heroism. Above all, these writers reveal the growing interest in the practice of power and kingship that an English audience had as a result of their country's burgeoning international standing.

A complex but generally positive account of Islam can also be found in Gibbon, which Chapter 5 examines. For Gibbon, the study of the decline and fall of Rome was above all a study in the origins of modern Europe. The study of the rise of Islam and its conquest of large parts of what had been the Roman Empire were of fundamental importance to his project. Not surprisingly, Gibbon's account is replete with classical comparisons and imagery. In part this is to give a sense of moral comparison between the ancient, the Byzantine, and the Muslim to enable his readers to assess how the Islamic world fits in with his overarching moral history. It was also perhaps because Gibbon used the rise of Islam as a mirror image of the decline of Rome to give a sharper focus to his account of the reasons for imperial decline and fall. These lessons were important for his own day, if his world was avoid falling into the barbarism that, to Gibbon at least, still seemed possible.

Chapter 6 looks at the way the increasing British involvement in India gave an urgent need for a new expression of the relationship between the English and the oriental. The discovery of the great cultures of India and China had to some extent shattered any sense of cultural superiority that the West had held and rendered obsolete the notion of the barbarian. Sir William Jones, for example, saw in Sanskrit a language that was "more perfect than the Greek, more copious than the Latin," and he saw near equivalence in his comparisons between ancient and Hindu cultures. Warren Hastings, the first governor-general, shared Jones's political aim of ruling India through understanding as well as arms, but this was not universally popular. When prosecuted for corruption, Hastings was likened to the venal Roman governor Verres, and thereafter a more hard-nosed approach to India emerged. This was perhaps most clearly expressed in *The History of British India* by James Mill, in which classical comparison was widely used to put the native world in its place. But not all Indians accepted this negative evaluation, and some even used classics to help them promote a more positive sense of local culture.

Chapter 7 looks at the dramatic change in European attitudes toward the East in the nineteenth century. The enthusiasm and sympathy that had characterized many descriptions transformed into colonial contempt. This development reflected a change in the power relations between the East and the West. The rise in British power and the feeling of superiority that industrial progress created both contributed to a new sense of hostility in the accounts of the Orient. The oriental was often portrayed as childlike, juvenile, and irrational, while England shouldered its White Man's Burden of governing the Orient and teaching it about liberty, freedom, and democracy. Classics was closely associated with the articulation of this sense of power and superiority. It also played a central role in justifying the maintenance of Western imperial rule, as can be seen in the work of the British consul-general of Egypt, Lord Cromer. Comparison with the Roman Empire allowed the British to understand their imperial project more fully and be aware of the potential pitfalls it faced. Classics gave a sense of permanence and tried to raise the rightness of British rule to the level of an eternal verity.

Chapter 8 explores some of the great nineteenth-century expeditions into Arabia, which was seen as one of the last unexplored regions. The very idea of penetrating the furthest recesses of the Arabian hinterland naturally reflected to some extent the degree to which European power now stretched into almost every region of the globe. But whereas writers like Cromer were fully confident in the righteousness of the British imperial project, many other English travel writers were far more positively disposed toward the Arabs. Classical writers had already created an image of the free-thinking, independent, and, above all, uncorrupted Arab, which contrasted with what they saw as the moral decay of their own societies. Nineteenth- and twentieth-century British travelers to Arabia, such as Charles Doughty, Richard Burton, and T. E. Lawrence, used these classical references and models to paint a highly sympathetic and positive picture of the area and its peoples, in particular groups such as the Bedouin. Motivated by a more idiosyncratic, individualistic set of causes, many of these travelers were personalities who were to some extent outsiders in Britain itself but who felt at home in the desert and believed they had a natural affinity with the Arabs.

Part III ends the book by considering the role of classics in oriental image-making over the past half century. It might be thought that the decline in the teaching of classics since World War II would have led to a fall in the importance of classics in the shaping of ideas about the East. This is undoubtedly true in some areas, such as travel writing, but has been at least in part compensated for by the continued use of classics in film and political analogy. Using both British and American examples to reflect the *translatio imperii* over the Atlantic, Chapters 9 and 10 briefly examine how images of the Orient and the classical past have combined to play an important role in helping modern Britain come to terms with its loss of power and in helping America consider its own identity and its relationship with the increasingly important East.

The texts and culture of the classical world have played an important role in English writers' creation of the image of the Orient. Said's monolithic distinction between East and West has now been tempered with some sense of hybridity: it is generally recognized that Western writers generated a wide range of oriental images, both hostile and well disposed. This only serves to emphasize how useful a tool classics has historically been in helping writers fashion such variety. It was the great advantage of classics that it could be so flexible as a reference point. Rome, for example, could function as a "revolutionary alternative to the existing order," provide a symbol of cosmopolitan multiculturalism, or act as a beacon of law and order.[47] English authors could always find an appropriate classical reference, whatever their agenda. For centuries, therefore, the classical past has helped justify, sanction, and authenticate the English present. References to antiquity have allowed, and continue to allow, the English and the English-speaking world, throughout the many upheavals they have undergone, to find in their images of the East new values and identities to meet their immediate social and political needs.

2

The Uses of Classics

England has had a close relationship with the classical past. At first glance it is not obvious why this should be. After all, England does not have much affinity with the Mediterranean world that was at the core of classical culture. Cold, damp, cut off, Germanic, and beer-drinking, England is a land very different from the vine-growing regions of the southern parts of Europe, the Middle East, and North Africa. This contrast of climate, history, and culture contributed to an English idea of the classical world that "often combined admiration with a sense of otherness."[1] But of course, much of Britain was for an extended period of time a part of the Roman Empire and for almost a thousand years looked to Rome for its spiritual leadership. An appreciation of the benefits of distance has therefore often been combined with aspiration to emulate.

There are various ways in which the English have tended to "classicize"—to use classical antiquity to make authoritative sense of the present.[2] The classical past was put to a variety of social and political uses in different periods, and some classical texts and authors were more favored in certain periods of English history. The classical past also performed many different functions in English historical and travel texts. The discussion in this chapter might tentatively be seen as offering a typology of the tropes and tactics of classicizing orientalisms, but no such typology could ever be exhaustive or complete. The classical past has fulfilled an unlimited range of purposes for English writers, and no general analysis of them is ever going to cover them all. Instead, this will provide us with a template within which to locate the various types of classical reference employed in English texts.

Themes

Three principal themes have dominated the use of ancient reference in English historiography and travel writing: the nature of empire, the notion of civilization, and the pursuit of self-knowledge.

Trying to understand what it means to wield power overseas, beyond the confines of the homeland, is something that permeates English texts. Classics has consistently offered a vehicle to bear the burden of reflection upon England's international situation. At the time of Elizabethan travelers, the English yearning for empire had to confront the realities of dealing with established powers, such as the Ottoman Turks. Later in the nineteenth century, when overseas possessions seemed to fall almost effortlessly into English hands, comparison with the great Roman Empire gave a way of understanding the potential limitlessness of power. English power, it seemed, was based upon an innate, racial superiority, something that made the English the natural rulers of the world. Because they understood power—even better than the Romans, because they had learned the lessons of Rome's decline—there was a certain naturalness to their rule. The late nineteenth and early twentieth centuries were particularly rich periods for imperial comparison.[3] This partly took the form of emphasizing the moral qualities of British rule in comparison with the relative brutality of the Roman regime. The British were keen to show that their empire could be seen in some historical sense as progressive. The corruption of many oriental rulers in areas that had once sat within the Roman world was thought to emphasize how right the British were to reintroduce forcibly their own version of Roman good-governance. But at a time when Germany was posing a threat to the Pax Britannica, discussions about the Roman Empire also served to convey contemporary concerns about the long-term viability of the British Empire and the possibility of its more imminent decline or overthrow. By reflecting upon the ways in which the Romans assimilated so many different peoples and, indeed, were themselves assimilated into so many other cultures, the British were also able to articulate concerns about the watering-down effect that a loss of their own perceived racial purity might have on their empire. In such a context, the attempt to highlight the supposed value of the British Empire can also be seen as an awkward attempt to drive doubts about the worth of the whole of the imperial project into the long grass.

If thinking about the value, purpose, and longevity of the British Empire found a ready means of expression in comparative analysis of the ancient world, so too did antiquity furnish the modern imperialist with firsthand practical knowledge of how to go about his purpose. Moreover, the English felt they knew from direct contact with the Romans how to conquer and govern. The English could look to the way the Romans had settled in small military encampments within their land as a model for how they should occupy foreign realms themselves. The Roman model educated the English in the everyday practicalities of foreign rule: how to administer, dispense justice, maintain order, and, in a more diffuse way, keep an appropriate distance. This is despite the fact that the Roman model was not always a particularly good example to follow. Often Roman examples were applied to regions that had never been under Roman rule, most notably India. The dominant view in the Victorian era favored the benefits of learning from classical examples over studying the history or culture of the particular region itself. As Robert Irwin has pointed out, colonial administrators in the East were much more likely to be "familiar with the campaigns of Caesar than those of Muhammad."[4]

Antiquity did not just help the English to consider the implications of empire, it also acted as a sounding board for English thought concerning the organization of domestic authority. In part this was because the whole notion of overseas expansion was at odds with democracy, betraying the contradiction of a liberal empire in the way that the Athenian-dominated Delian League had done. Looking at the ways in which power had been exercised, abused, and corrupted in the ancient world allowed the English at various periods to debate what kind of government their own land should have. Those who favored reform tended to prefer Athenian democracy, for all its faults, over the unforgiving regime of Sparta. Those who favored a monarch with strictly limited powers found ample examples in antiquity of despotic rulers who had used their unconstrained position of power to commit all manner of atrocities. Likewise, discussions of the nature of slavery provided not only a view of the horror of the institution in modern times but a metaphor for the potential political servitude into which the English could fall if they were not to keep a careful eye on their leaders.

Finally, especially once Britain was feeling the heat from German pressure by the late nineteenth century, the decline and fall of ancient empires was thought to offer valuable lessons and insights into how best the British could themselves avoid such a fate. The collapse of Rome, in particular, demonstrated the limits and impermanence of imperial power, however eternal it might once have seemed. It gave warning of what would happen to the British Empire if it did not learn from the Roman example. Many British writers therefore tried to analyze the end of Rome to discern the underlying causes of Roman decline. Richard Hingley has shown how the domestic examples of Roman ruins, most notably that of Hadrian's wall, acted as physical portents of the collapse of Britain's North West Frontier in India.[5]

The second theme is that of civilization. The growth in England's international presence from the Elizabethan period meant that English writers were often concerned to see how their homeland stacked up against more prestigious and long-established rivals, not just in terms of military or economic power but in terms of culture and civility. The classical world provided an important yardstick against which to measure the aspirations of a global power. Such comparisons also helped to justify England's attainment of such power. That the Romans could be seen as having Romanized the ancient Britons served to emphasize the passing of Roman civility to the English.[6] The English, in other words, had achieved power and sophistication because they had been taught how to by their Roman ancestors. More importantly, such comparison with the great Roman empire builders was to underline how colonization was almost hardwired into the English psyche, having been learned so long ago from the classical masters. They knew how to civilize. Texts such as Tacitus's *Agricola* were thought to emphasize how powerful the idea of civilization could be as a tool of imperial control. Once empire had been established, the comparison of Roman frontiers and walls also took on considerable significance as a metaphor for the imperial frontier of civilization.[7]

Classical comparison functioned to legitimate the whole imperial project, from the military to the cultural. Yet it also served as a means for the English to think about their own level of civilization.

Ancient exemplars showed what constituted moral behavior and virtue, and provided archetypes of rationality and physical proof of the benefits of material progress. In the eighteenth century, in particular, antiquity was both the mirror and the measure of English progress. By contrast, the fall of Rome gave clear demonstrations of civilization's antithesis, barbarism. Ancient barbarians could be cautionary symbols of the fragility of civilization, or indeed of its underlying strength and durability. Classics, therefore, represented civilization and itself was believed to hold civilizing powers. But antiquity had also shown that ancient civilization was not impregnable. Whether from barbarians or internal strife, such as at the fall of the Roman republic, ancient societies showed how easily a virtuous society could fall into the hands of unscrupulous tyrants. Classics was in this way able to provide examples to the English of the dangers of empire. Empire brought power and wealth, but at what cost to public morals and virtue? But if the eighteenth century was to see an innate plasticity in the concept of civilization, by the late Victorian era this had hardened under the influence of the racial model. Civilization now seemed to be inborn to the ruling British, the almost genetic result of generations of evolution within the perfect environment of the British Isles. This was not a quality that the British were likely to lose easily or rapidly and, in the eyes of its imperialist proponents, merely served to underline just how long the empire could be expected to persist. From a distance, of course, these racial notions seem to be no more than the desperate prejudices of those fighting to resist the slow ebbing away of their own power.

The third theme that recurs repeatedly throughout the later case studies is that of identity. Classics gave the English a means to explore their own Englishness and its characteristics in the context of the Orient. From the first contact with Islam, classical texts helped Christians identify the new form that the East had taken. It was possible to see Muslims as the latest in a long line of ancient heretics, and, from there, to locate the relationship between Islam and Christianity within the long battle between Christians and their pagan oppressors in the Roman world. In such a worldview, Christian writers asserted their unity with the classical past, thereby staking a claim on its supposed rationality. Islam was seen as having an identity that inherently clashed with that of the Western Christian, thereby serving to establish a clearer idea of the latter. Many English writers were to draw on these traditions and approaches to establish a sharper outline of their own identities by means of an opposition to an imagined Asia and an affinity with its classical past. Classics therefore allowed many writers to understand a place by looking at its ancient appearance, however much later developments had altered it. The East could be portrayed as a terrifying antithesis of English ideals. And when the racial model acquired greater explanatory power in the Victorian imperial period, the East offered clear examples of the unbridgeable differences between the English and their oriental subjects, and warned of the perils to that identity that any attempt at assimilation would bring.

Linked to this English tendency to see the East as an exotic and dangerous "other" is to see the East and classical antiquity as places of alternative sexual identities. Many authors have constructed the East as a place of alluring sensuality, a place far removed from the pruderies of Victorian sexuality, and the very different mores of the ancient world helped them to achieve this. Earlier English travelers were less obsessed with social customs such as polygamy, harems, and veil-wearing, but it would be wrong to say that they did not find such practices interesting. The Sultan's harem, in particular, was frequently reported in seventeenth-century travelers' tales as a way of sexing-up their accounts. But there is little or no sense in these accounts that the authors are on a personal mission to expand their own sexual identity. Differences in sexual practice come to the fore once travel writing has come, in the Victorian period, to represent a process of individual self-actualization, a way to find the self, which was accessible to both men and women keen to avoid the norms of English gender stereotyping.

Victorian travel accounts became less intent on educating the reader about the facts and customs of foreign lands. Rather they evolved into vehicles for the expression of individual identity development. The author, whether male or female, took center stage of the text, which itself became a metaphor for the struggle of the individual throughout life. Battling against the almost absurd difficulties they sometimes faced, these travelers stood as exemplars of the Romantic reaching personal fulfillment through individual struggle. The desert also took on a metaphorical function in these texts. A geographical carte blanche, the desolate landscapes represented the individual persona laid bare, ready to flourish anew and in new ways once the nourishing waters of experience had been applied. The desert became the perfect place to find the self. And the nomadic Arab himself came to represent the kind of free-thinking, free-roaming character that such a barren landscape could be expected to produce. These were individuals truly untouched by the stifling constraints of Victorian England, who went where the whim took them. Yet they were bound by one thing: tradition. And to many English travelers this seemed peculiarly comforting in an age that had seen so much change in the form of industrialization and domestic urbanization. The timeless quality that these Arab nomads seemed to possess to many conservative-minded English travelers represented the virtues that England had lost during rapid development. What they saw as the noble simplicity of the nomad stood in stark contrast with the kind of degraded, repressed, and subservient individual that England now seemed to produce. These simple and tough wanderers represented nothing less than a modern refashioning of the highest personal virtues of antiquity.

There is also a fourth theme to English historiography and travel writing concerning the Orient, which, though certainly less voluminous, is no less important for that: resistance. Resistance to the genres of history and travel writing; resistance to the tendency to use classical references for conservative purposes; and resistance to the self-congratulatory imperial texts that many British writers produced. Even in the early seventeenth century some writers found the exaggerated claims of early travel accounts ridiculous and mocked their claims. Joseph Hall, for example, wrote spurious accounts of his travels to such places as Pamphagonia, an imaginary land of gluttons, or New Gynia, where women actually ruled.[8] He reminds us not to fall into the trap of thinking that English readers of the day always believed everything that they read. They were perfectly capable of adopting a more skeptical attitude than that of the author they were reading. We also find a few rare examples of writers using classical reference to help them reject the claims of British imperialism. In India, some native writers educated in the Western classics used that knowledge to try to reassert the worth of traditional Indian culture. Bholanauth Chunder's *Travels of a Hindoo* used plentiful classical references to guide the English tourist through the highlights of India, while rejecting the denigration of traditional Indian culture found in many British writers.

Purposes

It is also worth considering why some classical texts were favored at different periods. For when looking at the use of classical examples in English writing, it is clear that certain writers, forms, and indeed literatures have gone in and out of fashion according to the demands of the day. In much of the early anthropological Latin literature of the Middle Ages, for example, Pliny's *Natural Histories* provided an easy recourse to those looking for a classical precedent by which to assert both European superiority and oriental animality. Likewise, during the Crusades, when the Kingdom of Jerusalem was in terminal decline, William of Tyre turned to quoting Juvenal to underline how it was the poor morals of the men of his day that had caused such a situation. He became a satirist, who could do nothing to save his mother city save issue blistering tirades against the softness of the fighting men of his own generation in comparison with the heroes of the First Crusade. How texts were used, therefore, was a matter of purpose.

When we look at the range of purposes for which different periods deployed classical texts, we find that these can be categorized into three broad areas. The first purpose was to help the cause of political conservatism. Many English writers have sought to maintain the status quo and looked to the classics to help them justify this stance. Sandys, for example, was a man who liked to be guided by the past in both social and political matters. But using classical sources to aid stasis was not an act we should see simply as a cynical attempt to bring in any authority that might be thought to help the cause. Sandys believed that classical texts were a source of eternal truth about human society. Any views for which support could not be found in the ancient past were, therefore, untenable. Many other conservative writers were attracted to authors who shared a similar approach in antiquity. It is fair to say that Tacitus heads this list. A source of political wisdom, Tacitus could be used to undercut both the weaknesses of more populist movements and the autocratic tendencies of strong leaders. Likewise, Roman writers such as Horace could be interpreted as a source of conservative public moralizing. Emphasizing his stanzas on moderation and knowledge was a way for political conservatives to resist the claims of more reform- or even revolutionary-minded Englishmen.

Conservatives did not turn only to Latin texts for inspiration and legitimation. In the late Victorian and Edwardian periods, in particular, it was the writers of classical Athens who were thought to show the importance of resisting political reform. Drawing from the Athenian aristocratic class, writers like Plato and Thucydides had always been hostile to the power of the Athenian democracy, seeing democracy itself as being a tyranny of the poor over the rich. Democracy allowed the poor to force the state into funding public pay and entertainments. Democracy allowed the uneducated to rule the wise. This was an approach that appealed to many English aristocrats who had seen so much political power transfer to the middle classes of the male populace during the period. It also attracted many of those upper-class Englishmen who were actively involved in governing Britain's colonies and could see the benefits of texts that propounded the rule of the dangerous masses by a small, classically literate elite.

It is fair to say that the cost of a classical education has generally meant that the rich have benefited from it most, and that this has in turn created a tendency for classical texts to be used to further political conservatism. But this is by no means the whole story. Classics has also been used widely for a second purpose: to push the claims of reform and revolution. In the revolutionary turmoil of the late eighteenth century, for example, Latin authors who had formed part of the emperor Augustus's literary circle, such as Horace and Virgil, came to seem stuffy and politically suspect in comparison with the freedom and naturalness of Homer. The democracy-loving Greeks seemed to provide a far more suitable set of texts for those looking to overthrow the anciens regimes of Europe. The Swiss adventurer Carsten Niebuhr, for example, was the first European to travel across the interior of the Arabian Peninsula and produce an account of it. What for him characterized the Bedouin was their love of liberty. The desert itself seemed to generate the space for individual expression to flourish away from the constraints of social norms. It was a freedom that could be found as far back as antiquity: Niebuhr relates, "There is a striking analogy between the manners ascribed to the ancient *Ichthyophagi*, and those of these Arabs. . . . They prize liberty as highly as do their brethren in the desart."[9]

The third broad purpose to which classics has been put by many English writers has been what we could call "anthropological." Authors who were looking to analyze foreign peoples and customs found it natural to turn to ancient sources such as Herodotus and Tacitus for models of how to achieve this. Tacitus's *Agricola* was especially popular as providing an example of the benefits of civilization, albeit in an account that found some virtues in the barbarians' warlike natures. Writers such as Tacitus and Thucydides were used to provide models of objective history, an objectivity that could be claimed as their inheritance by English writers steeped in these texts. This in itself helped justify their claims about and accounts of far-off cultures by emphasizing the supposed independence of the English recorder. That this could be a problem can be seen in the fact that the highly influential historian of British India, James Mill, never traveled to the subcontinent.

One other area where classical texts have frequently been useful is in debating the role of the individual within society. The Romantics rejected the Romans' carefully contrived refashioning of Greek originals in favor of the originals themselves. Apart from suiting the Romantic taste for the new and creative, Greek texts seemed to possess greater spontaneity and self-expression. They expressed personal emotions in a more natural, freer, and less artificial way than the imitative texts of Roman authors. In particular, they seemed to be the unique works of individual artists, exuding personal sincerity, rather than flattering texts fashioned for some greater imperial purpose. But the nineteenth century also saw classics used for a more conservative expression of thinking about the individual. Many British high imperialists saw Homer as their key text. This was not because they focused on his originality and primitiveness, but because the age of empire looked for heroes to express its highest social ideals. The British Empire had, in their view, been built by great men such as Clive of India, and foundational texts such as the *Iliad* shone with examples of the kind of hard-fighting, high-minded heroes that many British imperialists felt themselves to be. And when the empire was starting to weaken, it was to classical heroes that some British travelers, like Charles Doughty, turned in an attempt to inspire a regeneration of British morals and reinvigorate the flagging Pax Britannica.

What is clear, of course, when looking at these different purposes, is that classical texts were open for reinterpretation. Imperialism sought texts that could be seen as legitimating colonial projects, such as the *Odyssey*. During the expansion of commerce in the Renaissance, by contrast, interpretations of the *Odyssey* focused on its maritime wanderings.[10] In fact, Odysseus can equally be seen as exile, hero, adventurer, or wanderer, to name but a few of his possible interpretations. As in the classical literature itself, what is also apparent from the range of ends to which classics has been deployed as an assistant, is that it is always necessary to examine the political or class agenda of the author and the text.[11] Both social conservatives and radicals have found support from their different readings of the same texts.

Modern writers who have used classics to help them create an image of the East have mostly resisted attempts to impose a single reading onto classical texts. The ancient text now becomes a text within a text, something that problematizes any notion of a single reading. Classical reference also becomes more difficult because it is no longer possible to assume the same level of knowledge in a readership or viewing audience. Writers who know their Herodotus, therefore, have a problem when it comes to utilizing such knowledge. On the one hand, they cannot avoid the classical tradition that has influenced so much of the Western literary canon. On the other, its influence often has to be expressed in an oblique, concealed manner to maintain access among a less classically aware readership. This kind of indirect, or even negative, referencing of the classical past means that even when modern works have no explicit or obvious classical quote, we cannot be sure that there is in fact no classical voice to be heard. As we shall see in Chapter 10, an architectural work like the Vietnam Veterans Memorial defines itself largely in opposition to classical war monuments, while expressing in its reflection of the Washington Monument's Egyptian obelisk an affinity with the republican ideals of the past. The memorial seeks to create a new kind of modern hero, an individual who has lost none of his or her individualism in the pursuit of military and political objectives.

Whatever the purpose or purposes of a classical reference, such usage implicitly and often explicitly establishes a comparison with the ancient world. When used in creating images of the East, such a comparative method sets up a three-way process of measuring English, classical, and oriental cultures, texts, and histories. This process of triangulation, often employed by classical Greek authors, whereby two "others" were used as a kind of adjustable mirror to produce an image of the Greeks, has been a common method of English writers.[12] The side effect of this has been to make the image of the East highly mobile and plastic. Depending on the purpose of the text, the Orient could be adapted to contrast with modern decadence or modern progress. The ancient Persians could, for example, be seen as set in stone—an unchanging and undeveloped empire—as a tactic to emphasize a positive comparison with modern Persia, and so a negative comparison with the modern West. Or classical precedents could be used to highlight contemporary concerns, such as the place of kings in a democracy, as was the case in seventeenth-century England. But just as it would be overly simplistic to see only one orientalist discourse, so there was never any one simple, uncontested view of the ancient past.

The Tropes and Tactics of Classicization

Writers have used classical references to perform multiple tasks in their oriental texts. The following outline of some of the principal of these functions is not in any way exhaustive or closed. One of the reasons ancient sources have been so useful to English writers is precisely because they have been able to bear the burden of such diverse functionality.

To begin with, it is worth remembering that exactly what constitutes a classical reference is not always clear. Often quotations are paraphrased or inaccurate, and allusions are vague or even parodies of the original. We should also bear in mind that references can be experienced variously by the reader: some will interpret the allusion quite differently from the author's intended reading.[13] Above all, it must be realized that attitudes toward conscious imitation of the texts of earlier generations of writers have changed enormously over the past century. Direct imitation is not now admired as a literary quality. Classical referencing still continues, but it is, as we have seen, less explicitly based on earlier models. By contrast, classical authors held quotation, literary recycling, and imitation in the highest regard. Repeated episodes, replicated metaphors, translations, and extended similes were all common. Earlier texts were treated as a shared literary resource for writers to draw upon, and such use revealed respect and even reverence for tradition. Seneca explains that the skilled imitation of earlier forms and models was admired, "not so as to steal but to borrow openly in the hope of being recognised."[14] This was not a question of copying; rather, writers were hoping to improve and reinterpret their forerunners incrementally.

When later English writers, therefore, play the same literary game as their classical forebears of quoting, imitating, and referencing, they are locating themselves and their audience within that same classical tradition. This was a way to establish a textual community that transcended narrow cultural and historical boundaries. Instead, English writing could be seen as being part of the long civilized tradition dating right back to antiquity. Bruce Lincoln has shown how the repeated evocation of sentiments via the invocation of select moments from the past can be used to establish social identities and construct social formations.[15] Modes of literary discourse based on careful quotations from ancient authors therefore helped to construct English society in a form that established a close affinity and attachment between its audiences and their classical predecessors. The purpose was nothing less than to situate England as the rightful inheritor of the classical tradition. Not that the English were simply replicating what the ancients did, but that they were in their own way improving on tradition and the past. It also created a community within the English between author and reader through shared classical knowledge. But this sense of community itself opened up the possibility of more disruptive readings being made. Classical references made with the greatest sincerity could be received in tones of irony or even rejection.

For many writers, to quote the classics was to turn to a store of explanatory truth. When people encountered strange new practices and customs in the East, it was often a natural, knee-jerk response to see what light the ancients could shed to help discern the truth of what was going on. The classics represented the accumulated treasure house of wisdom encapsulating the eternal verities of human nature and it would have been folly to ignore this guide. Closely connected with this view of classics as the accumulated insight of the past, classical reference also often functioned to establish authority within a text and to charter particular views or actions. Credible and revered simply on account of their age, classical sources gave weight to a text and to its author's voice. Lincoln suggests that literary authority is "the capacity to produce consequential speech, quelling doubts and winning the trust [of the audience]." It is a "posited, perceived, or institutionally ascribed asymmetry between speaker and audience that permits certain speakers to command not just the attention but the confidence, respect, and trust of their audience," or make an audience act as if this were so.[16] By helping to generate such authoritative speech, classics helped authors manipulate the responses of their readers toward certain desired ends. Authority must be seen then as an aspect of discourse, in which access to what are perceived as the legitimate instruments of expression is restricted by inequalities such as wealth, education, and status. Creating classically authorized texts was a way to articulate ideas within a larger and more culturally privileged context, so as to help persuade the reader to the appropriate view. In a comparable way, the use of biblical quotations helped set the narrative of events in the context of the unfolding destiny of God's continuing plan. Bringing in the external authoritative classical voice tried to locate the present in the firm embrace of the past. Breaking out from that grip is presented as something akin to foolishness. But that is not to say that such authority and credibility could never be contested. It was always possible to counter such classical references with alternative interpretations or texts.

Alongside such functions as lending veracity and authority, classical quotation provided a source of morality. This was particularly useful when encountering new cultures in the Orient, which might otherwise have challenged the English way of doing things. We therefore find classical imagery used at points of moral emphasis to reinforce the structure of the English view of worth—or at least of the writer's view of the English view of worth. For, as always, we cannot assume that the moral views being expressed are more than the author's own private opinions or simply those of the dominant discourse of the day. We now see that the power of classics stems not from its relationship with the past or truth but from its relation to the contemporary social, political, and moral values that it helps legitimate. In general, classics has been closely associated with many of the core beliefs of Western civilization, however disputed these might be, and so bringing their force to bear in a text has been a way to assert the superiority of Western values over the often imagined values of the Orient.

The great cultural weight that classical sources possessed in English writing meant that they were open to abuse. Often texts were peppered with quotations in what is surely no more than intellectual showing off. Sometimes these references seem to be simply the leftovers of an earlier education, a veneer of learning designed to lend polish to the work, or perhaps worse still, a little learning to give the appearance of more profound classical knowledge. The function of such use is partly self-aggrandizement, but it also highlights another use of classical knowledge, which is to exclude. Works bristling with quotation and allusion to ancient sources are usually understandable only by the educated few, although there are exceptions such as tales that borrow classical stories. That is not to say that "the few" was always synonymous with the English aristocracy. The English elite has historically been permeable, and classical education offered a path by which the upwardly socially mobile might fulfill their aspirations. Classical quotes, in this context, became a bourgeois commodity to be traded en route to social enrichment. For many, of course, classics has acted as a genuine inspiration. The power of the ideas contained within the strongest classical texts has undoubtedly made some see antiquity as a privileged moment in history and Greek and Latin as superior languages: classical inspiration has meant that many writers felt moved to refer to the classics.

Certainly classical antiquity has frequently been employed to highlight and mark off a small elite of white European males and, conversely, to marginalize whatever sections of society that group saw as culturally unacceptable. But it is also clear that not everyone has used classics to support the status quo. Classics has been used in both assent and defiance, to praise authority and to challenge it. Edward Backhouse Eastwick, for example, was a Victorian who did not believe in the glory that was Greece. In his account of his three years' residence in Persia, in 1864, he complains how "young Europe is whipped and schooled into admiration of Greece, till no one dares give a candid opinion. Otherwise, how can men in their senses affect to believe all that stuff about the invasion of Xerxes?"[17] As in this instance, classics itself has brought some to question the overweening importance of classical learning within English culture. Above all, this quote also shows how such contestations of Greece as the privileged locus of civilization were part of the process by which Persia and the Orient were to become, to some extent at least, deorientalized. By applying to oriental cultures the standards of study that the discipline of classics had helped establish, it became clear that places like Persia could no longer simply be dismissed as the barbarian other found in the most ethnocentric of classical Greek literature.

Within the text, classical reference has performed a huge variety of functions. It has entertained, amused, and provided simple ornamentation. It has provided insight but also been used to obscure and deflect the reader from possible readings. It has performed straightforward rhetorical tasks, such as reinforcement through repetition and historical parallel. Classical analogy has also performed a range of roles to propel the narrative of texts forward. Stephen Nimis has argued that analogies and similes should be seen as performing a productive function by offering solutions to specific textual problems.[18] To some extent, then, classical images served as an index of the textual and thematic difficulties the writer had to overcome. Classical reference allowed authors to say things that otherwise would not be said well or not be said at all. It was thought to improve the persuasiveness of the argument with respect to content, clarity, and expression. Or it was used to raise an issue to a higher plane. Often such reference occurred when it was no longer possible for the author to let the subject matter speak for itself. It appeared at points where it was difficult for the writer to generate meaning or get the message across. As such, classical referencing frequently helped to grease these textual blockages. Its appearance may alert us to the possibility that the writer is either creating a smoke screen to prevent the reader from seeing the truth of the argument, or is trying particularly hard to establish some supposed interpretation. Sometimes it is found when texts are in danger of falling apart and helps to cover over the cracks. Often, of course, a text is doing all these things at the same time.

The use of metaphor, simile, and analogy attempted to create close proximity between contemporary England and the ancient world but also sought to regulate the degree of that attachment. To employ metaphor was to make the English become, even momentarily, the Romans and the Greeks. Most commonly this was a tactic used by those seeking to embrace aspects of antiquity wholeheartedly, but it was also adopted by writers seeking to highlight the vices of the

English as being every bit as degraded and degrading as those of the ancients. To use simile, though, was to establish the English as like the ancients in important respects but also to maintain a safe distance in certain others. This was a tactic Sandys used in reverse in the description of the Janissaries we saw earlier: they were troops that retained "something of Antiquity." Sandys is keen to limit the comparison between the Ottoman troops and the heroes of ancient mythology, an undercutting that we have seen was emphasized by using the "not so spirited Paris" as the comparator. Often this desire to maintain distance was driven by the difference in religious outlook between the pagan world of antiquity and Christian England. Many writers were fearful of aligning themselves too closely with what seemed the dangerously relaxed social morals of antiquity. Instead, they wished to keep a clear sense of England's future being a distinct part of God's plan. Likewise, the use of analogy maintained important differences between the classical world and that of the English. This was particularly important for those who sought to paint an image of the future of the English empire that was more optimistic than comparison with the Roman world would otherwise create. British imperialist writers in the Victorian and Edwardian periods were particularly fond of this approach. By comparing ancient and modern empires, the British were established as analogous to the Romans in important areas—their virtue, their discipline, their civilization—but fundamentally different in others, above all their political system and their morals. Again it is worth noting that it was in discussions of religion and morality that comparison with antiquity generated the greatest difficulties for many English writers. Radically different ancient attitudes toward sexuality posed great difficulties for many English writers seeking to draw parallels between these two eras. The British were also keen to establish their rule as being far less corrupt and so less likely to end in failure.

3

Classics and Medieval Images of Islam

English views of Islam did not arise from a vacuum. The previous chapter highlighted some of the many, varied purposes and uses to which classical texts were put by English authors in their own writings. But the English were not the first to approach the challenges of dealing with Islam and the Orient. Well over half a millennium of contact between Islam and Christendom had taken place before English travelers first encountered Islam. And despite a great deal of military, religious, and cultural conflict with each other, most Christians in Northern Europe as a whole, let alone England, had little direct experience of Islam. Unlike the Byzantines, whose empire was most affected by the Arab invasions and who had to live with this new reality on their doorstep, most Northern Europeans were either ignorant of or indifferent to the rise of Islam during its first three hundred years or so. But as Arab power spread and Christendom was pushed back farther north into the European mainland, fear, awe, and curiosity about this dangerous new arrival grew. These largely hostile early opinions were to have a long-lasting and widespread influence on many subsequent English views of the Orient and Islam. This chapter examines the kinds of images that arose in Christendom during the Middle Ages—and in particular the period of the Crusades, as these wars were to disseminate such hostile opinion more widely in Northern Europe—and shows how these views often relied on ancient sources for their strength and were influenced by classical precedent.

In his famous book on Western views of Islam in the Middle Ages, Richard Southern argued that in understanding Islam, the West "could get no help from antiquity, and no comfort from the present. For an age avowedly dependent on the past for its materials, this was a serious matter."[1] He was right to emphasize the fact that this was an age where people tried to understand the world by transporting it into the medium of respected classical authorities, searching for truth via dependence on the revered texts of antiquity, which remained the "surest guide" available.[2] I think, though, that he attached too little importance to the role that the classical past still had to play in constructing an image of this new religion. Christian perceptions of Islam were filtered through a combination of the biblical and the classical, so that in the end they came to be based less on Islam itself than Christian preconceptions of divine history and antiquity. Assessed within such a framework, Islam was seen variously as a Christian heresy, a resurgence of paganism, a punishment sent by God to scourge the impious Christians, a fraud, and a monstrosity. The use of classical sources played an important part in the establishment of all these medieval images.

For many Christian writers the appearance of a new religious group in the East was nothing new or remarkable. Arabia lay on the edge of the Christian world, and it seemed natural to view Islam as yet another of the numerous heresies that had arisen over the centuries in the theological hothouse of the Eastern Mediterranean.

Muhammad was certainly not the first prophet Christians had encountered who worshipped one almighty God but denied the existence of the Trinity. The long-running Arian controversy had rumbled on in the eastern half of the Roman Empire for centuries after it first arose in Egypt in the early fourth. Christian thinkers were well versed in dealing with what they saw as heretical religious sects of this kind, and they possessed the great volumes of writings of the church fathers to help guide them in their refutation of each point of doctrinal controversy. In many ways the Muslims appeared to possess a close intellectual parallel with the Jews, a religion about which Christian theologians had written many detailed rebuttals. Islam fitted neatly, therefore, into a preexisting heretical framework for interpreting the religious other. The classical-era precedent and model for all such heresiarchs was the ancient false prophet Simon Magus: a demonically inspired false messenger who impressed the emperor Nero and allegedly indulged in all kinds of sexual debauchery.[3]

Islam was also labeled as a resurgence of ancient paganism. If the Christian writer could successfully portray Muslims as a continuation of the classical tradition of idolatry, this would show that this upstart religion, far from being new, was nothing more than a more recent form of backward-looking superstition. Ecclesiastical writers schooled in the Latin classics had a "vivid image of pagan worship, an image they transposed to create a portrait of the religious error of the 'pagan' Saracens."[4] Muslims, therefore, were commonly portrayed as worshipping various gods, in medieval art often shown as classical stone statues encrusted with jewels: Apollo, Jupiter, Juno, and Mars all feature, as do Diana, the Devil, and the Antichrist. Or they are shown adoring a divine trio of Tervagan (also called Termagant), Mahomet, and Apollo, a kind of false trinity set up in opposition to the true Christian Trinity. The account of the life of Thiemo, archbishop of Salzburg, who died in the Crusade of 1101, describes how he encounters the Saracen pagans, who are led by three brothers from Corosan, "who in their ferocity were more tyrannical and in their cult more pagan than Decius." How better to emphasize their fanatical anti-Christian paganism than to liken them to that Roman emperor who had first systematically tried to stamp out Christianity and reassert the values and worship of the traditional Roman Pantheon? Like all good Christian missionaries against the pagan, Thiemo then embarks on a campaign of smashing idols and preaching against the worship of Saturn, Jove, and, significantly, Priapus, the ancient god of fertility.[5] This is not to say that medieval Christian writers had a wholly negative view of the Roman Empire. Far from it. Rome had obviously made a significant positive contribution to Christian history. Some even argued that the emperor Philip the Arab, who ruled from 244 to 249, had in fact been the first, closeted, Christian emperor and had clandestinely furthered the Christian cause.[6] But that role was now over. The world had moved into a new stage of God's plan for humanity, and any new religion that was seen to be turning the clock back to the times of pagan supremacy was both theologically flawed and potentially highly dangerous.

Some saw Islam as lacking the support of philosophers, especially Aristotle, and as being deficient in internal logic.[7] Others saw Muhammad as a religious fraud who sought to facilitate his desire to expand his power and so gain opportunities to satisfy his unnatural lusts. In the same way that some writers suggested that the Muslims worshipped Priapus as a way of emphasizing this, there were frequents attempts to link Muslims with Venus worship. All these connotations of lewdness drew on ancient perceptions of the East as a place of loose sexual morality, the idea being that the physical heat of the place must necessarily result in human beings of certain sexual proclivities. Various myths in the Middle Ages promoted the idea of Muhammad being associated with homosexuality, prostitution, and adultery. In this way the sensuality associated with the East was concentrated onto the personage of Muhammad in order to generate an anti-ideal of the morals of Christ. The supposed facts of the Prophet's life were presented as "an essential disproof of the Islamic claim to revelation."[8] How could he be the successor to Christ when his private morality was the very opposite? Of course, these claims had no basis in any evidence. Rather, as Islam became more successful and expanded farther westward, it was no longer sufficient to see it as a short-term divine punishment sent to whip the Christians into shape: Islam was here to stay, and it posed a threat to the Christian communities on and within its borders. Within the conquered lands, many Christians—in Syria and Egypt, for example—had started to convert, attracted by the desire to keep in with the new powers-that-be or to avoid paying tribute, or by the simplicity of the religion itself. There was an urgent need, therefore, to forge polemical, hostile Muslim stereotypes in order to put off apostasy.

As a result, the Christian image of the Muslim degenerated into a caricature of the antithesis of Christian values. Islam was portrayed as a material religion whose followers were in the thrall of power, wealth, and sex. Muslims were thought to be naively credulous to believe so obvious a set of lies as were peddled by Muhammad, who was himself ridiculed as being an epileptic, demon-possessed fraud. The Quran was dismissed as being repetitive and disorderly, lacking the kind of rational logic supposedly found in the Christian Bible. A new biblical tradition was created, one that saw the Saracens as claiming to be descended from Abraham's wife, Sarah, when in fact they were the offspring of his slave girl, Hagar, also known as Ishmael, hence polemical writers often addressed them as Hagarenes or Ishmaelites.[9] Islam was now for many the very opposite of all the Roman church stood for, a view that was only encouraged by the Arab sack of Rome and St. Peter's in 846. In the 850s, the Spanish writer Paul Alvarus went so far as to present Muhammad as the precursor of the Antichrist, following on from the Roman emperors Domitian and Nero. And in the French chronicler Aimoin's account of the removal of the bones of those who had died resisting the Arabs in Spain, the process has become the equivalent of the translation of the relics of those who had been martyred by the Romans in their persecutions of the early Christians, with the Muslims taking on the role of the pagan oppressors.[10]

In this process of demonization, the Muslim was held up as a terrible warning to Christian souls of the degenerate state that awaited them if they failed to stay acutely vigilant against the temptations the devil put before them. The alleged sensuousness of Islam could easily entice the unsuspecting believer into a vortex of physical decay that would see them end up as the helper of the Antichrist itself. This notion of the transmutability of the body was also expressed in terms of the animalization of the Saracens.[11] As in classical thought, the monstrous was also linked to place, so the Arabs were seen as a product of their geography. The heat made them crude and violent. The third-century Latin writer, Solinus, describes the harsh deserts stretching to the Gulf of Arabia. At the extremity of the eastern part of this region live a people with a monstrous appearance: some have no noses, others drink through a straw because of their small mouths.[12] The desert itself became a physical stage for the Western Christian unconscious to act out its fantasies of wildness.[13] A widespread link was imagined between the Saracens and Cynocephali, a monstrous race who, instead of a human head, had that of a dog.[14] In medieval art, dogs often stood for the Jews and Christian heretics, those who knowingly rejected the truth of Christ, and so it seemed natural to link Muslims in with this group.[15] In classical interpretations, the appearance of the monstrous was generally treated as a portent, a disruption of the natural order that boded ill for the wider community. In the Christian mind, though, the monstrous beast acted as a sure sign of God's power over the natural world and his ability to adapt it for didactic purposes. The representation of the Muslim as a dog-headed beast was therefore closely connected with the idea of his being sent as a divine spur to better Christian behavior. Much of such writing, however, is concerned primarily to boost Christianity by creating an anti-ideal and to debase Islam by ridiculing its beliefs. We can see this most clearly in some accounts of Muhammad's death. In Christian accounts of the lives of saints, the exact mode of death was always of the highest significance as, through its extreme suffering, it bore out in the most perfect manner possible the saint's utter rejection of the physical world in favor of the love of Christ. Muhammad's death, therefore, became equally important and in the cacographies created for him, it was claimed that he had been eaten by dogs or even, in a supremely offensive twist, devoured by pigs.

Hostile images such as these were created at a time when Christendom was unable to defeat or even contain Islam militarily, and so was reduced to trying to control it intellectually. Symbolically, they represent Christian powerlessness rather than strength, nothing more than the vicious slurs and insults hurled by the weak against the strong. By denigrating Islam they hoped to reaffirm the Christian values which were so palpably under threat. They were aimed, of course, primarily at a domestic readership—such texts would not have circulated in the Muslim world—and have the explicit aim of trying to ward off apostasy. They reflect a growing disquiet at the loss of both Christian territory and believers to the new religion and a fear that this was a trend that would gather pace. The harsh image of Islam was a consequence of a worldview that saw truth as eternal and Christian, and any deviation from that as the work of the devil. It divided the world into "us" and "them."

No simple division can be drawn for this time, however, between what constituted the East and the West. Indeed, concepts such as the "West" and "Europe" were in their infancy, with "Christendom" being a far more common term. Even this was problematic, though, as the Byzantine Empire did not recognize the authority of the pope in Rome. The Byzantine Empire acted as a military, religious, and intellectual buffer zone between such conceptual polarities as East and West and mediated most Western engagement with the Orient. Before the Crusades, the Latin west of Europe was as much, if not more, concerned with dealing with the problems posed by the Byzantine Empire as with the more nebulous threat of a far-off new religion such as Islam. By the time of the First Crusade in 1096, the Byzantine Empire, usually then known as the Eastern Roman Empire, had already had over four hundred years of intensive contact with the Muslim world. The Byzantines had had to learn to live with a powerful neighbor, which had in early conquests taken great swaths of their territory. Some Byzantine writers saw the Arabs as a divine retribution for Christian sins, which was a model of barbarian agency they had already used to explain the fall of the Western Roman Empire in the fifth century.[16] Because this did not signal any divine approval for Islam, merely God's wish to use these terrifying warriors as a means to bringing about a Christian end, such a view did not entail evaluating the worth, if any, of Islam. But as it became clear that Islam posed a far more fundamental threat, Byzantine writing became more openly hostile in an attempt to stem the flow of conversion that was happening in previously Byzantine-controlled provinces. Islam was portrayed as an extreme heresy with heavy pagan overtones. Yet close contact brought with it greater knowledge and some more sympathetic response. For example, the Byzantine emperor Alexius I wrote to Robert, Count of Flanders, appealing for help for Constantinople, "a miraculous city and a second Rome which is worthy of having the whole world come together to help it." He describes how the Arab conquerors had mistreated Christian holy sites: "After Christianity was driven out, the churches which the pagans held had been turned into stables for horses, mules and other animals." But being familiar with some of the details of the Muslim religion, he explains that even though it was also true that they had set up temples, which they called "Mahomeries," they "did not think that he was God" but a "just man and leader." Byzantine emperors also treated Arab guests well. The tenth-century emperor Constantius VII wrote a book of protocol for his son and successor; called *On Ceremonies*, it included formulae for welcoming ambassadors from Baghdad and Cairo. The importance of the Arabs in Byzantine affairs meant that these dignitaries were to occupy a higher place at table than the emissaries of the "Franks," as those from the west of Europe were known.[17]

Conflicts sometimes arose between Latin and Byzantine Christians over the meaning and ownership of the Roman inheritance. For example, in Liudprand of Cremona's account of his embassy to Constantinople in 968, on which he was sent by the future Holy Roman Emperor Otto II, we find the pope writing a letter to the Byzantine emperor Nicephorus in which he addresses him as "the emperor of the Greeks" and Otto as "august emperor of the Romans."[18] The Byzantines, Liudprand tells us, were livid. "The audacity of it!" they cried, "To call the universal emperor of the Romans, the one and only Nicephorus, the great, the august, 'emperor of the Greeks,' and to style a poor barbaric creature 'emperor of the Romans'!" Their rage was such that they shouted that if they were worth punishing, "we would sew them in a sack, and after giving them a sound beating with rods and plucking out their beards and hair, we would throw them into the sea." They blamed the pope's ignorance for this misallocation of the Roman title: "The silly blockhead of a Pope does not know that the sacred Constantine transferred to this city the imperial scepter, the senate, and all the Roman knighthood, and left in Rome nothing but vile slaves, fishermen, confectioners, poulterers, bastards, plebeians, underlings."

Byzantine writers also employed classical texts to help them create negative images of their neighbors, both eastern and western. Anna Comnena was a princess in the court at Constantinople, the eldest child of the emperor Alexius I, born in 1083 in the purple chamber of the imperial palace. Exiled after a clumsy attempt to assassinate her younger brother, who had inherited the throne, she was sent into a comfortable convent where she turned to scholarship and history. Her account of her father's reign, the *Alexiad*, is of interest not only because it is one of the first works by a female historian but also because it provides a view of the Crusades from a Byzantine point of view. An expert in the philosophy of Aristotle and writing in a highly artificial, classicalesque Greek style, she lets her work bristle with ancient references designed both to illuminate her arguments and show off her learning. Anna commonly refers to the Muslims in the text as barbarians, ascribing to them the same stupidity sometimes anciently assigned to the Persians. Although proximity meant that Byzantine scholars and aristocrats were much better acquainted with the Muslim world than the Latin West, that does not stop Anna from turning to pagan stereotypes when it suits her. The First Crusade, she wrote, would "bring dreadful afflictions upon the barbarian Ishmaelites, who were the slaves of drunkenness and wine and Dionysus. The Ishmaelites are indeed dominated by Dionysos and Eros; they indulge readily in every kind of sexual license, and if they are circumcised in the flesh they are certainly not so in their passions. In fact, the Ishmaelites are nothing more than slaves—trebly slaves—of the vices of Aphrodite."[19]

But Anna reserved at least something of the contempt she felt for the barbarian Turk for the Franks of the West. "[They are] an exceptionally hotheaded race and passionate, but let them once find a cause and they become irresistible."[20] The battle between the Muslims and the Franks in the First Crusade will be an epic one, and Anna appropriately turns to Homer for imagery to describe the drama. To underline the strangeness of the Arab mode of fighting, she mentions how their battle line differed from other people's: "It was not arranged, as Homer says, 'shield to shield, helmet to helmet, man to man.' "[21] It is, in fact, knowledge of Homer that seems in the *Alexiad* to mark out the Byzantines as being more civilized, both through their greater education and on account of their having had the torch of ancient Greek learning passed on to them. After the second battle of Ramla in 1102, a defeat for the Crusaders that came as a grievous shock to Anna's father, his imperial spirit was so sensitive to the heroic that "the thought of the Counts being held in captivity was intolerable. To him these men, in the prime of their life, at the height of their strength, of noble lineage seemed to rival the heroes of old." This thought drives him to action, and he decides they must no longer remain as prisoners in a foreign land. He therefore donated plenty of money to ransom them.[22]

Writers like Liudprand of Cremona and Anna Comnena show us that no simple East/West divide existed in the Middle Ages. The Byzantine world existed as a kind of intellectual hybrid that mediated the transition from the Occident to the lands under Arab domination. In fact, Anna's beloved and hard-pressed father, Alexius, had triggered the First Crusade by asking for help against the Arabs as they pushed to within striking distance of Constantinople itself. In many ways the Crusades created a more widespread and uncompromising image of the Muslim throughout Western Christendom as a polar opposite of the Christian. Edith Hall suggests that the

Crusades popularized an image of Islam and Muslims "comprising savagery, depravity, sexual profligacy, pagan darkness, and satanic evil—which has consistently resurfaced, in slightly modified forms, even to our day."[23] The Crusades created a demand back home for news about the enemy that Christian soldiers were facing in the East, and ancient negative stereotypes acted as a useful shorthand for people to readily understand this unfamiliar world. Muslim details were grafted onto images of ancient barbarism to form a powerful fusion of symbolic forms that combined familiar motif and contemporary observation.[24] The twelfth-century English historian William of Malmesbury gave an account of Pope Urban II's call to Crusade in 1095 at the Council of Clermont in central France. It shows how classical preconceptions helped shape some of the pope's ideas: the struggle is presented as a battle of a universal Christian civilization against narrow-minded barbarians who lived like brutes. Pope Urban's letter to Mahomet II also expressed what he saw as the superiority of the West in terms of its classical heritage.

An appropriate conclusion to this survey is to now turn to the writings of two of the chroniclers of the Crusades, to see how important a role ancient sources played in helping them establish their various images of the Islamic enemy. Classical imagery helped to validate the notion of Crusading. The idea of the Greeks and Romans battling with barbarians made the Crusades seem a natural part of historical continuity. It gave the Crusades an air of heroism and enhanced legitimacy. Guibert of Nogent composed his account, *Gesta Dei per Francos* [*The Deeds of God Done through the Franks*], in 1108. Although he relied heavily on a slightly earlier anonymous account, the *Gesta Francorum*, he added much material of his own and rewrote it in a far more highbrow Latin.[25] A deeply conservative, religious man, Guibert spent his whole life in northern France. His account, therefore, contains nothing that he himself had witnessed, though he had no difficulty with this: "hearsay is almost as good as seeing," he says. For, and here he quotes Horace, although " 'What has been thrust into the ears stirs the mind more slowly than those things which have appeared before reliable eyes', nevertheless, who doubts those historians who wrote the lives of the saints."[26] This highlights one of the tensions that run throughout Guibert's work: the tension between the classical and Christian traditions. As an educated man, Guibert respected the ancients and naturally turned to them for authoritative opinion. Many of their works he considered to be close to perfection. Yet Christianity must come first, even if that meant that the Christian sources could sometimes do no more than reproduce the achievements of antiquity. So regardless of what Horace says about eyes, it is the ears of the Christian hagiographers that must take precedent. Guibert's was a work where, however much he relied upon the comparative method and however much he held ancient achievements in esteem, they had been superseded by the Christian era.

Guibert, then, was no slave to classical sources. In the opening to the first book, he criticizes those who "have developed the foul habit of praising previous times and attacking what modern men do." Guibert concedes that "the ancients should be praised for the way in which they balanced good fortune with restraint, as well as for the way in which thoughtfulness controlled their use of energy." But he is adamant that "no discerning individual could prefer in any way the temporal prosperity of the ancients to any of the strengths of our own day." What made life so much better in his day was, of course, the possibility for salvation that the spread of Christianity allowed. However much people in his day "admire Philip for his merciless slaughter and victories everywhere," or "commend with resounding rhetoric the fury of Alexander, who emerged from the Macedonian forge to destroy the entire East," or "measure the magnitude of the troops of Xerxes at Thermopylae," yet "if the essence of these things were laid bare," while their bravery would be considered praiseworthy, what could not be overlooked, and in fact deserved reproach, would be "the relentless madness of fighting without good reason, only for the sake of ruling." Quoting Lucan, he emphasizes the stupidity of waging war "that could win no triumphs."[27] The only true triumph was the salvation of the soul. So none of the wars of the pagans of antiquity were "comparable in any way to ours." For "God ordained holy wars in our time" to give all the chance to "find a new way of earning salvation."

Many of Guibert's worst allegations are, in fact, reserved for non-Latin Christians. Eastern Christians are portrayed as possessing an ingrained tendency toward heresy: "We wonder at . . . the sordidness of the Egyptians, the instability of the Asiatics, as described by Trogus Pompeius and other fine writers."[28] For the faith of Easterners has never been stable, "but has always been variable and unsteady, searching for novelty, always exceeding the bounds of true belief." He attributes this natural leaning toward heresy to the climate: it is "because of the purity of the air and the sky in which they are born, as a result of which their bodies are lighter and their intellects consequently more agile."[29] The Latin west of Europe, however, was, in Guibert's mind, as it had always been, a place of solid orthodoxy: "Read through the catalogues of all heresies; consider the books of the ancients against heretics; I would be surprised if, with the exception of the East and Africa, any books about heretics could be found in the Roman world." Nor did heresy only spring up in the old eastern provinces of the Roman Empire; the whole of the East was characterized by these errors: "Out of Alexandria came Arius, out of Persia Manes"—Manes, the founder of Manichaeism, whose "fictions," although "ridiculous, nevertheless deceived the sharpest minds far and wide with its trickery." The East seemed to be a teeming torrent of heretical fervor: "What should I say about the Eunomians, the Eutychians, the Nestorians, how can I represent the thousands of hideous groups whose frenzy against us was so relentless?" It resulted in political discord and, to Guibert, was wholly attributable to "Asiatic instability" and "foolishness." The eastern provinces of Rome had, by losing sight of the true faith, therefore brought the Islamic yoke upon their own heads: "For since they fell away from faith in the Trinity, like those who fall in the mud and get muddier, little by little they have come to the final degradation of having taken paganism upon themselves; as the punishment for their sins proceeded, foreigners attacked them, and they lost the soil of their native land."

The heightened hostility toward Islam in Christian sources during the Crusades is particularly reflected in Guibert's scandalous account of the life of Muhammad. Guibert had looked for theological refutation of Muhammad in the early church fathers but had found none, which was unsettling for a man who liked to speak "from the security of patristic authority."[30] Guibert also had very few details about Muhammad and was forced to rely upon rumor: "According to popular opinion, there was a man, whose name, if I have it right, was Mathomus," who "gave them free rein for every kind of shameful behavior. I do not think that this profane man lived a very long time ago, since I find that none of the church doctors has written against his licentiousness." Linking him to the ancient heresies, he describes him as a hermit who was "like Arius" and, having been rejected as patriarch of the Alexandrian church, "began to think carefully how to take vengeance by spreading the poison of false belief, to undermine Catholic teaching everywhere." His account was not all ill-informed or scurrilous: only Guibert of writers of the time recognized that Muhammad was a prophet, not a divine figure, and that Muslims were not pagans but monotheists. But his hostility is clearly seen in his retelling of the story of Muhammad's alleged death: that while suffering an epileptic fit he was eaten by swine who left only his heel. For added emphasis, he also associates the Prophet with the teachings of Epicurus to emphasize the sensuousness of his beliefs, so problematic to the Christian thinker: "While the true Stoics, that is, the worshippers of Christ, killed Epicurus, lo, the greatest law-giver tried to revive the pig, in fact he did revive it, and, himself a pig, lay exposed to be eaten by pigs, so that the master of filth appropriately died a filthy death." It was as if being eaten by pigs was simply divine retribution for all the previous heretical beliefs of the Greeks. Guibert concludes that it is fitting that only Muhammad's heel was left, as Muhammad had "fixed traces of false belief and foulness" everywhere, and goes so far as to "make an epitaph for his heels in four lines of the poet" by adapting Horace's famous lines:[31] " 'He who has lived by the pig is chewed to death by the pig and the limbs which were called blessed have become pigs' excrement. May those who wish to honour him carry to their mouths his heels, which the pig has poured forth in stench.' " Relishing these "comic remarks intended to mock" Muhammad's followers, Guibert speculates about whether there is "some truth in what the Manicheans say about purification?"—that there is a part of God in all food that is turned into angels when it leaves the body in belching and farting: "How many angels may we believe were produced by the flesh eaten by these pigs and by the great farts they let go?"[32]

Such offensive abuse reflects Guibert's robust joy in the Crusaders' early successes. It is clear from his polemical account what the Crusades were trying to achieve: in the context of the aftermath of a fallen Roman Empire, they were both reclaiming Christian land and damning heretics. It is interesting to compare Guibert's work with that of a later and more influential chronicler of the Crusades, William of Tyre.[33] His *History of Deeds Done beyond the Sea* was written between 1170 and 1184 and is particularly notable because it is the only source for this period produced by a native of the Kingdom of Jerusalem. Although being from the coastal city of Tyre by birth, William received an expensive education in Europe, which is reflected in the elegant Latin style of the text. It is also evident in the many classical influences in his work.[34] Although written only two generations after Guibert's account, it has an altogether less triumphalist tone. The steam had run out of the Crusades, and a combination of European indifference and Muslim revival under Saladin meant that the pressure was beginning to tell on the Kingdom. William is trying to analyze the cause of this decline and, as a result, be in a position to propose a means for reversing it.

William is keen to locate himself within the classical tradition. As a citizen of Tyre he may have felt out on a limb in comparison with most of his intended readership. He takes great pains to underscore the city's Western links, its heritage, and its loyalty: quoting the Latin lawyer Ulpian in the start of the thirteenth book, he describes how the city "with its commanding position, great antiquity, and prowess in arms, held tenaciously to the treaty which she had made with the Romans. The divine Severus, our emperor, granted Italian rights to the city as a reward for its signal loyalty towards the republic and the empire of Rome." It is a city, he claims, that has been at the heart of Europe ever since its mythological foundation: "To this city, if we hark back to ancient stories, belonged king Agenor and his children, Europa, Cadmus, and Phoenix. It is from the latter as the Phoenicians claim, that the whole region derives its name. The other son, Cadmus, founded the city of Thebes and was also the inventor of the Greek alphabet. . . . The remaining child, a daughter, gave her name to the third part of the globe, which is called Europe." It is the city where the Greek alphabet itself, the building blocks for so much Greek cultural achievement, was invented. It is worth noting that he is equally keen to distance himself from the Eastern Romans, although on the whole his attacks on the Byzantines are of a lesser ferocity than most. He describes how the Greek emperor had "always envied the successful advances of the Christians. For it is well known that the Greeks have always looked with distrust on all the increase of power by the Western nations (as they still do), especially by that of the Teutonic nation, as rivals of the empire." As Liudprand had earlier discovered, "They take it ill that the king of the Teutons calls himself the emperor of the Romans. For thereby he seems to detract too much from the prestige of their own emperor."[35]

The main issue that William was trying to understand was why the early successes of the Crusaders had not been repeated. He wonders "why it was that our fathers, though less in number, so often bravely withstood in battle the far larger forces of the enemy and that often by divine grace a small force destroyed the multitudes of the enemy." In contrast to this, he muses, "the men of our times too often have been conquered by inferior forces."[36] One explanation is that their forefathers had been heroes of an epic kind. They were "religious men and feared God." But in their place, "a wicked generation has grown up, sinful sons. . . . From such, because of their sins, the Lord justly withdraws His favour, as if provoked to wrath." It is life in the East that he argues has softened them: "Such are the men of the present age, especially those dwelling in the East. One who would undertake with careful pen to portray their morals, or rather their monstrous vices, would succumb under the vast amount of material; in short, he would seem to be writing satire rather than completing history." He has, in other words become a latter-day Juvenal, watching in horror the degraded behavior of his people, powerless to correct it save by writing satire. And the result of such softness and decay is, for William, an inevitable loss in military capability. So the reason the Christians besieged the fortress of Harim without result was that "they were given over to frivolity and paid more attention to games of chance and other evil pleasures than military discipline or the rules of siege operations permitted." They succumbed to the urban delights of Antioch, where "they spent their time at the baths and at banquets and indulged in drunken debauches and other pleasures of the flesh. . . . Even those who seemed to be assiduous in attendance there became lazy and careless and accomplished nothing of importance. They passed their time in idleness and led vicious lives."[37]

By the preface to the twenty-third book, William is discussing the likelihood of Jerusalem being saved. In his view it is a moral decline, akin to that which affected ancient Rome, that is the issue. He is in "utter detestation of the present, amazed at the material which is presented before our eyes and ears"; he hears tales of sexual immorality that would be "unfit to be told even in the songs of a Codrus," one of the rustic poets of Virgil's *Eclogues*, poems full of the political turbulence of late republican Rome.[38] William believed the situation had become very bad. "We have now reached a point where, [quoting Livy] 'We can endure neither our evils nor their remedy.'"[39] In despair, William must stop writing and "draw the shades of night over our failures." He recognizes, however, that some people wish him to carry on recording the history of the Kingdom of Jerusalem, so that every phase "adverse as well as prosperous, might be recorded in this work for posterity." They encourage him by citing examples of the "most distinguished historians, namely Titus Livius, who recorded in his history not only the successes of the Romans, but also their reverses," and also Josephus, who made known "not only the brilliant deeds of the Jews, but also those shameful things which were done to them." Such classical allusions freshen his resolve to continue with his previous determination, but the book stops at this point.

What these chronicles show us is that the simplest approach to explaining the rationale of the Crusades was to place it in the ancient context of the struggle between Christian and pagan. Crusading represented in some ways a radical new form of piety, a combination of pilgrimage and military ardor, but it also reflected a desire to continue the struggle of the Apostles and martyrs of the early church who died to free Christians from the oppression of pagan Rome. In the accounts of the First Crusade it is clear that it is "as much a fight over time as it is over space"; it is a struggle to "reestablish the age of Christ and His Apostles in the land in which they lived, preached, and died." As such, the crusaders defeat the Muslim "pagans" by purifying the holy soil, polluted by the pagan occupation, with the blood of new martyrs and by destroying the pagans' idols in order to get history back on a Christian timeline.[40] The Muslims, therefore, were cast in their role as the new pagans and persecutors so that they might play their part in the fulfilling of God's plan for humanity. The polemical, almost jingoistic, accounts that accompanied the successes of the First Crusade have by William's time given way to a more pessimistic outlook. Both found inspiration in the ideas they had inherited from antiquity.

The Crusades had another side effect, which was that they brought cultural contact as well as military conflict. From the mid-twelfth century, more accurate Western observations about Islam can be found alongside such hostile accounts. In 1143, at Cluny, Peter the Venerable arranged for the first translation of the Quran into Latin. In Spain, the long, drawn-out process of *reconquista* meant that some writers, like Ramon Llul, wished to engage with Islam on intellectual terms. By the start of the thirteenth century, when it was clear that the Crusades were struggling, the effort against Islam was slowly transferred toward the first missionary efforts.[41] The replacement of military action with mission was a slow process, and also risky, given that it was known that Islam prohibited attacks on the Muslim creed. It is not surprising that few wanted to go. And by the early fourteenth century when it had become patently clear, especially after the fall of Acre in 1291, that neither crusade nor mission had worked, a more pessimistic view of Christian relations with Islam prevailed. For many, no possibility of positive engagement seemed left.

Given the long period of hostilities, it is perhaps not surprising that many of the more offensive images of the earlier traditions became an easy fallback for early English writers. As far back as Bede, the distant and obscure Muslims were described as Saracens and Venus worshippers who were punished for their *perfidia*, their religious error.[42] Katharine Scarfe-Beckett rightly argues that it was the appealing solidity of concepts such as Hagar and Venus that helped "crystallise notions of Saracen illegitimacy or venality repeatedly around the same 'factual' core."[43] Assumptions of an equivalence between Islam and Roman paganism were common: the Middle English version of the travels of John Mandeville, written in about 1356 in the tradition of pilgrim guides to the Holy Land, describes a Roman idol of Jupiter as a "maumette."[44] Also common were accusations of heresy: Gerald of Wales compares Muhammad to the great heretic of the Roman Empire, Arius.[45] Lydgate's *Fall of Princes*, written in the 1430s in rural England and adapted from Boccaccio's *De casibus virorum illustrium*, provided an instructive account of the falls of great men throughout history. It relies of stock images of Islam for its polemical effect. The Saracens worship Venus and hence the text has them worship Friday, the *dies veneris* in the Roman calendar, to emphasize their sensuality.[46] At about the same time, one medieval tale, *The Sowdone of Babylone* (The Sultan of Babylon), included descriptions of Muhammad worshipping characters as diverse as the pharaoh, Herod, and the emperor Augustus.[47] And with gratuitous offensiveness, Lydate resorts to that old claim that Muhammad had "Lik a glotoun deied in dronkenesse" and that he "Fill in a podel, devoured among swyn."[48] But such bigotry did not stem from direct contact with the East. These views had been imported from hostile sources from overseas. Greater interaction was to bring a far more sophisticated and nuanced range of English responses to the East, which continued to rely heavily on classical models for their image creation. But the negative stereotypes that classical texts had helped establish in the Middle Ages never completely went away.

PART II

Texts

4

Traders and Travelers

Islam posed a double threat to early modern Europe. Militarily it could not be defeated; religiously, it could not be converted. Many of the more unreconstructed medieval views of Islam survived into this period. Christendom was now coming into conflict with the Ottoman Turks, and generally coming off the worse, and unsurprisingly the medieval corpus of Muslim-hating crusading literature had great appeal. It is easy to find endless chronicles of Turkish brutality: carnage, sacrilege against Christian holy places, the brutal enslavement of Christian children, and the rape of Christian women abound. This polemic shared the same objective of its antecedents: to make conversion to the religion of the Mediterranean's most powerful and wealthy state less attractive to its Christian audience. It served up vicarious victory to a readership hungry for success and fearful of what the seemingly endless advance of the Turk would mean for the inhabitants of northern Europe. With the fall of Constantinople in 1453, that great buffer zone between the central regions of Europe and the Muslim empire had finally been swept away. There was now a new power for Western seafaring nations to deal with. Moreover, Europeans had to adapt to growing Turkish power at the same time as it was undergoing great convulsions of change itself. The Reformation and the invention of the printing press were having enormous repercussions throughout the continent. The end of the Eastern Roman Empire also meant the end of any meaningful attempt to reunite the Roman and Orthodox Christian Churches. Greek culture now lay in the trusteeship of the Latin West and defined itself even more sharply in opposition to the so-called barbarian conquerors from the East.

Despite all this anti-Turkish rhetoric there was a very practical need to deal with their empire. The best that could now be hoped for was peaceful coexistence and military containment. Any thoughts of crusade or missionary conversion were gone. One of the main problems of coming to terms with the Turk was the fact that it was such an unstable identity. Were they upstart usurpers of the old Arab empire or sophisticated imperialists? People in the West just did not have sufficient information about these strange new Easterners to be able to form a comfortable opinion. In some ways, though, the lack of a coherent image of the Turk simply reflected an equal lack of coherency in the idea of what it meant to be a Christian. The ideological drive in Europe for a sharper focus on what the Ottoman Empire symbolized marked a parallel push to identify the values and goals that could be termed specifically European, a process that was paralleled by a struggle in England to isolate the meaning of Englishness. Some of these competing images of the Turk that operated in England during the sixteenth and seventeenth centuries can be found in the accounts that came back from the travelers of the day. For the English were becoming increasingly interested in the possibilities offered by the Ottoman Empire, and the accounts of these engagements offered their writers the means to discuss how best to organize the nascent English nation.

The Sublime Porte, as the empire was known, named for the great gate at the entrance to the Topkapi Palace where the Sultan met foreign dignitaries, was no longer seen as simply an evil threat to Christian Europe. Turkey now offered a market opportunity. In the early modern period, the English were "acutely conscious of their own marginalization on the fringes of European mercantilism," and they sought to correct this by engaging in the lucrative trade in oriental luxury goods.[1] The Ottoman enemy became a business partner. And for London, the Orient became above all a place of profit. The English were not only hungry for trade. They were greedy for empire. Empire at this stage meant something different from what it was to come to mean in later centuries. Empire was less to do with a civilizing mission and more to do with the power that was reflected in the nexus of influence, space, and commodities that controlling new lands could bring. But whatever it was, the English had what Gerald MacLean calls "imperial envy."[2] A nation with increasing imperial ambitions had to get involved in imperial affairs, and that meant active engagement with the Ottomans, both directly in terms of trade and politics and indirectly in the form of cultural and intellectual examination. So successful was this policy of involvement that by the middle of the seventeenth century, "Islam was no longer viewed as a religion with which Christians were engaged in distant lands but as an intellectual and social matter at home."[3]

It is tempting to see a close link between the increase in Eastern commerce and the rise of a nascent orientialism. But power relations did not favor the Europeans at that time. Quite the reverse is true. Between the Crusades and the eighteenth century, the Ottoman Empire conquered large parts of Christendom. European military activity against the Muslim world consisted largely of small-scale raiding by plunderers. Islam was actually seen as culturally superior by some. Elizabethan travelers often comment on the cleanliness of the Turks, their good manners and politeness toward strangers. Many Britons were enslaved by Muslim slave traders operating out of the North African coast. The phrase *alla Turchesca* came to mean a kind of deportment, carrying oneself in a disdainful way, looking haughtily down at others. Persia was seen as a place of enormous wealth, an image that in part writers inherited from ancient sources. As Samuel Chew says, "The Elizabethan conception of the luxury, gorgeousness, and voluptuousness of Persian life was part of their heritage from the classical past."[4] Operas from the eighteenth century, such as Handel's *Serse (Xerxes)*, have typical oriental themes: corruption, tyranny, internecine succession conflicts, the threat posed to Christian women by oriental lust. The North African coast, with its close links to the slave trade and captivity, was known generally as Barbary, emphasizing its association in the English mind with the cruelty, injustice, and inhumanity of barbarism. But such stereotyping did not represent a colonialist discourse, as it did, as we shall see, to some extent in the nineteenth century. To quote Nabil Matar, in early modern relations "English writers did not express either the authority of possessiveness or the security of domination" that later gave rise to Orientalism.[5] There is no simple postcolonial model that can be applied retrospectively. It had become clear in the first half of the seventeenth century that England's resources were insufficient for providing an adequate living for its population. The burden had fallen on trade to solve this dilemma.[6] Much of the English discourse about the Turks, therefore, is less about colonialism than about generating visions of commercial success.

Christian Europe and the Ottoman world began to develop a far more serious relationship with each other. As Alastair Hamilton puts it, "The fear of a powerful religious antagonist advancing ever further north, the prospect of alliances of value, the awareness of the Arab contribution to culture and to science, curiosity about an exotic neighbour, all contributed to the ambivalent fascination of the Levant and North Africa."[7] Engagement with the Muslim world was extensive: pilgrims, merchants, captives, ambassadors, academics, and adventurers all interacted with the Orient. The range of these contacts meant that the encounter between the Christian and Muslim worlds was not entirely, or even primarily, adversarial. It also meant that early modern attitudes toward the East lacked consistency. Neither East nor West had yet been properly defined. They were certainly not only polemical, instead often reflecting a high degree of ambivalence. These texts, therefore, reflect the wide range of attitudes the English were developing toward the East: not just dominating and exploiting, but also inquiring, understanding, and admiring. It helped train them for the greater global role they would acquire in the future.

Many of our records are literary representations of actual encounters. The growth of interest in travel texts of this kind acted as a register of more widespread domestic interest in the Orient. They show a fascination with the politics, climate, and customs of the East. To some extent these new travel texts were based on more accurate first-hand observation, but they still leaned heavily on the authority of the ancients. They still integrated their discoveries into a preexisting intellectual framework, which would be more readily understandable back home. The need to win domestic market share also meant that these travel accounts were also often highly competitive in providing colorful, perhaps too colorful, scenes of the Orient.

Classics played an important role in helping to create a clearer European idea of the Turk. Once the Turks had become the main power in the Eastern Mediterranean, it was a matter of vital interest to gather some intelligence about them. This was a very different matter than in modern espionage, and writers looked backward for ideas about where the Turks had come from. In the fifteenth century, for example, Theodore of Gaza, in his *On the Origin of the Turks*, emphasized the parallel between the Turks and the barbarians of antiquity and tried to discover links between them.[8] Some saw Turks as descended from the Scythians, those arch-barbarians who lived to the north of the ancient Greeks. But by far the most common means of explaining where the Turks had sprung from, and how they had managed to be so successful, was to trace their ancestry back to the Trojans. The Turks, it was argued, drew their name from being the sons of Teucer, the son of the Greek Telamon and the Trojan princess Hesione. Robert Schwoebel argues that the Trojan legend was invoked "to identify the Turks and assign them their place in history."[9] Turkish power was effectively "Europeanized" by legitimating their rule in both Asia and Europe on account of their being the descendants of both sides in the Trojan wars. In 1484, Felix Fabri went even deeper in his search for the ancient origins of the Turks. He traced their genealogy back to Priam's father, Laomedan. Many, he explains, think that the Turks come from Teucer. In fact, he argues, after the war ended, Telamon went to Cyprus where he founded the city of Salamis. But there was another Teucer, who lived at this time, one of the many sons of Priam and not therefore the son of Telamon, but he was mauled by a bear and died childless. The Turks, he declares, are therefore descended from Turcus, a son of Troyas, the son of Priam. In 1190 BCE, when Troy fell, two groups of its inhabitants fled. One, led by Franco, the son of Hector, migrated to Germany and become known as the Franks; the other party of Trojans, led by Turcus, traveled into Asia, to Scythia to be exact, where they lived like beasts. So savage and barbarous were they that Alexander the Great shut them up with the Jews in the mountains. Later a group of them journeyed into Persia, but the Persians treated them cruelly because they feared their growing number. Eventually the Persians drove out these Turks, who went on to conquer the whole Orient. It was therefore the Turks who were truly Trojans, merely Trojans who had converted to Islam.[10]

Such convoluted genealogies were important to identify the nature of the dangerous new culture that confronted Christendom. Discovering the Turks' true descent was in some ways a relief, as it showed that they came from, in some sense, a common stock, however mythological. It lent them a kind of respectability. But it also made clear just how dangerous they could be. The Trojans were no pushover, after all. It took an epic struggle to overcome them. But overcome they were by those to their west, and the fact that the Trojans were also seen as the common ancestor of the French and Germans emphasized that these nations should therefore recover their rightful lost inheritance by asserting that they and not the Turks were the true Trojans.[11] Others turned the myth of Trojan descent on its head. Mario Filelfo's epic of the 1470s, *Amyris*, contained four thousand verses on the Turkish sultan Mehmet II. Filelfo defends this verbosity by antique precedent, saying that the topic was as worthy as the deeds of Hannibal, Pyrrhus, Cyrus, and Philip of Macedon. He praises the sultan as being anything but barbarian. And he makes great use of Mehmet's Trojan ancestry, representing the Turkish subjugation of Greece as a triumph of justice: at last the aggressive conquest of Troy by the Greeks had been avenged.

Finding Trojan lineage was a routine piece of nation building. Denys Hay notes that it was thought that most nations derived their origins from Troy.[12] Even the British commonly adopted the idea of the Trojan Brutus as the founder of Britain.[13] Others tried to emphasize the warlike, expansionist aims of the Turks by comparison with the conquerors of old. Jean de Lastic, grandmaster of the Knights of St. John the Hospitallers on Rhodes, when pleading for help from the rulers of Christendom, claimed that the Grand Turk saw himself as another Alexander or even greater, as he planned to conquer not only Italy but the whole of Europe.[14] Many saw the Turks as a threat to high learning and culture. Cardinal Bessarion, the unofficial leader of the Greek exiles in Italy after the fall of Constantinople, in supporting his claim that Mehmet planned to invade Italy, "again fell back upon his store of historical knowledge, in this case that of ancient Rome. . . . He recalled the examples of the Gauls, of King Pyrrhus, of Hannibal, the Huns, and several German tribes."[15] One of the first eyewitness accounts of the siege of Constantinople, that of the Florentine merchant Jacopo Tedaldi, ends with remarks on Mehmet II, that he is "more infamous than Nero" when it comes to spilling Christian blood, and that the Grand Turk is "bold and ambitious, and desired more than Alexander or Caesar to conquer the whole world."[16] These writers were no mere bigots. As Schwoebel points out, the list of fifteenth-century humanists who wrote orations against the Turks would include "many of the most distinguished men of learning."[17] They were motivated by a powerful internal logic. By the early modern period, the Turks had become synonymous with Islam. Moreover, the image of Islam and Muhammad had become synonymous with the pagans of antiquity, hence the Turks were equated with the Scythians and Trojans, and English plays of the period even have Alexander the Great and Julius Caesar worshipping statues of Muhammad. The promotion of classical culture by translating ancient authors was therefore justified as it provided examples of past achievements to inspire present-day Christians to march against the Turks.[18] The result was that the love of classics and the desire for renewed crusading now went hand in hand.

Some sense of this link is found in the work of Sir Anthony Sherley, whose *Relation of Travels into Persia* was published in 1613. His journey through the Ottoman Empire makes for depressing reading for a classicist. On reaching Cyprus and Paphos, he "found nothing to answere the famous relations given by ancient histores of the excellency of that Iland," because the monuments of antiquity had been defaced by "the barbarousnesse of the Turke, and time." Instead the people had become "Slaves to cruell Maisters," "so grievous is the burthen of that miserable people."[19] Sherley is outraged that the West had left the holy lands in the hands of these barbarous Turks and turns to ancient history for an analogy:

> Romulus, when his people fled before the Sabines; so that the victory shewed it selfe undoubtedly on their side, and overthrow on his: the very remembring them of leaving Iupiter, and the rest of the Gods in the Capitoll, to the possession of their enemies, was sufficient to turne that desperate fortune. And the French had sacked and burnt a great part of Rome; the same awfull reverence to their Gods, and love to their Countrey, could binde them rather to re-build their ruinated Citty, then to go to Vejes, a Towne ready, and magnificently builded. But we can leave, in the Turkes possession, not onely the Countrey of our Saviour, (which should be deerer unto us then our owne, for his great name sake;) but this the Sepulcher of his precious bloud.[20]

Yet Sherley's deep-rooted hostility toward the Turks is balanced by his high opinion of the Persian king. Describing his "vertues," he lists his "iustice, wisedome, temperance, liberalitie, valour, mercifulnesse, and generality" and protests that in spite of all these excellent qualities he is still "esteemed by us barbarous."[21] Sherley elsewhere proclaims that "he is both one of the mightiest Princes that are, and one of the excellentest"; moreover, he adds that his rule is so perfect it could serve as a classical model: "the fashion of his government differing so much from that which we call barbarousnesse, that it may iustly serve for as great an Idea for a Principality, as Platoes Common-wealth did for a Government, of that sort."[22]

Sherley's account gives a clear sense of how differentiated English views of the East could be. There was no all-embracing discourse lurking behind every attitude. Comparison with antiquity, however, did provide a common cause to disdain the Turk. William Lithgow, a Scot who traveled in the Ottoman Empire in the years 1611 and 1612, titled his account *A Most Delectable, and True Discourse, of an Admired and Painefull Peregrination from Scotland, to the Most Famous Kingdomes in Europe, Asia and Affricke.* He starts with a brief description of the ancient monuments of Rome, beginning with that "speciall obiect of Antiquitie," the pantheon and the "Auncinet Amphitheatre beautiful with great Columnes, of a wonderfull bignes and height." But once he has reached the Morea, "called auunciently Sparta, where, that sometimes famous Citty of Lacedemon flourished, but now sacked, and the lumps of ruines and memorie onely remeines,"[23] he too is shocked by the "barbarousnesse of Turkes" and "deformed" state of "that once worthy Realme." He naturally concurs that "the originall of the Turkes, is said to have beene in Scythia."[24] He travels to the site of ancient Troy, and his pride in reaching it is shown in his affixing to his text a likeness of himself in Turkish dress. Because the area was dangerous, he hired a Janissary as a protector and guide. After seeing the "many Toombes, which were mighty ruinous" of the Trojan heroes as well as Priam's palace, he returned to base and tried to settle his bill with the Janissary. The Janissary forced him to double his previously agreed pay and Lithgow warns other travelers that "they make no account of conscience, nor ruled by the Law of compassion, neither regard they a Christian more than a dogge."[25] Mind you, that was not the worst position to be in. "The inhumane policy of Turkes, to avoide civill dissention is such, that the seede of Ottoman (all except one of them) are strangled to death: wherefore, as Augustus Caesar said of Herod in the like case, It is better to be the great Turkes dogge, then his sonne."[26]

The contrast between the glory of the city of Troy, where epic heroes fell, and these modern tyrants was stark. It is easy to see why Lithgow fell back on inherited prejudices: "The Arabians are for the most part Theeves and Robbers."[27] But it should not be supposed that Lithgow only hated the Turks. As a vehement Protestant, his real hostility was aimed against Rome, by which of course he meant the Catholic Church. At one point he recounts the story of a priest killed in a brothel, when "lying with a whoore." "O! If all the Priests which do commit incest, adultery and fornication (yee, and worse, il peccato carnale contra natura) were thus handled and severely rewarded; what a sea of Sodomiticall irreligious bloud, would overflow the halfe of Europe, to staine the spotted colour of that Romane beast."[28] By comparison his views on Islam are remarkably restrained.

The years 1611–1612 also found the Englishman George Sandys traveling leisurely through the East. His *Description of the Turkish Empire,* published in 1615 as part of his *Relation of a Journey,* set a new benchmark in accuracy and detail for English travel writing on the Orient. Sandys, as we have seen, was a highly educated man and it came naturally and easily to him to enrich his narrative with a plentiful supply of references to the classics. There was a new kind of formality to his work, perhaps best evidenced by the frontispiece, which pictured various allegories of tyranny in the context of a classical temple.[29] The sultan of the time, Ahmed I, is described in Latin as *Tyrannus,* with the Christian virtues of Truth and Firmness (*Veritas* and *Constantia*) seated above him, flanking an image of an ascending Christ. Below lie symbols of injustice such as a lamenting virgin. The early seventeenth century was a period when new notions of national identity were being fashioned across Europe. Sandys uses the image of the tyrannical sultan to emphasize that an English king could never be a true tyrant, even though that is exactly what some accused James I of being. Sandys was a royalist, and the book is dedicated to James's son Charles, a statement of confidence in the dynastic stability of the Stuarts that is supported by predictions of the image of Virgil's Sibylline oracle on the frontispiece. It is a clear visual statement that, in Sandys's view, an English king could never share the attributes of a real tyrant, the best example of which was to be found in the East. It tries therefore to create an image of the king as both just and divinely guided at a time when these qualities were being contested, but it does so at the expense of the Turk. In this process of self-fashioning, therefore, the Ottomans become the excluded other, consigned to the extremes of tyranny and injustice.

Sandys was a social and political conservative who liked to be guided by tradition and stereotype. It seemed unlikely to him that a statement unsupported by classical authority could be true. But although he uses ancient sources to lend his work authority and authenticity, that is not to say that classical texts created an interpretation so fixed that it could not be molded. In fact Sandys sought to create a new style of travel writing, which looked backward to help narrate lessons relevant for the contemporary reader. English power was growing and the country was becoming increasingly involved in overseas matters, so it seemed appropriate that this wider world should be represented to it "with proper sophistication and rhetorical pomp."[30] Whereas many earlier ancient and medieval travel books concentrated on simply accumulating a variety of information to emphasize the foreignness of other cultures, Sandys adopted a far more literary form. The Latin poets served as treasure chests of basic information and higher meanings, and as means to create heightened literary effects.[31] Each had his own uses: Ovid for intimate landscapes and analyzing character; Virgil for epic, Horace for public moralizing, Juvenal for satire. They established a body of opinion in relation to which Sandys could situate his own opinions. They functioned as the props for his views, a fact reflected in their physical location in the margins of the text, buttressing and supporting the messages of the text between. His carefully crafted prose was replete with quotations from antiquity because these texts acted as windows though which he could see the East more clearly and also as part of the subject matter of his book. As Jonathan Haynes suggests, for Sandys, "traveling the world and reading about it are inseparable."[32] His work was part of a humanist endeavor, whereby to understand and to know a place was to gather together all available information about it. In this view, the literary tradition associated with a place was the surest guide to its significance. Both past and present knowledge were pressed together to form an alloy that served to construct a solid framework of understanding. Classical quotation, therefore, was neither merely ornamental nor the "debris of a humanistic education, but [. . .] an absolutely central element in the understanding developed by the *Relation*." It turns what might otherwise be just a set of private views into a public, authoritative document, a collective view of the East formed from the shared cultural memory.

It was for this reason that the classics played such an important role in his text. They spoke to him not of ancient history or mythology but of the real meaning of a place. Everything that came after served merely to show what a fall had occurred. The contrast between the glory and grandeur of antiquity and the degradation of the modern world pervades Sandys's work. It is a tale of the struggle between civilization and the forces of barbarism, revealed in this contrast with the past, in the battle between Christian Europe and the Ottomans, and in the internal struggle between virtue and vice. Examples of these contrasts abound. When reaching Smyrna, which had been reputable "in the title of one of seven primitive Churches of Asia," he notes how it is "now violated by the Mahometans, her beautie is turned to deformitie, her knowledge into barbarisme, her religion into impietie."[33] The change at Troy is profoundly symbolic, and Sandys composes his own verses:

> Old Troy by Greeks twice sackt: twice new Greece rued
> Her conquering ancestors. First when subdued
> By Romes bold Troian progenie: and now
> When forc't through Turkish insolence to bow

It is placed at the heart of the historical conflict between East and West, a conflict which in Sandys's day, after the battle of Lepanto in 1571, seemed to be taking a significant turn in Christian Europe's favor. The Turks' low state was such that they deserved to lose their empire, because they were reduced to carting off their classical remains: "But now the ruines beare not altogether that forme, lessened daily by the Turkes, who carried the pillers and stones unto Constantinople to adorne the buildings of the Great Bassas."[34] The Turks are portrayed as inherently unworthy of possessing so great a heritage.

A common theme is the Turks' failure to care for their classical inheritance, acting as a symbol of their lack of civilization. Sandys lists the remains of Constantinople, "the relikes of the Pallace of Constantine, now made a stable for wilde beasts."[35] Ruins such as these are all that is left of "so many goodly buildings" and the "congested antiquities, wherewith this soveraigne Citie was in times past so adorned." He muses, "I thinke there is not in the world an obiect that promiseth so much a farre off to the beholders, and entred, so deceiveth the expectation. The best of their private buildings, inferiour to the more contempible sort of ours. For the Turkes are nothing curious of their houses" because "possessions are not hereditary." Constantinople has become a place that suffers fires and earthquakes and the plague, which "miserably infesteth this Citie"; and matters are "increased by the superstition of the Mahometans" and the "scepter of a Tyrant." How then, he asks, "O New Rome how are thy thus balanced profits and delights to be valued!"[36]

Sandys sees history as the story of civilization.[37] It is a story of founding cities, manly heroic effort, the display of public morals and virtue, a very classical model of history. The Turks act as the foils to all these standards. He describes, for example, the island of Lesbos, the home of one of the Seven Sages, of Sappho and Alcaeus. He follows it with a portrait of the town's capture by "Mahomet the Great." He recounts how, after the siege, individuals were brought to the lowest state because the Turk, "distinguishing the inhabitants according to their degrees, the better sort he leadeth away with him." He "giveth away those of the middle condition, (afterward sold as they do sheepe in markets,) and leaveth behind the dregs of the people," but "reserving to himselfe eight hundred boyes and virgins, excelling the rest both in birth and beautie."[38]

The Turkish world is a world of sensuousness. He claims Mahomet promises in paradise "pallaces spread all over with silke carpets" and "flowry fields, and christalline rivers; trees of gold still flourishing," the kind of thing seen in the mythology of Virgil's sixth book of the *Aeneid:*

> Which being pluckt, to others place resigne,
> And still the rich twigs with like mettall shine.[39]

But even such glories are, in Sandys's view, derived from classical sources as his Virgilian borrowing perhaps suggests: "It is to be more then coniectured, that Mahomet grounded his devised Paradise, upon the Poets invention of Elisium. For thus Tibullus dscribeth the one":

Love shall conduct me to th'Elissian fields
There songs and dances revell: choice birds fly
From tree to tree, warbling sweete melody . . .
Youths intermixt with maids disport at ease,
Incountring still in loves sweete skirmiges.[40]

He notes that the Turks love baths. These "Bannias" are "in such request with these nations (as once with the Romanes)," and while he accepts that "after exercise and travell restoreth to the wearied body a wonderfull alacrity," he adds Juvenal's warning that,

Yet punisht strait, if you disrobde, and full
To the bath do undigested viands bring,
Hence sudden deaths, and age intestate spring.[41]

For the Turks are suffering from that same internal weakness that laid low the Romans: they have a propensity to luxury and vice.

They devote themselves to the perils of leisure: "Not far from the Temple of Sancta Sophia, there is a spacious place surrounded with buildings, like to that of Smithfield; and anciently called the Hippodrom, for that there they exhibited their horse-races." Here he quotes a line from Martial, again suggesting a classical equivalence, "The swift hoofe beates the dustie Hippodrom." And the Turks now likewise "play every Friday at Giocho de Canni; which is no other then Prison bace upon horseback, hitting one another with darts. . . . Nor is it the least contentment to the Christian to behold the terrible falls that they often get (not rarely costing them their lives)."[42] The Turks drink strange liquids: they "sippe of a drinke called Coffa (of the berry that it is made of) in little China dishes, as hot as they can suffer it: black as soote, and tasting not much unlike it (why not that blacke broth which was in use amongst the Lacedemonians?)."[43] And they debase the once fine wheat of Greece: traveling in Lesbos, he finds "the South and West parts mountainous and barren, the rest levell and fruitfull, producing excellent corne," and then is moved to quote Horace: "And Lesbian floure, more white then snow." But what is now become of this fine flour? It is the stuff "whereof the Turks make their Trachana and Bouhourti; a certaine hodgepodge of sundry ingredients."

Sandys's fascination in the nature of tyranny finds a particular expression in the notice he takes of slavery. The act of enslavement seems to be, for him, the ultimate mark of an unjust tyrant and the experience of being enslaved is the lowest condition to which a human being can sink. And being a Christian slave to a Turkish master is the worst of all. He describes how people buy slaves, how they are "sold as horses in Faires" in weekly markets in the City, mainly Christians "taken in the warres, or purchased with their money"; these slaves "endevour to allure the Christians to buy them, as expecting from them a more easie servitude and continuance of religion." When the buyer "hath agreed of the price (but yet conditionally) they are carried aside into a roome."

> [Those] Who horses cheapen, search them, and make proofe,
> Lest a good shape, propt by a tender hoofe,
> Cheate him that should uncircumspectly buy,
> For that short headed, broad-spred, crested high
>
> So, T'allure you of deceitlesse women, they shew
> All that they sell: nor boast they of the best,

> Nor hide the bad, but both give to the test:
> even to the secret of her mouth, and assurance (if so she be
> said to be) of her virginitie.[44]

Horace is able to provide him a suitable picture of what the realities of the slave-trade were like. Things will still be the same. And just as slavery could lead the Romans into immoral behavior, so Sandys sees the same degrading effects on the Turks:

> Many of the children that the Turkes do buy (for these markets do affoord of all ages) they castrate, making all smooth as the backe of the hand, (whereof divers do die in the cutting) who supply the uses of nature with a silver quill, which they weare in their Turbants. In times past, they did but onely geld them: but being admitted to the free converse of their women, it was observed by some, that they more then befittingly delighted in their societies. For according to the Satyre,
>
> With feeble Eunuchs some delighted are:
> Kisses still soft, chins that of beards despare:
> Who need force no abortments.[45]

If the Turks share the capacity for immorality of the Romans, they lack the capacity for reason of the Greeks. "They study not Rhetorick, as sufficiently therein instructed by nature; nor Logick, since it serves as well as to delude as informe; and that wisedom (according to the opinion of the Epicures) may be comprehended in plaine and direct expressions."[46] Instead, Sandys portrays them as possessing a passive fatalism: "With the Stoicks they attribute all accidentes to destinie, and constellations at birth," and then quotes Seneca as being in agreement with them:

Fates guide us: unto Fates yeeld we
Care cannot alter their decree
For what we suffer, what we do,
Coelestiall orbs proceeds from you.
All go in a prefixed way:
the first prescribeth the last day

Such passivity is not a virtue likely to result in civilized creativity. In fact, it seems to lead to mindless violence. It affirms to them, says Sandys, "that their ends are written in their foreheads" and quotes Lucan, to emphasize their frenzied warlikeness:

Thereby freed from deaths affright,
The worst of feares, thence take they heart to fight
And rush on steele.[47]

Some of Sandys's strongest contempt is reserved for those who have fallen under the Turks' dominion. Egypt seems to create a sense of disgust. It is the archetype of the foreign. It seems to be a country that is in a permanent state of decline. Its religious practice of worshipping animals, attacked by Juvenal in his fifteenth satire, seems to sum up their superstitious nature, a religious folly that is now reflected in their belief in Islam.[48]

What honour brain-sick Aegypt to things vile
Affoordeth, who not knowes? A Crocodidle
This part adores: that Ibis, serpent fed.
Monkie of gold they there divinely dread

Likewise, the Greeks are a nation that has been overcome by this corrupting influence of the Orient, a negative influence that has been working on them for millennia. Sandys notes the impact on their eating habits: "The antique Grecians used to lie along at their meales, from whom the Romanes received that custome, as they from the effeminate Asians, upon beds that circled three parts of the table." And "[although] the Greekes do now for the most part imitate the Turkes (I meane here in Turkie) in sitting at their meate, yet retaine they still that vice of immoderate drinking."[49] The example of the "Grecians" is a powerful one for Sandys as it reflects a fall from the apogee of civilized humanity to enslavement under the Turk: they were a "Nation once so excellent, that their precepts and examples do still remaine as approoved Canons to direct the mind that endevoureth vertue. Admirable in arts, and glorious in armes; famous for government, affectors of freedome, every way noble: and to whom the rest of the world were reputed Barbarians." But now their decline is such that "their knowledge is converted . . . into affected ignorance, (for they have no schooles of learning amongst them) their liberty into contented slavery, having lost their minds with their Empire." Instead of high culture and learning, they now "delight in ease, in shades, in dancing and drinking: and no further for the most part endevour their profit, then their bellies compell them."[50] It is a series of images aimed at the empire-hungry English to warn them of the perils of wealth and power, and to make them see how lucky they are to have such an enlightened, just ruler, a king who is very far from being a tyrant. The perils of political change are laid out for the English reader to see, and it is classical texts that provide the tools with which to force this message home.

If Sandys saw in the Ottoman Empire the lessons of barbarism and decay, other English writers of the time found in it inspiration. Richard Knolles, in his *Generall Historie of the Turkes*, first published in 1603, exalted the Turks for their religious unity, in contrast to the Christians, as well as their courage and toughness. He turns to ancient history for images of decline and fall. Struck by how all worldly things are subject to change, he declares, "What small assurance there is in mens affaires, and how subiect unto change even those things are wherein we for the most part repose our greatest felicitie and blisse." Not even "the great Romane empire, or the proud citie of Rome itselfe (sometime the mistresse of the world) herein found any exemption." Instead it became corrupted by success, "growne great with continuall triumphs," and it "converted the forces of itselfe upon itselfe, to the overthrow of the antient libertie thereof, together with the utter subversion of the state."[51] Likewise, in his *Politicall Reflections upon the Government of the Turks*, of 1656, Osborne says that it was merely a question of historiography that Muhammad has such a bad reputation in the West, claiming that "the main difference between Alexander, Caesar, and Mahumet consists in a Feather, or the Quill of a Goose."[52] He condemns the fact that thousands "bury their Talents" in "an implicit adhering to the writings of the Ancients." He sees Turkish ignorance of classical literature as a positive boon because it allows them to focus on the business of government: "The Turk's want of knowledge in our Learning or Religion, leaves him neither so Imprudent or Wicked, but that he is able to promote his owne Interest, and willing to make his Subjects so far happy, as may suit with an Absolute power."[53]

Paul Rycaut went so far as to see in the Turkish government a model form of rule. His *The Present State of the Ottoman Empire*, published in 1668, includes a book describing "The Maximes of the Turkish Politie."[54] Like Osborne, he thinks the Turks have benefited from being written off by Europeans: "It hath been the happy fortune of the Turk to be accounted barbarous and ignorant; for upon this perswasion Christian Princes have laid themselves open and unguarded to their greatest danger." He plans to reverse that by producing a study that traces "the footsteps of Government in the best formed and moulded Common-wealths."[55] When he looks at the Turkish government and "the absoluteness of an Emperour without reason, without virtue," he cannot but admire its success and achievements, and wonders if the Turk has been sent by God as a "chastisement of the sins and vices of Christians." But he has no faith in being able to understand God's plan for the world, if such a plan exists at all, and quotes Tacitus's observation that "the more I reflect on the past and present, the more ridiculousness all human affairs seem to be."[56] The appeal of Turkish power is such, though, that he would not be surprised if "the ignorant and vain amongst Christians . . . should be catched and entrapt with the fancy and enticement of the Turkish Mode"; this, after all, is what had happened in Britain before: "for so the Britains, and other Nations, after Conquered by the Romans, began to delight themselves in their Language and Habit, their Bankets and Buildings, which they accounted to be humanity and refinement of their manners," even if the truth was, as Tacitus says, that these were actually signs of their subjection.[57]

Rycaut served as secretary to his excellency the Earl of Winchilsea, ambassador extraordinary to the Sublime Porte for Charles II. Coming so soon after the restoration of the monarchy, it is perhaps not surprising that the more authoritarian regime of the Ottomans held attractions for one close to the heart of royal power. It also explains something of his interest in the usurpations that were a recurrent feature of Ottoman politics. When he considers the general premise of usurpations, he reflects that "it hath always been the Misfortune of unlimited powers to be subject to dangers and violence, arising from the discontents and inconstancy of the Souldiery." He finds parallels for this in the Roman world: "Thus we see in the time of the latter Roman Emperours, who usurped a power unknown in the dayes of the pure and happy constitution of that Common-wealth, and governed all by the Sword and their own lusts"; but because of this tyranny, "few of them ended their dayes fortunately, or died in their beds and peace, without becoming a Sacrifice to the same power that first proclaimed them Emperours."[58] By contrast, he argues that the Turks are loyal to Ottoman blood and to their religion: "And may all Christians learn this Lesson from the Turks . . . who no sooner threw off her Obedience and Religion to her Prince, but (as if that vertue had been the only bar to all other Enormities and Sins) she was deprived of all other Ecclesiastical and Civil Rights, and in all her capacities and relations deflowred and prophaned by impious and unhallowed hands."[59] If the English have not already learned their lesson from their own recent past in the civil war, they can take their instruction from the superpower of the East.

Rycaut's position may also account for some of his interest in the court politics of the Ottomans. He praises the custom of selecting captured Christian youths for the imperial seraglio, from which the best are selected for high office. He notes that "this was always the custom in the Eastern countreys, as Q. Curtius reports."[60] Life for the high-ranking official was perilous, though. "It is the fate of great Favourites with barbarous Princes to be but short-lived. For either the Prince delights to exercise his power in debasing some," quoting the Latin of Tacitus again: "So rarely is it the fate of power to be long-lived."[61] Similarly, "emulation and flattery are likewise great, and the factions are commonly many in the Ottoman Court, whereby the State of the first Minister is endangered," a statement for which he again turns to Tacitus for verification: "They act on the instincts of human nature, which makes men scrutinize those who have been promoted, and demand a temperate use of good fortune from them all the more since they see them on a level with themselves."[62] Viziers were often brought down by factions because their "power and greatness being only borrowed from his Master [the Sultan], and depending on anothers pleasure, by its short continuance and mutability, verifies that true saying of Tacitus": that "the most precarious and transitory thing in human affairs is a reputation for power which has no support of its own."[63] Some few, lucky viziers survive for as much as eighteen or nineteen years in post and die peacefully in bed, "from whence this question may arise, whether the favour or displeasure of the Prince depends on the destiny or fortune we are born to, or whether humane Councel can assign a way between contumaciousness and flattery, wherin to steer free from danger and ambition." Again Rycaut quotes Tacitus.[64] He concludes that few survive to a peaceful end: "For if viziers have been evil, their own cruelty and covetousness have hastened their fate; if good, their merits have been their ruine, least the great benefits their merits have procured to their Prince should seem to want reward, or be dangerous or difficult to requite."

The dispassionate and cynical analysis of power found in Tacitus appealed to a conservative like Rycaut. Here was a source of political wisdom perfectly matched for the needs of his day. The nature of the power of kings had been a matter for great dissension in England during the seventeenth century, and in looking for a model of strong government in combination with a realistic assessment of its weaknesses, what better pairing could he find than the sultan and Tacitus? If a firm monarch was good for England, it was also true that he needed to be prevented from becoming a tyrant, if those who served him were to sleep at night. Otherwise the result would be the kind of fierce internal political struggles that were one of the Ottoman Empire's weak spots. The resultant political assassinations, with the bowstring about the neck were, to Rycaut, reminiscent of the Roman emperor Tiberius, that most loathsome example of imperial rule. He relates that great men are often "barbarously put to death" having been sent a few days before on some great mission to make room for others with the "least noise."[65] He goes on: "And this methinks is somewhat agreeable to the crafty policy of Tiberius, who sometimes would Commissionate men for Government of Provinces, to whom before-hand he had designed not to permit license to depart the City."

Like Sandys, Rycaut is fascinated by Turkish slavery because he too is interested in setting limits for a stronger form of monarchy. He notes how slavery among the Turks goes right to the top of society and denotes a condition of "entire resignation to the will and command of the Emperour." He adds, "They that should have been where they have seen and known the manner of this blind obedience, may well cry out, *O homines ad servitutem paratos!*," the phrase, according to Tacitus, that Tiberius uttered in disgust at the servile attitude of Roman senators.[66] And so Rycaut, concurring with Aristotle's view of barbarians, concludes that the Turks are naturally slavish, a characteristic he attributes to the fact that the Turks have more children by their slaves than by their wives. This, in combination with the rich slave trade, "fills Constantinople with such a strange race, mixture, and medly of different sorts of blood, that it is hard to find many that can derive a clear line from ingenious Parents: So that it is no wonder that amongst the Turks a disposition be found fitted and disposed to servitude, and that is better governed with a severe and tyrannous hand."[67] This is a key difference between the Turks and the English. The English, being less slavish, will not need a despot to keep them in order.

Another difference is that the Turks are rougher and more militaristic. The Ottoman Empire "had Mars its only Father" and "that rude temper they brought with them out of Scythia."[68] Their troops are brave to the point of recklessness, which brings with it a political threat: the Janissaries have "an imprudence," "which may equal the levity of the Roman Souldiery, until they shamelessly set their Empire to sale, and forgot both their old obedience to the Senate, and reverence to their new Emperours."[69] But not even the Turks are so rough as to mistreat envoys, a fact that was close to the heart of this secretary to an ambassador extraordinary to the Sublime Porte: for, as Cicero had agreed, "There was no Nation in the World ever so barbarous, that did not acknowledge the Office of an Embassadour sacred and necessary."[70] In fact, the Turks do not always behave as well as they should to dignitaries, such as Rycaut: one ambassador "contrary to the custom of the ancient Romans" was "in a most undecent and barbrous manner dragged . . . to a Dungeon so loathsome and moist, that the ill vapours oft-times extinguished the candle."[71] Rycaut acknowledges that access to Eastern princes was "always difficult, and not permitted with the same familiarity as hath been practised amongst the Romans."[72] This again is in contrast to England, where "the sight of the king is his own glory, and the satisfaction of his subjects."

By the 1660s, when Rycaut was writing, England was starting to fulfill some of its imperial ambitions, in places as diverse as North America, the Far East, and the Caribbean. Rycaut is keen to learn from the Ottoman experience. By analyzing the dynamics and mechanics of what was still the most powerful European polity, he hoped to set out lessons for the aspiring English. It is nothing less than a study in the theory of empire. And it is a theory that draws heavily on the ancient empires to provide comparative insight. He recognizes that "there was never any people that laid Foundations—Designs of a great Empire—but first thought how to make it populous." He concedes that "it is true, that Alexander did with an army, for the most part, composed of Macedonians, as it were in a rank, make a Conquest of the best part of the Eastern World"; but such an empire was unstable: "this Empire, like a ship that had much Sail and no Ballast, or a fair Tree over-charged with boughs too heavy for its stem, became a windfall on a sudden."[73] The Romans, by contrast, were far more adept at populating their conquered lands with citizenry: they "well knew the benefits of receiving strangers into their bosome. . . . The English call it Naturalization . . . the Turks call it becoming a Believer." The Turks, he believes, are far harsher masters than the Romans ever were, which is one of the key reasons the Romans were more successful imperially: the jurisdiction and dominions of the Roman conquest "were far larger than this present Empire," "and yet we do not finde that they so studiously endeavoured to dispeople." Unlike the Turks, whom he sees as having a policy of desolating their own provinces in Asia in order to keep them subjugated, the Romans "rather encouraged industry in plantations, gave priviledges to Cities meanly stored, invited people to inhabit them, endeavored to improve Countries rude and uncultivate with good Husbandry, and Maritine Towns with Traffick and Commerce." Not only that but they "made Citizens of their Confederates, and conferred on their conquered subjects oftentimes greater benefits then they could expect or hope for under their true and natural Princes." It was a policy that bore great fruit: "and certainly the Romans thrived and were richer and more powerful by their policy; and therefore why the Turk might not proceed in the same manner . . . is worth our consideration."[74]

He concludes that the principal reason for this divergence in the treatment of their subjects was the "vast difference in the original, foundation, progress and maximes each of other." For the Romans "built their City in peace" and "made Laws by which the arbitrary will of the Prince was corrected"; and once their empire had been gained, "they accommodated themselves often to present necessities and humours, and constitutions of the people they had conquered"; they "used proper Arts to keep them in obedience"; and "by their generosity and wisdom won those nations to admire and imitate their vertues, and to be contented in their subjection." Conversely, the Turks "have but one sole means to maintain their Countries, which is the same by which they were gained, and that is the cruelty of the sword in the most rigorous way of execution, by killing, consuming and laying desolate the Countries." Even brave people such as the those "formerly called the Daci," "which withstood so long the Roman Arms," and "alwayes esteemed a Valiant and Warlike people"—as he finds evidenced in the eighth book of Virgil's *Aeneid* and Juvenal's sixth Satire[75]—are now slaves to the Turks, who exploit them and their resources: they "may well be compared to the industrious Bee and profitable Sheep," who are kept "for the sake of their Honey, and interest of their Wool."[76] Rycaut concludes that the problems of overexpansion are such that the Roman emperor Augustus "was a wise and judicious Prince" because he set limits to the extent of empire and so avoided having to rely on excessive brutality to keep his peoples in check.[77]

Rycaut pays close attention to the administration of the Ottoman Empire. He is aware that it is important to rotate office so as to prevent corruption. He finds that "long continuance in authority" is avoided by the Turks, which is similar to the situation that prevailed in Rome: "we finde that the Romans often changed their Governours." The Pashaw of Egypt was limited to three years tenure also, which policy he compares with that of Augustus, who "had that opinion of the wealth and power of Egypt" that he cut it off from senators, the reason for which is given by Tacitus: "from a fear that any one who held a province containing the key of the land and of the sea, with ever so small a force against the mightiest army, might distress Italy by famine."[78] It is the failure of these checks on office that for Rycaut are a sure sign that the peak of Ottoman power has now passed. Bribery and corruption, he argues, are now "run out of course; a manifest token in my opinion of the declension and decay of the Ottoman Empire," for which opinion he quotes Livy for support: "prosperity constantly went alongside submission to the gods, and adversity with the neglect of them."[79] People now buy themselves into Ottoman office but often borrow from the court eunuchs at rates as high as 40 to 50 percent per annum. The consequences of this are all too obvious to Rycaut, who has Tacitus to rely on: "Think then . . . what oppression, what rapine and violence must be exercised to satisfie the appetite of these men, who come famished with immense desires." And he quotes Tacitus's description of the Roman general Fabius Valens, whom the short-lived emperor Vitellius ordered to ravage the provinces of Gaul: "Poor for many years and suddenly growing rich, he could not help showing off the change in his fortunes, indulging without moderation the appetites which a protracted poverty had inflamed, and, after a youth of neediness, becoming prodigal in old age."[80]

For all Rycaut's respect for the Turks, other texts of the period rehash received stereotypes with an insouciance that talks of a nation that has fulfilled some of its imperial ambition and acquired with it an appropriately superior attitude. Richard Pococke, for example, was a clergyman traveler distantly related to Edward Pococke, the first holder of the Chair of Arabic at Oxford University. He published his *A Description of the East and Some other Countries* in 1743 but he has a low opinion of the Egyptian locals: "The natives of Egypt are now a slothful people, and delight in sitting still, hearing tales, and indeed seem always have been more fit for the quiet life, than for any active scenes: And this idle manner of living is probably one great reason of the fruitfulness of their invention, with regard to their antient Heathen religion, and of their making so many extravagant fables; out of which the Greeks might take some of the most beautiful, as a foundation for their religion and poetry, and so they passed to the Romans. This indolence may be owing to the great heat of the country, that enervates them, and inclines them to the unactive life."

He also finds that they are "malicious and envious to a great degree," and that they "love plunder" and possess a "natural cunning and artifice."[81] His account is illustrated with various drawings of the views at Baalbek, and these reflect his poor estimation of the Arab population. Against the dominant, domineering architecture of the Roman remains, they stand as small, insignificant figures who have no interest in the past greatness that surrounds them and are of no interest to those that do. Likewise, Thomas Shaw, relating the tales of his travels in Barbary in 1738, sees North Africa as fundamentally a part of the Roman Empire and so still a natural part of Christendom. He looks through the reality of the Islamic presence to see what for him is the true reality of the classical past.

As evidence of the decline of the Ottoman Empire became more apparent, there was less interest in England for works dealing with what had been the Turkish menace. Greater contact also brought better knowledge with it, a development that was reflected in more accurate and sympathetic academic investigations of Islam. George Sale published the first English translation of the Quran from Arabic in 1734, complete with notes and a preliminary discourse. He is well disposed toward the Arabs, drawing on ancient sources to reinforce his position: they "are commended by the ancients for being most exact to their words and respectful to their kindred."[82] The fact that "Arabia was of old famous for heresies" he believes "might be in some measure attributed to the liberty and independency of the tribes."[83] He tries to render seemingly strange practices as harmless by comparing them with ancient Roman customs: trying to account for the Muslims' march round the Kaaba, he notes that "the Romans had something like this in their worship, being ordered by Numa to use a circular motion in the adoration of the gods, either to represent the orbicular motion of the world, or the perfecting the whole office of prayer to that God who is maker of the universe."[84] Sale accepts that the Prophet Muhammad had weaknesses: he tells us that he was "a great lover of women, we are assured by his own confession"; but he balances this by explaining that, according to the Roman historian Ammianus Marcellinus, Arabs are so "by complexion."[85] And overall, he believes that Islam is a moral society, in part because it shares prohibitions that existed in the classical world. So, for example, when discussing the Quranic ban on gaming, he notes that "gaming, at least to excess, has been forbidden in all well-ordered states. Gaming-houses were reckoned scandalous places among the Greeks, and a gamester is declared by Aristotle to be no better than a thief: the Roman senate made very severe laws against playing at games of hazard, except only during the Saturnalia."[86] In fact, he praises the Quran for raising moral standards in some areas over and above those that prevailed in antiquity. Muhammad, he says, prohibited infanticide, which was "common among several of their tribes." But he reminds his readers that "the Arabs, in thus murdering of their children, were far from being singular; the practice of exposing infants and putting them to death being so common among the ancients, that it is remarked as a thing very extraordinary in the Egyptians, that they brought up *all* their children."[87]

The travel book had become an important part of English literary life during the early modern era. Increasing contacts and more accurate scholarship did help to weaken some of the old myths about the East, which the English had inherited from the Middle Ages, but rapid political change also saw efforts to perpetuate the traditional image of Islam for the benefit of domestic interests. Classical sources played an important role in these texts because they provided a sounding board for contemporary political ideas. They allowed English writers to think about what it meant to be part of the English polity. The Orient provided the backdrop for these debates because this was where the most influential power in Europe then resided. Many Englishmen recognized that this would be the place where they might make their fortunes and where a newly powerful English nation would make its presence felt on the international stage. Classics provided the means with which to analyze the Ottoman Empire, taking into account its organization, its morality, and the likelihood of its continued flourishing. The writers of antiquity, therefore, provided English travelers with the tools to learn the lessons that would be useful for what they hoped would be their own imperial future.

5

Gibbon's Islam

Prior to the eighteenth century, attitudes toward Islam had been predominantly, if not entirely, hostile. The term *Muslim* had become practically synonymous with the Turk and so was often thought to share the same presumed attributes of barbarity, despotism, and lustfulness. Much of this negativity can be ascribed to Christian Europe's need to maintain a healthy distance between itself and its greatest military, religious, and cultural threat. As Turkish power waned, though, and that of Western European nations rose, the need to maintain such a hard divide decreased. It became possible to consider the East in a more balanced, less fraught manner. Historians, such as Edward Gibbon, were able to make use of better-quality information to see Islam in a far more positive light, as is revealed in Gibbon's account of the rise of Islam in his *History of the Decline and Fall of the Roman Empire.* Gibbon's work, along with other writing on the Orient, was not, however, written in a void. All these texts expressed contemporary Western developments: the move toward greater individualism, the questioning of traditional political structures, the challenge to religious authority. The Orient, therefore, came to be seen in relation to these ongoing debates about the nature of power and how it should be organized and the development of ideas of progress and civilization. All of this had profound implications for how the inherited knowledge of the ancients should be treated. And classics, as the highest form of learning of the day, played a central role in all these debates.

Gibbon not only wrote about Rome but "cultivated certain Roman attitudes and sensibilities, and in this respect he was representative of the age."[1] Writers such as Gibbon admired not just the achievements but the outlook of the great men of the Roman republic, and they tried to imitate these habits of mind in their own feelings. The first half of the eighteenth century, therefore, saw Roman aristocratic ideals adopted in upper-class English culture and thought. This favoring of the neoclassical was partly a matter of aesthetics. Classics stood for what was decorous and tasteful. It was bad taste, asserted the Earl of Shaftesbury, that "makes us prefer a Turkish History to a Grecian, or a Roman; an Ariosto to a Virgil; and a Romance or Novel, to an Iliad."[2] It was also a question of morals: symmetry and proportion were seen as essential components to a good and well-lived life.[3] But self-interest was also at stake. Both political and social motives existed for looking to antiquity to provide suitable models for the eighteenth century. Rome, of course, had been both republican and imperial in its long history, but the English elite at that time had a preference for the republican model because it suited their privileged position in the new political settlement that had been established after the Glorious Revolution. By adopting some of the virtues of the Roman republic as its ideals, the English aristocracy sought to both justify the oligarchy they now formed and aggrandize it by historical parallel. Men such as these naturally turned to the heroes of Homer and Plutarch for inspiration, because they recognized in them the same qualities of rank and title they possessed themselves.

Roman models of political and moral behavior lent authority and legitimacy to the English elite's claim to good governance. Horace, in particular, with the emphasis on his moderation and wisdom, seemed to epitomize the kind of calm that was needed after the revolutionary crises of the previous century. His literary persona of the gentleman writer was also attractive to the landed gentry of the shires. Such men turned to garden architecture to help reinforce the elite's image of itself as guarantor of the nation's newly won liberty. The message was a simple one: the best moral and political values of classical antiquity expressed in a new harmonious relationship with nature. Tastes were to change, in particular in the late eighteenth century with a switch in fashion toward classical Greece.[4] At a time when more revolutionary models were needed, Greece offered a more fertile seedbed of comparisons and ideas. Writers like Horace and Virgil seemed artificial and lacking in the down-to-earth honesty of Homer. Greek religion seemed so much more sincere than the political manipulation that characterized dealings with the Roman pantheon. But whether the vogue was for the Greek or the Latin, the central importance of antiquity and its values remained the same.

To be fair, the elite also had more altruistic motives for turning to the past. The Roman republic had been based on the individual's duty to serve and defend it. They tried to use the image of Roman republican ideals to establish a more unifying image of individual freedom that was not incompatible with the notion of either aristocracy or constitutional monarchy. To read the classics was, therefore, to publicly express devotion to freedom. Gibbon was later to point out that it had been loss of freedom, of virtue, and of honor that had been central to Rome's decline and inseparable from it. The Glorious

Revolution had also enshrined religious toleration, save for Catholics, and ancient Rome was able to furnish a "model of toleration" and a "rational and natural religion whose *pietas* underpinned civic-minded *virtus*."[5] The importance of morality to the aristocratic idea of government meant equally that they saw it as a prime mover in the rise and fall of nations. Hence, Gibbon's image of decline and fall "stressed the need for the British to consider morals for the survival of their own empire."[6] The cause of that decline—luxury and corruption stemming from immoderate greatness—had resulted in a loss of liberty and a move toward absolute monarchy. The flow of wealth and power to Britain from its oriental acquisitions and business interests posed a direct moral threat to the survival and health of the polity.

The genuine sense of nostalgia for the ancient past that many English gentlemen so clearly felt went hand in hand with the knowledge that they were far removed from it. This was brought painfully home to them when traveling in what had once been the eastern and North African provinces of the Roman Empire. The true classical Orient lay hidden beneath the surface detritus of the modern Ottoman Empire and its postclassical religion. These needed to be swept away—literally in the case of archaeology, metaphorically when it came to conceptualization—if the eternal truth of the classical world was to be rediscovered and recreated. Collecting antiquities was not just some quaint pastime; it was a way for the gentleman to generate a network of tangible reconnections with the ancient fonts of knowledge.

The present-day Orient was to some extent written out in this concentration on the classical past. But London had also developed a fascination with the East on account of the growing trade contacts Britain had established there. Ellen Harris has argued that the board of the Royal Academy of Music may have subsidized operas with oriental themes, such as Handel's *Giulio Cesare* and *Serse*, because many of its members had investments in the East India Company, and that staging such works had great value as a marketing tool to help keep the image of the East in front of those who might be of assistance politically, especially in the period 1724–1728 after a rival Austrian company had been established.[7] These operas, therefore, are unreservedly supportive of the current domestic political regime; they were "written for the benefit of their elite audiences as a celebration of monarchy and an exhibition of ideal conduct."[8] But the Orient was also rewritten into a form that established it as a kind of anticlassical ideal. Authors refigured characters from the ancient Orient to be foils for classical heroes in a way that shed new light on modern political issues. Xerxes, for instance, was adapted to illustrate the "dangerous sway that harem women are thought to exercise over oriental rulers . . . an influence brought about through the combined deployment of physical ornament and verbal dexterity."[9] In discussing how a king should act, it became useful to adopt a more polar stance that saw the Eastern style of government as excessively feminized and the European, as characterized by Julius Caesar, as possessing the internal moral strength to let public duty prevail over personal desire. Suetonius describes Caesar as a notorious debauchee, but regardless of the accuracy of these observations, these were not the details that Handel and contemporaries chose to focus on. Rather, the Orient provided an easy opposition to Roman stoicism, the purpose of which was not primarily to disparage the East—although it can easily be argued that these texts reflect a nascent Orientalism, which sought to portray the Orient as something inherently in need of Western interference—but to highlight domestic political issues.

The image of Islam and the East was also affected by changes in the way classics was perceived among the educated class in Britain during this period. The advances that were being made in science and technology, as well as the growth in trade and political power, combined to make some feel that the ancients had for the first time been superseded. In what become known as the "Quarrel of the Ancients and the Moderns" (and later as "the Battle of the Books"), British writers reenacted a debate that had initially taken place in France in the 1690s. In one camp were those who believed that the modern nation had progressed to the stage where it was patently superior to classical predecessors in many areas of knowledge and reasoning; in the other were ranged the forces of reaction who believed that ancient authors represented the pinnacles of what humanity was capable of achieving and so could only ever be imitated and, at best, matched. At stake were fundamental issues of whether truth could be discovered or merely rediscovered, whether history could be seen as progressive or simply cyclical, and whether traditional authority should be respected or overtly challenged. Interestingly, most of the supporters of the ancients were educated gentlemen of private means who were opposed by some of the most cutting-edge classicists of the day.

Sir William Temple was very much a gentleman on the side of the ancients. A well-known diplomat and historian, he published in 1690 *An Essay upon the Ancient and Modern Learning,* in which he reaffirmed the manifest superiority of classical civilization over the modern world in the face of a growing feeling that antiquity had been surpassed. "How much we owe," he claimed, "to those learned languages of Greek and Latin, without which, for aught I know, the world in all these Western parts would hardly be known to have been above five or six hundred years old, nor any certainty remain of what passed in it before that time."[10] It might be imagined that such a conservative would have been hostile to the Orient, but although he could hardly be expected to place them on a par with classical writers, he does not discount all oriental knowledge: "It may look like a paradox to deduce learning from regions accounted commonly so barbarous and rude, and 'tis true, the generality of people were always so in those Eastern countries, and their lives wholly turned to agriculture, to mechanics, or to trades": but he believes this "does not hinder particular races or successions of men (the design of whose thought and time was turned wholly to learning and knowledge)" from "being esteemed." In fact, he believes that the physical attributes of the East, the qualities of its peoples, and its governance are all extremely beneficial to the acquisition of learning: "I know no circumstances like to contribute more to the advancement of knowledge and learning among men, than exact temperance in their races, great pureness of air, and equality of climate, long tranquility of empire or government: and all these we may justly allow to those Eastern regions."[11] Orpheus himself "is said to have brought out of Aegypt all his mystical theology."[12] Temple's view parallels his view of European nations, that tradition is what has conserved and protected knowledge: "in the Eastern regions there seems to have been a general custom of the priests in each country having been . . . the perpetual conservers of knowledge and story." In "Aethiopia, Aegypt, Chaldea, Persia, Syria, Judea," the priests were diligent in "the study and successive propagation thereby of all natural science and philosophy." They were like the "ancient colleges, or societies of priests," in that they were "mighty reservoirs or lakes of knowledge, into which some streams entered perhaps every age from the observations or inventions of any great spirits or transcendent geniuses that happen to rise among them."[13] Their behavior, though lacking the logic and art of the Greeks and Romans, was still comparable at a baser level. The ancient "Brachmans" of India, for example, "frequently ended their lives by their own choice, and not necessity, and most usually by fire; some upon sickness; others upon misfortunes;

some upon mere satiety of life: so Calanus, in Alexander's time, burnt himself publicly upon growing old and infirm."[14]

If we hope to find more enlightened attitudes among the moderns, though, we will be disappointed. In fact, the opposite seems to be true. William Wotton rebutted Temple's claims in his *Reflections upon Ancient and Modern Learning*, published in 1694.[15] His view of the Arabs is a poor one: "the Arabs were not a Learned People when they overspread Asia."[16] And he held that what improvements they had subsequently managed to achieve was mainly thanks to the classical world: "the Arabs borrowed the greatest part, at least, of their Knowledge from the Greeks"; and this was despite the fact that "they had much greater Advantages of Communicating with the more Eastern Parts of the World, than either Greeks or Romans ever had."[17] The traditional aspect to oriental learning that Temple found so appealing is a negative for Wotton in that he believes it hinders other forms of progressive study: "if the Philosophy of the Eastern Nations was all Traditionary, 'tis plain their other Learning could not be profound." Disciplines such as physics, geometry and natural history "will naturally teach Men into Enquiries into the Causes of the Phaenomena which daily occur. Those Enquiries will necessarily produce Principles and Hypotheses."[18] By contrast, in the East, "Tradition, the Fountain of all their knowledge, is only the Effect of Memory. And as it shews, that there is no Inquisitive Genius (the Mother of all Knowledge) in the People who content themselves with it, so all Acquiescence in it is utterly inconsistent with great Progresses in Natural Learning."[19] He concludes by emphasizing how it was this difference between science and tradition that distinguished the Greeks in terms of their achievements and in relation to the Orient: "I cannot possibly see how those who allow the Greeks to have been chief Advancers of Science as opposed to Tradition amongst the Ancients, can deny that Natural Learning, in every particular, was carried to a greater height by them, than by any of the Oriental Nations." These were countries where in some there has never been "any solid Learning originally."[20]

What, then, accounts for this divergence in opinions about the East between the supporters of the ancients and those of the moderns? What seems to be happening is that as the idea of progress took hold in Europe, so a reciprocal image of regression developed concerning the Orient. The East came to represent something of a mirror image of the developing countries of Europe, a place where time stood still and traditional authority reigned unchallenged. Ironically, the traditionalists used classics as a way to narrow the gap between East and West. They saw both as traditionally minded societies, where the accumulation of knowledge was a backward-looking, drawn-out affair. By contrast, the moderns saw thinkers in the classical world take the first steps on the very path of progress along which Western society was now striding with such confidence. The Orient in this view had long since been left behind by Western creativity and its natural propensity for critical thinking and the acquisition of knowledge.

The different views of the East that were created in this process reflected internal English debates about the nature of contemporary social developments. Other texts from the period operate in a similar way: using the Orient, past and present, as a foil against both the classical world and modern England so as to discuss domestic change. One such development was the place of women in society.

According to Simon Ockley, elected professor of Arabic at Cambridge University in 1711 and sometime inmate of the prison at Cambridge Castle for debt, the women of South Barbary were kept almost under lock and key by their husbands: "they are Jealous to that degree, that the Husband will not trust a Brother with his Wife."[21] But, like Ovid, he does not believe this will have any effect: "Yet. In spite of all the Strictness and Caution they can use, the Women have Will and Invention enough to procure a great many Opportunities favourable to their Inclinations." For as Ovid says, and he quotes him here in Latin—"we try to get what has been forbidden us, and we always want whatever we have been refused."[22] He believes that "these Barbarians with all their Suspicion and Jealousie" are wasting their time because "Restraint and Prohibition naturally excite Desire, and quicken our Appetites." At home, however, women can be relied on to behave more morally because, as he reckons, "we are generally more secure of the Chastity of our Women in England, where their Vertue and Innocence are their only Guards." For as he and Ovid both understand it, a woman's only armor is her virtue. By allying himself with the classical past and what he sees as its superior understanding about how the female mind works, Ockley establishes a comparative image of Muslim society as being both oppressively patriarchal and ineffective with it. England, by contrast, is a place where not only do the men operate a kind of benevolent oversight of the women, in that they allow them enough freedom to act as they please, but do so in the context of a restrictive moral code that condemns inappropriate behavior. It is, therefore, a country of both greater freedom and higher virtue.

Lady Mary Wortley Montagu was perhaps the embodiment of this ideal. She accompanied her husband to his appointment as ambassador to the Sublime Porte, and the fifty-two literary letters she wrote from Istanbul provide arguably "the first example of a secular account by a woman, on the Muslim Orient."[23] They represent a new kind of travel memoir, where autobiographical detail was included both to entertain and to convince the reader of the authenticity of her account, and also because it focused on some of the more intimate, homely aspects of Turkish life to which she, as a woman, was able to gain better access than earlier male travelers. To reach these domestic scenes of Istanbul, though, she had to journey through some of the rougher border regions of the Ottoman Empire. On 16 January 1717, she wrote to Alexander Pope while preparing for the journey from Vienna to Istanbul, "I am threaten'd at the same time with being froze to death, bury'd in the Snow, and taken by the Tartars who ravage that part of Hungary I am to passe." She survived her trip but was disappointed to find that she found few classical remains: "You will expect I should say something to you of the Antiquitys of this Country, but there are few remains of Ancient Greece. We pass'd near the piece of an Arch which is commonly call'd Trajan's Gate . . . but I rather beleive it the remains of some Triumphal Arch (tho I could not see any inscription)."[24] She discovered one of the reasons the ancient remains were in such a poor state of repair on a trip to Troy: "here are many tombs of fine Marble and vast pieces of Granite, which are daily lessen'd by the prodigious Balls that the Turks make from them for their Canon."[25] But this disregard for the relics of antiquity was not confined to the Turks. She relates how she has "made some progress in a Collection of Greek Medals." She had acquired "some very valuable of the Macedonian Kings, particularly one of Perseus. So lively I fancy I can see all his ill Qualitys in his face. I have a Porhyry Head finely cut of the true Greek Sculpture, but who it represents is to be guess'd at by the Learned when I return, for you are not to suppose these antiquarys (who are all Greeks) know any thing. Their Trade is only to sell."[26] The Ottoman Empire is in this way established as a place lacking in the taste necessary to appreciate these fine historical artifacts and has corrupted even the Greeks into such an attitude too. It takes an aristocratic English traveler to see the inherent beauty, and not just the value, in them.

Lady Mary presents the Ottoman troops as oppressors. She writes complaining of the "Theeves" in the woods of Serbia and how she had need of her guard: "Indeed, the Janizarys had no mercy on their [the poor villagers'] poverty, killing all the poultry and sheep they could find without asking who they belong'd to, while the wretched owners durst not put in their claim for fear of being beaten. Lambs just fall'n, Geese and Turkeys big with Egg: all masacre'd without distinction." So dreadful is the scene that she fancies she "heard the complaints of Moelibeus for the Hope of his flock."[27] Poor Meliboeus, in Virgil's first Eclogue, is a shepherd who has been forcibly dispossessed. Referencing him seems to have served two purposes: the first was to establish Turkey as a place of injustice, violence, and poor governance on a par with that of the late Roman republic, the time when Virgil too had lost his lands; the second was to implicitly set up Lady Mary as Tityrus, Virgil's other shepherd, who, like Virgil himself, has recovered his land and is rejoicing in his newfound leisure in a place where justice has returned. The Ottoman Empire, in other words, is a place where political morality has been lost, and is a society that needs an Augustus to restore it to its previous glory.

This is not to say that Lady Mary does not recognize that there are fine qualities to Ottoman life. Writing to Pope in 1717, after the publication of the second volume of his translation of the *Iliad* in 1716, she refers to some poetry written for a Turkish princess and finds "there is a good deal of Beauty in them." She warns Pope that, like ancient poems, these verses cannot be judged by their sound alone: "You are so well acquainted with Homer, you cannot but have observ'd the same thing, and you must have the same Indulgence for all Oriental Poetry."[28] But the East has become a place where time has stood still, ever since the time of the mythological heroes of Homer. She says, "I read over your Homer here with an infinite Pleasure and find several little passages explain'd that I did not before entirely comprehend the Beauty of, many of the customs and much of the dress then in fashion being yet retain'd." Here, it is the longevity of the domestic details she highlights:

> the Princesses and great Ladys pass their time at their Looms embrodiering Veils and Robes, surrounded by their Maids, which are allways very numerous, in the same Manner as we find Andromache and Helen desrib'd. The description of the belt of Menelaus exactly resembles those that are now worn by the great Men, fasten'd before with broad Golden Clasps and embrodier'd round with rich work. The Snowy Veil that Helen throws over her face is still fashionable; and I never see (as I do very often) halfe a dozen old Bashaws with their reverend Beards siting basking in the Sun, but I recollect Good King Priam and his Councellors. Their manner of danceing is certainly the same that Diana is sung to have danc'ed by Eurotas. The great Lady still Leads the dance and is follow'd by a troop of young Girls who imitate her steps, and if she sings, make up the Chorus. The Tunes are extreme Gay and Lively, yet with something in 'em wonderfull soft.[29]

Likewise, she recounts a trip she made to a Turkish bath in one of the towns where she "had the opportunity of seeing a Turkish Bride receiv'd there and all the ceremonys us'd on that Occasion, which made me recollect the Epithilamium Of Helen by Theocritus, and it seems to me that the same Customs have continu'd ever since."[30] But for all its traditional rustic simplicity, which shares some of the virtues of Homeric times, the Ottoman Empire is a place where standards of governance have declined. The torch of political freedom and moral virtue has been passed on to the English aristocracy, whose higher standards of taste are far better able to appreciate such classical elements as are still to be found in Turkish culture.

There can be no better writer to show how much more sophisticated the image of Islam and the East became during the eighteenth century than Edward Gibbon. His influence on Western perceptions was substantial because, as Bernard Lewis says, "From recondite and learned books, most of them in Latin and little known outside the narrow world of clerics and scholars, he was able to present a picture of the Prophet and the rise of Islam that was clear, elegant, and above all convincing."[31] It was perhaps the first account to give a reasonably balanced account of Muhammad's achievements, and it is hardly surprising that a man so steeped in the classics should make great use of them in the creation of it.

Gibbon had spent long hours studying the works of Cicero and Tacitus as a young man, and when he finally traveled to Rome it was already a kind of homecoming. Such study had not been easy: he notes how "the painful though necessary attainment of two languages, which are no longer living, may consume the time and damp the ardour of the youthful student."[32] But once acquired, knowledge of the ancients granted membership to an exclusive club. As Peter Gay comments, in such an environment free allusion to the ancients was a popular literary device, which "placed the author in a mutually congratulatory relationship with his readers, whom he thus complimented for not forgetting what had been drilled into them in their youth."[33] Gibbon saw great benefit in such learning for "students of the more perfect idioms of Rome and Greece." Antiquity, for Gibbon, was a world of "light and science," of the "free and polished nations of antiquity," where men "spoke the sublime language of eloquence and reason"; in his view, "such an intercourse must tend to refine the taste, and to elevate the genius, of the moderns."[34] Such statements make Gibbon sound more like one of the Ancients in the Battle of the Books than one of the Moderns. And he undoubtedly had the highest regard for the Roman Empire: "The name of Rome must yet command our involuntary respect."[35] Yet Gibbon was far more than just a traditionalist. Gibbon was concerned to use the classical inheritance to understand the modern world better. He was not simply writing a chronicle of events but using Roman history to get at the root causes for why the world was like it was. The past, in Roy Porter's words, was "pressed into service as offering solutions to constitutional conflict by revealing the *origin*, and thus the authentic *nature*, of institutions, titles, offices, privileges."[36] It was not that Gibbon thought the answers simply lay in the past, rather that parallels and comparisons with antiquity could generate a better idea of what could happen in the future given the current state of affairs. But it could only ever be a world of possibilities, not certainties. Gibbon was far too skeptical a historian not be aware of the radical uncertainty of things and the "unfathomable complexity of motivations" that the past reveals.[37]

What Gibbon admired perhaps above all was Rome's civilization. But his sense of the complexity of history meant that he did not see anything inevitable about Rome's rise. Roman civilization had been the product of a happy series of historical developments and individual actions that could easily have been derailed far earlier in its history. It is this fragility that was perhaps the main lesson for Gibbon's readers: that the progress that had been attained in the eighteenth century could not be relied upon to continue indefinitely or inevitably. Civilized Europe, under the Romans, had fallen before to the forces of barbarism, and it could not be ruled out that it would fall again. Indeed, Rome's fall from the heights of a society that excelled in so many fields to barbarity served only to emphasize just how possible such a transformation was.

It is in the context of Gibbon's concentration on the polarity of civilization and barbarism that his description of the rise of Islam needs to be read. Gibbon's barbarians are based on Tacitus's Germans—nomads who lack the civilized arts, laws, property, and money. They are great warriors who, like the Goths, "had humbled the pride of Rome."[38] Once they had settled within the boundaries of what had been the Roman Empire, they lost this ferocity that had been their one unique advantage. So Spain, "which, in a more savage and disorderly state, had resisted, two hundred years, the arms of the Romans, was overrun in a few months by those of the Saracens."[39] For Gibbon, barbarism was nothing but a merry-go-round of violence, whereby each new turn brought into play the latest terrifying tribe of barbarians to oust the last winners now enfeebled and softened by the very fruits of their victory. Gibbon describes how when the barbarian Musa beheld the works of Roman magnificence—the bridge, the aqueducts, the triumphal arches, and the theatre of the ancient metropolis of Lusitania—he said, "I should imagine that the human race must have united their art and power in the foundation of this city: happy is the man who shall become its master!"[40] Yet with happiness and prosperity seemed to come danger. For it was these that threatened to decay the prime attribute of the barbarian: their military prowess.

Barbarians did have one other great quality, which was their love of freedom. Like Tacitus, Gibbon is well able to admire the barbarians, particularly when they display the very qualities that were valued by his own society. His overall idea of what constituted a barbarian can be seen in his description of the "Curds": "a people hardy, strong, savage, impatient of the yoke, addicted to rapine, and tenacious of the government of their national chiefs." Gibbon recognizes in them a resemblance of name, situation, and manners with the Carduchians of Xenophon's *Anabasis*.[41] He recalls how "the ten thousand suffered more from the arrows of the free Carduchians, than from the splendid weakness of the great king." He also admires them for continuing this role in his day: "they still defend against the Ottoman Porte the antique freedom which they asserted against the successors of Cyrus."[42] It is this love of political liberty that Gibbon loves also in the Arabs. Describing the "National independence of the Arabs," he notes how "the arms of Sesostris and Cyrus, of Pompey and Trajan, could never atchieve the conquest of Arabia." Instead, "the legions of Augustus melted away in disease and lassitude."[43] This simple freedom of the Arab was "of a very different cast from the nice and artificial machinery of the Greek and Roman republics, in which each member possessed an undivided share of the civil and political rights of the community"; but above all, they disdain "a base submission to the will of a master."

Of course Gibbon can also see many failings in Arab society, many of which he recycles from Roman texts. Their friendship, he asserts, was "venal, their faith inconstant, their emnity capricious." He explains that the heat inflames the blood of Arabs and makes them libidinous.[44] Quoting Pliny, he recounts how "the Arabian tribes are equally addicted to theft and merchandise: the caravans that traverse the desert are ransomed or pillaged; and their neighbours, since the remote times of Job and Sesostris, have been the victims of their rapacious spirit."[45] Both they and their language "have ever been the same." But Gibbon realizes that certain kinds of society produce specific kinds of leaders, and in the same way that the second century could be seen as the pinnacle of Roman civilization because it produced the Antonine emperors, Muhammad's virtues would have been instilled in him at birth by the type of society into which he was born. Muhammad's grandfather and ancestors are portrayed as the princes of their country, "but they reigned, like Pericles at Athens, or the Medici at Florence, by the opinion of their wisdom and integrity."[46] The freedom-loving, yoke-impatient Arabs were never going to bow down sycophantically to some weakling despot.

It was the change in Arab behavior under Muhammad's leadership that was so noticeable to Gibbon: as the deputy of Mecca said when seeing the city's inhabitants collecting his spittle and hair that "dropt on the ground," "I have seen the Chosroes of Persia and Caesar of Rome, but never did I behold a king among his subjects like Mahomet among his companions." As Gibbon observes, "The devout fervour of enthusiasm acts with more energy and truth than the cold and formal servility of courts."[47] Gibbon is slow to level the charge of fraud at Muhammad because he recognizes that it is often hard to tell it apart from keenness: "From enthusiasm to imposture, the step is perilous and slippery: the demon of Socrates affords a memorable instance, how a wise man may deceive himself, how a good man may deceive others, how the conscience may slumber in a mixed and middle state between self-illusion and voluntary fraud."[48] By using the comparison with one of the founding fathers of Western philosophy, Gibbon is able to distance himself from traditional views that treated Muhammad as a kind of fraudulent magician. He is able to look at him as a historical figure who influenced Europe. Classical reference gives him the space to form a more detached, more sympathetic view of Islam's founder as a clever and charismatic thinker. But the effect of this intelligence and charisma on Muhammad's followers disturbed Gibbon profoundly.

Gibbon hated fanaticism. The fanatic, in his view, represented the confluence of religious fervour, superstition, and barbarism into one destructive force. He sees how the Muslim soldiers in the first siege of Constantinople, in 668–675 CE, were "animated by a genuine or fictitious saying of the prophet, that, to the first army which besieged the city of the Caesars, their sins were forgiven."[49] Gibbon also notes that their motivation was to become Rome's successors, in both military glory and wealth: "the long series of Roman triumphs would be meritoriously transferred to the conquerors of New Rome; and the wealth of nations was deposited in this well-chosen seat of royalty and commerce." But Gibbon recognizes that the material and spiritual benefits that might be transferred to the Arab armies were incompatible with the maintenance of Roman civilization, because for Gibbon, Rome's values, and the great moral figures they produced, were partly the result of a state that was free of the encumbrance of the church. Religion, by contrast, grew out of fear and ignorance, which could only encourage sycophancy and servility. People would be far more willing to accept tyranny and accept loss of liberty if they were in awe of their religious-political leaders. As Porter says, Gibbon saw that no civil polity can "ultimately withstand the destructive forces of the Church Militant."[50] It was religious fanaticism that had weakened the Roman state and left it vulnerable to attack: while Byzantium was "exhausted by the Persian war, and the church was distracted by the Nestorian and Monophysite sects, Mahomet, with the sword in one hand and the Koran in the other, erected his throne on the ruins of Christianity and of Rome."[51] And so, in a typically ironic twist, Gibbon presents a picture of a Christian empire so fervent in its sectarian beliefs that it turns upon itself and falls prey to its greatest religious rival.

Islam's strengths act, in Gibbon's eyes, as the mirror image of Rome's failings. It is a religion that has retained its simplicity, having no caste of priests or central organization. Rome's empire had fallen increasingly into the grip of a hierarchical state church. Of course, Gibbon's sympathy toward Islam also served as an oblique criticism of contemporary Christianity. Portraying Muhammad as, in part, a wise and tolerant lawgiver, leader of an undogmatic and priest-free movement, was implicitly to condemn all these traits in organized religion in Europe and especially in Roman Catholicism. Likewise his adoption of a Tacitean model in the writing of history was itself a rejection of the Christian view of history, which saw history as an inevitable progress toward the triumph of the Cross. To use Tacitus was to adopt a cynical view of power and its abuses, but one that was founded on a very moral view of the world.

Islam's success parallels Rome's demise. The early victory of Muhammad in recapturing Mecca is compared to the return of the generals Marius and Sulla to Rome. But whereas Muhammad was merciful and spared the lives of those who had opposed him, the Romans stained the capital with the blood of their compatriots.[52] A crucial moment in Rome's history, where power transferred to greedy generals in violation of senatorial authority, is directly contrasted with the bloodless and generous character of Muhammad's early rise. Similarly, Muhammad's uncle Abbas, who "like the heroes of Homer, excelled in the loudness of his voice," single-handedly turned the battle of Honain valley.[53] But such mythological associations, harking back to the events that were to lead to the foundation of Rome, did not mean that the Muslims were to retain their traditional free-spirited virtues. The fact that Islam and the sword went hand in hand meant that, for Gibbon, Islam's success meant a rise in barbarism just as it had in Rome's fall.

When Gibbon looks at the forces ranged facing each other at Aiznadin on 13 July 633 CE, the ghost of Rome seems to hover in the background. The Byzantine emperor, Heraclius, has assembled a force of seventy thousand of what could still be self-styled "Romans," "from the proud appellation which was still profaned by the successors of Constantine." The Arabs opposing them are led by Derar, who is inspired by a barbaric concoction of the hatred of Christians, the love of spoil, and the contempt of danger and death. He single-handedly fights off thirty Romans, killing or unhorsing seventeen. After the defeat, the Byzantines are forced to make a liberal offer of peace, but Derar contemptuously rejects it with these words: "Ye Christian dogs, you know your option; the Koran, the tribute, or the sword. We are a people whose delight is in war rather than in peace; and we despise your pitiful alms, since we shall be speedily masters of your wealth, your families, and your persons."[54] Here are the self-styled "Romans" laid low by heroic Arab leaders, compelled to sue for peace from a power that lacks civilized values. It is not, in Gibbon's view, a battle between the Arab barbarians and the civilized Byzantines we are watching, but a battle in which both sides have been barbarized by religious fanaticism.

Gibbon makes repeated use of this kind of triangular comparison of the Roman past, Byzantine present, and Arab future. When he describes the resistance of Pope Leo IV to the Arab attack on Rome in 846, he describes how "the courage of the first ages of the republic glowed in his breast; and, amidst the ruins of his country, he stood erect, like one of the firm and lofty columns that rear their heads above the fragments of the Roman forum."[55] Flashes of the old Roman brilliance were all that seemed to stand in the way of Arab conquest. In chapter 57, he recounts the efforts of the eleventh-century Byzantine emperor Romanus Diogenes to resist the Muslims. In the palace, says Gibbon, "Diogenes was no more than the husband of Eudocia," but when in the field "he was emperor of the Romans, and he sustained that character with feeble resources and invincible courage. By his spirit and success, the soldiers were taught to act, the subjects to hope, and the enemies to fear."[56] Three laborious campaigns Romanus undertook for the deliverance of Armenia. He launched a "bold invasion" but the Muslim commander, Alp Arslan, responded with great skill and exploited the "imprudence of the emperor." In the battle, Romanus was a single solid phalanx, pressing with vigour and impatience the "artful and yielding resistance of the Barbarians," whereas the sultan, according to some Byzantine writers, "committed his forces to an eunuch" and "retired to a distance."[57] Romanus fought with desperate courage but was betrayed by the "base cowardice, or the baser jealousy, of Andronicus, a rival prince, who disgraced his birth and the purple of the Caesars," and, as a consequence, "in this fatal day the Asiatic provinces of Rome were irretrievably sacrificed."[58] But in the aftermath of the defeat it is also clear than the civilized/barbarian polarity, which had been so clear in the glory days of the Roman republic, had all but melted away. The captured emperor is taken "despoiled of his arms, his jewels and his purple," this "successor of Constantine" was taken wearing "a plebeian habit" before the Turkish Divan and "commanded to kiss the ground before the lord of Asia." Reluctantly he obeyed. Alp Arslan is said to have planted his foot on the neck of the emperor, but Gibbon doubts this and in fact believes that he instantly raised up the prostrate emperor, thrice clasped his hand in "tender sympathy," and treated him with "pomp and reverence." The Turk then "severely censured the unworthy subjects who had deserted their valiant prince in the hour of danger."[59] It is Alp Arslan who shows a more Christian forgiveness than Romanus himself says he would have shown.

The Arab conquerors' dismissive attitude to the classical inheritance they acquire is particularly significant for Gibbon. The Muslims, he says, "deprived themselves of the principal benefits of a familiar intercourse with Greece and Rome, the knowledge of antiquity, the purity of taste, and the freedom of thought."[60] He refuses, however, simply to regurgitate the inherited misinformation of old. He discusses the tale of how the caliph Omar had supposedly ordered the burning of the great library at Alexandria with the words, "If these writings of the Greeks agree with the book of God, they are useless and need not be preserved: if they disagree, they are pernicious and ought to be destroyed." So many books were burnt that they fed the boilers of the city's four thousand bathhouses for six months. Gibbon is "strongly tempted to deny both the fact and the consequences," arguing that it is not what the Quran commands, because it says that Muslims should protect the holy books of Christians and Jews. Instead he argues that that the library had already been run down according to ancient sources, a reflection of the decline of the civilized arts in the Byzantine Empire. Moreover, he says, "if the ponderous mass of Arian and Monophysite controversy were indeed consumed in the public baths, a philosopher may allow, with a smile, that it was ultimately devoted to the benefit of mankind."[61] But even if Gibbon rejects the accuracy of such stories, he believes that the classics would probably have been suppressed anyway: "The mythology of Homer would have provoked the abhorrence of those stern fanatics." Instead, lacking any interest in great literature, the Arabs "possessed in lazy ignorance the colonies of the Macedonians, and the provinces of Carthage and Rome: the heroes of Plutarch and Livy were buried in oblivion."[62]

The classics, Gibbon believes, would have done nothing less than civilize the Arabs, both damping down their religious fervour and restoring them their traditional freedom, now lost under the tyranny of the caliph:

> Our education in the Greek and Latin schools may have fixed in our minds a standard of exclusive taste; and I am not forward to condemn the literature and judgment of nations, of whose language I am ignorant. Yet I *know* that the classics have much to teach, and I *believe* that the Orientals have much to learn: the temperate dignity of style, the graceful proportions of art, the forms of visible and intellectual beauty, the just delineation of character and passion, the rhetoric of narrative and argument, the regular fabric of epic and dramatic poetry. The influence of truth and reason is of a less ambiguous complexion. The philosophers of Athens and Rome enjoyed the blessings, and asserted the rights, of civil and religious freedom. Their moral and political writings might have gradually unlocked the fetters of Eastern despotism, diffused a liberal spirit of enquiry and toleration,

> and encouraged the Arabian Sages to suspect that their caliph was a tyrant and their prophet an imposter.[63]

Indeed, it is only once their fanaticism has subsided that Gibbon can trace the first dawning of the restoration of science, when the Muses were invited from their ancient seats. Then the caliphs aspired to conquer the arts, rather than the provinces, of the empire: "their liberal curiosity rekindled the emulation of the Greeks, brushed away the dust from their ancient libraries, and taught them to know and reward the philosophers, whose labours had been hitherto repaid by the pleasure of study and the pursuit of truth."[64]

Gibbon trusted civilization and doubted empire in equal measure. Peter Brown calls Gibbon a "sociologist of empire" who was "always prepared to see in the Roman Empire a paradigm of the universal dilemma of empires."[65] That dilemma concerned the internal distribution of power between the requirements of individual liberty and official authority. For, as Porter notes, *Decline and Fall* is "at bottom a study of the workings of power." It is power that is the unseen hand of history.[66] This is what makes Rome so worthy of Gibbon's admiration—that it managed to balance the demands of law, liberty, and empire for so long. It was a matter of great reassurance that he could also see the Roman political structure reflected in the famously mixed British constitutional settlement. The problem with empire was that it ossified society. In Gibbon's view it took international competition to generate progress, a situation that had been best observed in ancient Greece and again was reassuringly present in contemporary Europe: "The cities of ancient Greece were cast in the happy mixture of union and independence, which is repeated on a larger scale, but in a looser form, by the nations of modern Europe: the union of language, religion, and manners, which renders them the spectators and judges of each others merits: the independence of government and interest, which asserts their separate freedom, and excites them to strive for pre-eminence in the career of glory." He did not see Rome as equaling this level of perfection; in fact, he accepts that "the situation of the Romans was less favourable"; but Rome had acquired good habits early in its history: "in the early ages of the republic, which fixed the national character, a similar emulation was kindled among the states of Latium and Italy; and, in the arts and sciences, they aspired to equal or surpass their Grecian masters."[67] The problem with empire, then, was that it curtailed freedom, stopped competition, and weakened community. The power and wealth that came with empire encouraged flattery and sycophancy and so weakened society's constraints on its leaders.

It is in this context that Gibbon sees the Eastern empires. In his view, Constantine's "orientalization of imperial power was an unmitigated disaster," a long slide into "servility, superstition and sexual abuse."[68] The free spirit of Rome was transformed into the blind faith of theocracy, and the humility of Christianity was turned into a hotbed of high politics. This view did not just apply to the Islamic world. The surviving Eastern Roman Empire is portrayed by Gibbon as a fetid and stagnant pool of corruption. The emperors are all so uniformly worthless that he covers fifty reigns in a single chapter.[69] Likewise the Arab empire was to fall to the overcentralization of power and lack of social cohesion that empire encouraged: "We should vainly seek the indissoluble union and easy obedience that pervaded the government of Augustus and the Antonines."[70] The Arabs had started off with an impressive energy and determination, which outdid even the Romans, though it also displayed a certain recklessness: he recounts how in the victorious days of the Roman republic, "it had been the aim of the senate to confine their counsels and legions to a single war, and completely to suppress a first enemy before they provoked the hostilities of a second. These timid maxims of policy were disdained by the magnanimity or enthusiasm of the Arabian caliphs. With the same vigour and success they invaded the successors of Augustus and those of Artaxerxes."[71] But if the Arabs had a reckless streak, they also showed admirable discipline: "We must applaud the moderation and discipline of the Arabian conquerors."[72] Similarly, in their dealings with the Saracens, the princes of Constantinople "too often felt that these Barbarians had nothing barbarous in their discipline."[73] But once powerful caliphs had recruited large numbers of Turks to protect themselves, these guards, "ambitious and apprehensive," were "tempted by the rich promise of a revolution."[74] In four years of disorder, these troops "created, deposed, and murdered three commanders of the faithful. As often as the Turks were inflamed by fear, or rage, or avarice, these caliphs were dragged by the feet, exposed naked to the scorching sun, beaten with iron clubs." It was only later that the Turks' insolence was curbed, but by then the damage had been done. The "nations of the East had been taught to trample on the successors of the prophet; and the blessings of domestic peace were obtained by the relaxation of strength and discipline." None of which is remotely surprising to Gibbon, for "so uniform are the mischiefs of military despotism, that I seem to repeat the story of the praetorians of Rome."

The fall of the Roman world into general barbarism is nowhere better illustrated than in Gibbon's account of the Crusades. François Furet rightly argues that the principle of the Crusade was a savage fanaticism, which would always be intolerable to Gibbon. He would always prefer a "pre-Christian civilization rather than a Christianized barbarism."[75] The crusading army was like the innumerable hordes with which the ancient Persians had sought to conquer Greece: "The ancient hosts of Darius and Xerxes labour under the same doubt of a vague and indefinite magnitude; but I am inclined to believe, that a larger number has never been contained within the lines of a single camp than at the siege of Nice [Nicaea], the first operation of the Latin princes."[76] But size was no replacement for discipline and military rigor: the First Crusade and its hundred thousand knights and martial attendants cannot compare with the conquest of Asia that was "undertaken and atchieved by Alexander, with thirty-five thousand Macedonians and Greeks; and his best hope was in the strength and discipline of his phalanx of infantry."[77] The Crusaders soon fell into barbarism, with some knights, during the siege of Antioch, resorting to eating the flesh of their infant or adult captives, something which made them "more odious" to the Turks and Saracens.[78] Eventually these "Barbarians of the West"[79] turned against the heart of the Eastern Roman Empire itself, when, in 1204, the Fourth Crusade sacked Constantinople. Their "unfeeling avarice" meant that the Crusaders desecrated the city's great classical heritage: shrines and books were destroyed, as were many incomparable statues, of charioteers, the Sphynx, of the wolf suckling Romulus and Remus, of Bellerophon, Pegasus, Venus gifting her prize, Hercules, and an incomparable statue of Helen, with "a beauty that might have moved her Barbarian destroyers to pity and remorse."[80] Nor did the Latins of Constantinople show any interest in the idiom of Horace or even the Greek of the Gospel, even when "the same grammar would have unfolded the sense of Plato and the beauties of Homer."[81]

Eventually the Crusades fell into the, for Gibbon, ironical situation where King Louis IX of France died besieging Tunis: "It is thus," he says, quoting his fellow ironist Voltaire, "that a Christian king died near the ruins of Carthage, waging war against the sectaries of Mahomet, in a land to which Dido had introduced the deities of Syria."[82] But the end of crusading meant only a respite for Constantinople. That great city where the "power of the Romans was combined with the art and science of the Greeks," a "free idea" that had been "formed and executed by a single mind" when Constantine was inspired to move the capital from Rome,[83] was steadily weakened until in the last years of Byzantium, when the "Roman world was now contracted to a corner of Thrace." Even then, the religious fanaticism which gripped the empire would not loosen its hold. The two Byzantine factions "displayed the ambition and animosity, with which Caesar and Pompey had disputed the empire of the world."[84] Until at the end, only the last vestiges of the ancient Roman spirit lived on and the last Constantine, with his noble band of volunteers, was "inspired with Roman virtue" to defend the city against the final Muslim onslaught.[85] But with their failure, the East's long decline from civilization and fall into barbarism was complete.

6

The Roman Raj

Europe was of modest importance to the world's economy before the Industrial Revolution. China and India probably dominated global output. The Far East, however, began to register significantly in English perceptions only during the early modern period. The traders and travelers we encountered earlier opened up whole new worlds of commercial opportunities and cultural contacts. As those contacts developed, India began to play a far more central role in the English conception of what constituted the Orient. Whereas the English idea of the East had been dominated by the looming figure of the Turk, as the Ottoman Empire weakened and European horizons expanded, it was these farther-flung regions that increasingly fascinated the English imagination. Interest in India became notably more acute after Clive's victory at Plassey in 1757 and was to burgeon in the wake of Napoleon's Egyptian campaign of 1798–1801. English writers used various classical references to both exaggerate and reduce Indian "otherness," sometimes challenging comfortable English assumptions about English superiority. In the eighteenth century, in particular, there was a far less stable sense of the English self than we are to find in the later imperial period.[1] But governing India generated anxieties as well as feelings of satisfaction, and this is reflected in many English texts. The pressure of ruling so large a territory as India with so thin a force as the British possessed seems to have generated harsher, more overtly imperialist texts, particularly in the aftermath of the 1857 rebellion. With their fascination for historical precedent, the British were helped by the classics in shaping their developing relationship with their Indian subjects.[2] Once again the Roman Empire was able to meet many of these imaginary demands.

The Romans knew a lot about India, although not much of it was true. In fact, as Balsdon says, "no story about India was too fantastic to be true."[3] The Roman geographer Strabo had a similarly low opinion of what had been said about India: "All who have written about India have proved themselves, for the most part, fabricators," they speak of "men that sleep in their ears" and "men without noses" and "ants that mine gold."[4] He says that according to the historian Megasthenes, the people who inhabit the Caucasus "have intercourse with the women in the open and . . . eat the bodies of their kinsmen"; also that it is a place of tough sophists who stand on one leg and hold logs over their heads.[5] But he also describes Megasthenes as the second worst liar, so he probably did not take these stories too seriously.[6] According to the orator Dio Chrysostom, India had rivers of flowing milk and olive oil, its people lived to be over four hundred years old but stayed young and beautiful and had no disease.[7] Such fantastical images show just how exotic a place India came to be in the Roman imagination. This aspect of the Roman image of India was no doubt created and influenced by the trade in luxury commodities between the two regions.[8] India was also seen as a place of special knowledge, a land where Eastern sophists and religious fanatics endured great hardships to improve their wisdom and strange medicine men peddled even stranger treatments and cures. India was particularly symbolic as representing the limit of Alexander the Great's conquests and so came to represent the ultimate extent that empire could ever achieve. Above all, it was a place of contradictions. The Indians seemed to live both modestly and luxuriously. Said Strabo, "All Indians live a simple life . . . neither do they enjoy useless disturbances; and on this account they behave in an orderly manner. But their greatest self-restraint pertains to theft." But then, "contrary to their simplicity in general," they also liked to "adorn themselves; for they wear apparel embroidered with gold, and use ornaments set with precious stones." So strange a place was it that "they respect alike virtue and truth; and therefore they give no precedence even to the age of old men, unless these are also superior in wisdom."[9] Grant Parker notes that Indian virtue and barbarism are often mentioned together "almost as if one is dependent on the other."[10] In fact, this very strangeness seemed to be the key to understanding India. Only by recognizing its fundamental exoticism could the Roman fully appreciate how this alternative society functioned.

This recognition of the uniqueness of Indian society was shared by many of the early administrators sent to India by the British East India Company in the final quarter of the eighteenth century. They realized that if the Company was to govern so different and sizable a region with any degree of success, it was imperative that they understood its culture. Under its first governor-general, Warren Hastings, a significant effort was therefore made to translate and study Indian laws and social customs. The most talented of the individuals involved in these studies was Sir William Jones, founder of the Asiatic Society in 1784. Jones was profoundly sympathetic to the Indian tradition and sought to convey some of that sympathy to a European audience. He tried to Westernize the Arabic and Sanskrit literary traditions by translating some of their finest works into Greek and Latin meters, even though he found Sanskrit "more perfect than the Greek, more copious than the Latin."[11]

Jones based his knowledge on firsthand, direct experience, which he felt to be key to its attainment: "the justest description of the Asiatic manners must necessarily be given by those, who, besides a complete acquaintance with Oriental literature, have had the advantage of a long residence in the East."[12] Not even the great historian of Rome, Plutarch, who was "supposed to have resided in Rome near forty years at different times," ever managed this, because "he seems never to have acquired a sufficient skill in the Roman language to qualify himself for the compiler of a Roman history."[13] Jones challenged every preconceived Western notion of the East. Even the image of the Turk came in for revision: "There is no people in Europe, which has raised the terror, and excited the curiosity of the Christian world more than the Turks; nor any, I believe, of whose true genius and manners we have so imperfect a notion."[14] Jones also discovered a common Aryan heritage between the Hindus and their European governors, which seemed to bring the two regions into an almost familial relationship.[15] But Jones's sympathies with the Orient had its limits. Concerning Turkish histories of the Turks, he remarks that some were highly esteemed by the Turks themselves, "yet," he says, "it must be confessed, that the style of these writers . . . by no means answers to our ideas of the simple and graceful diction, the kind of writing which Cicero commends, diffused, expanded, and flowing with a natural smoothness." In fact, Jones finds their style unfathomable: "on the contrary, most of their figures are so extravagant, and many of their expressions so ridiculously bombast, that an European must have a very singular taste, who can read them either with pleasure or patience."[16] Jones believed that the higher authority of the Western literary tradition was based on its classical foundations. In his *Second Anniversary Discourse of the Asiatic Society*, he notes that "whoever travels in Asia, especially if he be conversant with the literature of the countries through which he passes, must naturally remark the superiority of European talents: the observation, indeed, is at least as old as Alexander." He draws the line at agreeing with Alexander's teacher, Aristotle, that "the Asiaticks are born to be slaves," yet he believes that "the Athenian poet seems perfectly in the right, when he represents Europe as a sovereign Princess, and Asia as her handmaid."[17]

Jones's image of India establishes the subcontinent's culture as static and unchanging. So stuck in the past is the Hindu tradition that it seems to go back to antiquity. In his comparative examination of the gods of Greece, Italy, and India, he affirms, "I am persuaded, that a connexion subsisted between the old idolatrous nations of Egypt, India, Greece, and Italy, long before they migrated to their several settlements, and consequently before the birth of Moses."[18] The modes of popular worship seems so similar, he sees a "parallel between the Gods adored in three very different nations . . . but, which was the original system and which the copy, I will not presume to decide."[19] And, of course, the fact that he is prepared to connect the classical European and the classical Indian traditions is a sure indicator of how much further he was prepared to go than most other Westerners either at that time or previously: he comments how "both are so complex, not to say absurd, however intermixed with the beautiful and the sublime." But for all its sympathy, it would be too easy to accept Jones's work at face value as simply the great work of a pure and disinterested scholar. It must be remembered that Jones's work helped the English by enabling them to adopt the mantle of traditional Indian authorities, whether legal or literary. It blurred the stark differences between the local and Western traditions and in doing so made it seem more natural for the English to be in control.

Despite this, Jones's approach was far too sympathetic for many in England. Edmund Burke saw the power that the East India Company placed in the hands of its young administrators as a corrupting influence. He was moved to prosecute Warren Hastings for misgovernment after he had returned home, during which Hastings was likened to Verres, the corrupt Roman governor of Sicily. Hastings was eventually acquitted, but the prosecution reflected a growing and more widespread feeling of superiority in Britain over its expanding colonial acquisitions. The empire now included many of non-British descent who had been conquered by the force of arms and had no representation in Parliament. This shift in the size and composition of its empire generated a debate in Britain about how the administration of these territories should be reformed to be more appropriate to this overtly imperial reality. But British control in India was fragile and rested mainly on the compliance of local elites. The questions of what kind of government India should have and what form its laws should take were, therefore, pressing. In the aftermath of the French Revolution, the domestic mood in Britain was both conservative and reactionary.[20] It was a well of feeling that James Mill, the father of the utilitarian philosopher John Stuart Mill and an employee of the East India Company, sought to draw on by writing a far more judgmental and critical history of India. His *History of British India* was highly influential, became the standard textbook at Haileybury, the training college for the East India Company's future administrators, and has been described as the nineteenth century's "hegemonic textbook of Indian history."[21] His own career in the Company blossomed after the work's publication.

In style his history is very different from Jones's literary works. For one thing, it is a history. It ascribes the degenerate state of Indian society to the static and cruel tyranny of both its political and its religious leaders, which has naturally led to a new more civilized European power taking control. By starting his history late he explicitly exaggerates the role of European and British involvement in India. As such, it very much represents an attack on the school of Hastings and Jones and their notion of sympathetic government based on an understanding of local traditions. Instead Mill sought to find a comprehensive legal code based on the principle of utility that could be universally applicable.[22] Trying to establish a universal system of government obviously entailed the examination of many different forms of government. Mill's approach, therefore, was inherently comparative. By looking at the various kinds of government that had existed throughout history, Mill sought by critical comparison to arrive at a more perfect solution.

Javed Majeed points out that "there is often a confusion between the diachronic and synchronic axes of comparison in these works."[23] Mill is keen to measure India against any cultural yardstick he can lay his hands on. Given Mill's high level of education and achievement in the classics at Edinburgh University,[24] it was natural that he should look to antiquity to provide many of these points of comparison. Allusions to Roman and Greek literature, philosophy, law, and history all provided valuable aid in considering the process of governing imperial subjects. This central role of the classical tradition to British thought concerning its possessions in India was reflected in the importance Latin and Greek were to play in the Indian Civil Service exams.[25] One parliamentary report recommended an allocation of 1,500 marks to English Language and Literature, 1,500 to Latin and Greek, and 1,000 to Mathematics. Modern European languages, Sanskrit, and Arabic were to receive 375 marks each. Such centrality established the study of Greece and Rome as one of the core features of Western culture and thereby excluded non-European traditions from playing any significant role in it. This was an important change in emphasis from the Jonesian approach. Rather than being seen as something assimilable, Indian culture was presented as something essentially different. Many of the binary oppositions that characterized some Greek thought about barbarians were transposed onto the natives: free versus caste-bound, rational versus mystical, progressive versus static. Mill tries to show how inferior this society, however ancient and venerable, was to modern Britain. But Mill did not see India as being inherently incapable of improvement. The great hope of British rule was that it would advance Indian civilization. In that respect, the model of simple binary opposition between Britain and classics on the one side and India on the other is inadequate. Like the provinces of the Roman Empire, India could, in theory at least, rise to the level of its colonial power, however long a road this might be and however much it would mean ridding itself of its traditional way of doing things.

One significant distinction that Mill draws early on between his approach and that of writers such as Jones regards the importance of knowledge derived from firsthand experience. Mill never went to India and had only "very slight and elementary acquaintance with any of the languages of the East."[26] Mill saw no difficulty in this: "A man who is duly qualified may obtain more knowledge of India in one year in his closet in England, than he could obtain during the course of the longest life, by the use of his eyes and ears in India."[27] Such distance was, for Mill, a sure sign of his reliable objectivity, unlike the oriental sympathizers who had been corrupted by long exposure to the seductive lures of the East. He turns to his historian hero, Tacitus, for support: "Tacitus, though he never was in Germany, and was certainly not acquainted with the language of our uncultivated ancestors, wrote the exquisite account of the manners of the Germans."[28] Mill complains of the problems of using evidence which has come from general opinion "borrowed, in succession, by one set of Indian gentlemen from another."[29] But equally he has no time for "rash and superficial travellers," who set down "lofty accounts of the riches of new countries." He wishes to be more like "the Arcadian who was sent ambassador to the court of the king of Persia, in the days of Agesilaus," who "saw through the glare of eastern magnificence."[30] And in order to further stake his claim to independence, he likens his dilemma to that of the first great "objective" historian, Thucydides: "The difficulty arising from this source of false information was felt by the very first accurate historian." Thucydides, however, he quotes in the original Greek.

This quote is placed not in the body of the text, but in a footnote. It is a noticeable feature of Mill's work that he packs his footnotes with classical references, often cited in the original language. The effect is to provide legitimacy and confer authority on the opinion of the text, even if the classical underpinning is literally subordinated to the text. The fact that he used footnotes, not endnotes, means that they act as physical supports for the superstructure of the text above. And whereas Gibbon's notes often subvert as well as support his account, Mill's are designed to help establish the eternal value and relevance of his new universal interpretation by locating it within a tradition that stretches back centuries. What he said was as true then as it had been in the works of the great writers of antiquity.[31] Mill is quick, however, to condemn this practice among other subordinate cultures: "Rude nations seem to derive a peculiar gratification from pretensions to a remote antiquity."[32] Referencing Herodotus, he notes that the Egyptians thought themselves the most ancient of mankind, "but the inhabitants of the further Peninsula of India make the boldest incursions into the regions of past times."[33] He says that these Burmans believe that the lives of the first inhabitants of their country lasted one *assenchii*, a period of time they explain thus: "If for three years it should rain incessantly over the whole surface of this earth," then the numbers of drops would only equal the number of years in one *assenchii*. The effect is twofold: to damn the locals as being simple and ignorant believers in mythological explanations, and to emphasize that this a timeless culture, even in its own myths of genealogical explanation.

This difference in attitude toward legend and history is, for Mill, one of the prime differentiators between the British and the Indians. It is that propensity "which so universally distinguishes rude nations, and forms so remarkable a characteristic of uncivilized society," the fact of their love of "filling the ages that are past with fabulous events and personages, and of swelling every thing beyond the limits of nature." Mill believes that this propensity may easily be accounted for: "Every passion and sentiment of a rude people is apt to display itself in wild and extravagant effects. National vanity follows the example of the other passions, and indulges itself, unrestrained by knowledge, in such fictions as the genius of each people inspires"—an opinion for which Livy's preface is footnoted as support.[34] He ridicules Indian mythology for its uselessness in tracing real events: if, in their fables and myths, even the Greeks, "the most accomplished people of antiquity, have left us so imperfect an account of the primitive state of their own country, little is to be expected from nations confessedly and remarkably inferior to them."[35] And he justifies his contempt for Indian mythology by locating it at the end of a long Western tradition of such views: "The people of the East have far surpassed the other races of men in the extravagance of their legends. The Babylonians, the Arabians, the Syrians, the Egyptians, have long been subject to the contempt of Europeans, for their proneness to invent and believe miraculous stories." And to emphasize the longevity of the oriental tendency to tell such tales, he notes that the ancient satirist Lucian "deems it a sarcasm, the bitterness of which would be universally felt, when he says of an author, infamous for the incredible stories which he had inserted in his history, that he had attained this perfection in lying, though he had never associated with a Syrian."

Not only is India presented as a place where legend is preferred over history, but as therefore a place which has no history. "From the scattered hints contained in the writings of the Greeks," he says, "the conclusion has been drawn, that the Hindus, at the time of Alexander's invasion, were in a state of manners, society, and knowledge, exactly the same with that in which they were discovered by the nations of modern Europe."[36] India's image is thus loaded with insinuations of inaction. It is a place with an unchanging essence, which gives the impression, as Mill sees it, that it is only natural for a more advanced society to step into the driving seat. A country that has no change has no history; its history begins with the arrival of the British. The British, in this view, were therefore vital for any progress India was to achieve. India needed the British to lead it out of the perpetual standstill in which it was trapped. It was consequently essential that the British maintain their distance from the local culture in case they too were sucked down into the quicksands of Indian tradition. There was no room for fusion between East and West; that would have to wait for the far-off time when Britain had managed to drag India out of its stasis.

Mill sees India's traditional legal framework as inadequate. He likens the system of Hindu judges to Herodotus's account of the king of Persia, for whom "it was law, to do whatever he pleased."[37] And in the public nature of judicial proceedings "common to rude nations," he sees traces of the murder trial depicted on the shield of Achilles in the Iliad.[38] Hindu law is certainly well below the level of English law, founded as it is upon Roman principles. Discussing the legal distinction between persons and things, he notes, "This was the groundwork of the arrangement bestowed upon the Roman laws. It is that of the arrangement which continues to prevail in the English; rude as it is, at once the effect, and the cause, of confusion. It will be seen, however, that even this imperfect attempt at a rational division was far above the Hindus."[39] The Hindus are even located a distance below the ancient Egyptians because they allow creditors to seize and bound their debtors and then beat their money out of them: "This mode of personal seizure had place at an early age among the Egyptians; but they made sufficient advancement to abolish it."[40] Property laws also, in Mill's eyes, locate the Hindus substantially below classical Greece and Rome: "It is only in stages of society considerably advanced, that the rights of property are so far enlarged as to include the power of nominating. . . . It was first introduced among the Athenians by a law of Solon, and among the Romans, probably, by the twelve tables. The Hindus have, through all ages, remained in a state of society too near the simplicity and rudeness of the most ancient times, to have stretched their ideas of property so far."[41]

The 1858 edition of Mill's history came out shortly after the shock of the Indian rebellion. It might be imagined that such an event would lead to, if anything, an increase in the degree of fervor of derogatory British rhetoric about traditional Indian culture. Interestingly, though, the opposite is the case. The edition comes with additional footnotes by Horace Wilson, the first holder of Oxford's chair in Sanskrit, who had continued Mill's history in the 1840s. Many of his comments obviously predate what the British called "the Mutiny," but they show that there was no simple slide in the nineteenth century from sympathetic observation of Indian culture to one of greater hostility. In fact, Wilson's comments on the Indian legal system are of the opposite end of the spectrum. Making equal recourse to classical referents, he notes that in contrast with Mill, "in the spirit of Pyrrhus's observation on the Roman legion, one cannot refrain from exclaiming, I see nothing barbarous in the jurisprudence of the Hindus."[42] Likewise, he refuses to accept that "the right of dividing property by will, is clearly no proof of advance in civilization by the instance given!" Both the Athenians under Solon and the Romans under the Twelve Tables were, he argues, "certainly less refined than the Hindus."[43] In fact, Wilson's comments show that the growth of the discipline of oriental studies was resulting in a far more balanced assessment of Indian culture in some academic work. Mill, though, has no such doubts or refinements: "Two principles therefore universally characterize the penal code of a barbarous people: severity; and retaliation. The early laws of the Greeks and the Romans were cruel; the laws of the twelve tables, says Mr. Gibbon, like the statutes of Draco, were written in characters of blood." Mill denies that "mildness which has generally been attributed to the Hindu character." Instead he finds that "hardly any nation is distinguished for more sanguinary laws," and is even able to quote Sir William Jones that they are "shocking to humanity."[44] He lists various examples in a footnote—a goldsmith who commits fraud is sentenced to be "cut piecemeal with razors"; a woman who murders her husband, son, or spiritual guide shall have her ears, nose, hands, and lips cut off and then be exposed to be killed by cows—and the parallel for Mill is obvious: "The same system of mutilation prevailed in Persia."

A sure sign for Mill of Indian barbarity is their sexual mores: "Among rude people, the women are generally degraded; among civilised people they are exalted. In the barbarian, the passion of sex is a brutal impulse, which infuses no tenderness."[45] The fact that Indian law on adultery "includes every unlawful species of sexual indulgence" leaves him disgusted: "If the laws are any proof of the manners of a people, this article affords indication of one of the depraved states of the sexual appetite." He is shocked to report, "There are even titles of sections in the code which cannot be transcribed with decency, and which depict crimes unknown to European laws."[46] Wilson's comments again deploy classics to help rebut Mill's claims: "The offences denounced . . . were not unfamiliar to Greece and Rome, in their most polished periods, if their satirists and historians may be credited."[47]

Mill can see some mitigating circumstances for the backwardness of Indian religion. "We find several nations," he says, "who make a considerable figure in the history of the world, who have not in this respect advanced beyond the Hindus."[48] For, although the Hindus "had made considerable progress beyond the first and lowest stage of human society," he thinks it "seems common, however, to retain for a long time the ideas which are then implanted." Hence, "the Greeks and the Romans did not reject their Jupiter, and Mars, their gods of the mountains, trees, and rivers, when they rose to more comprehensive views of the universe; they only endeavoured to accommodate to these primary conceptions their new apprehensions and conclusions." This is what explains and perhaps excuses the Hindu retention of the "long and splendid catalogue" of their 330 million deities.[49] But Mill ensures that his readers do not lose sight of just how backward such beliefs are in his opinion in comparison with the classical tradition: "it is well known how vile and degrading were the notions of the Divine Nature presented in the fictions of the Greek poets; insomuch that Plato deemed them unfit to be read." Plato, Mill argues, states that "the only practical inference the youth could draw from the accounts delivered by the poets concerning the gods was; to commit all manner of crimes, and out of the fruits of their villainy to offer costly sacrifices, and appease the divine powers." He sees nothing better in Indian religion, since "the Brahmens themselves do not surpass the Greek poets in elevated expressions concerning the Deity."[50] Like the "timid barbarian, who is agitated by fears respecting the unknown events of nature," the Indian "feels the most incessant and eager desire to propitiate the Being on whom he believes them to depend."[51] He groups Indian religious beliefs into an amalgam of barbaric beliefs, which are all characterized by their inferiority to ancient rationality: "It is remarkable that the Greeks and the Romans were forcibly struck with the similarity between the ideas of the Druids, and those of the Brahmens of India, the Magi of Persia, the Chaldeans of Assyria, and the priests of Egypt."[52] The absurdities of Hindu religion are, in Mill's eyes, comparable with the neo-Platonists of late antiquity who twisted allegorical readings from mythology, like Proclus who "borrows many exalted notions from Christianity; and blends them with the basest alloy, with the dregs of Pagan mythology."[53]

The Indian caste system was hard for a Briton like Mill to comprehend, but he sees it as fundamental to understanding Indian society: on it "the whole frame of Hindu society so much depends," and as "an object of primary importance," it merits a "full elucidation."[54] He needs to bring Plato in, though, to help him fathom so strange a hierarchy. He notes there is "a remarkable passage in Plato . . . in which he describes the effects which would be produced on a small number of men left alone in the world, or some uncultivated part of it." They naturally divide themselves into four classes according to their types of labor. "The Hindus," he suggests, "appear to have had similar opinions, though without the reasons."[55] He gives other ancient examples of a fourfold division: "It is worthy of observation that the Colchians and Iberians were also divided into four castes, whose rank and office were hereditary and unchangeable."[56] Indeed, the classical evidence points to the distinction of castes belonging to the most antique periods: "There is a passage in Herodotus which leads us to conclude, that the distinction of castes existed among the Medes at the commencement of the monarchy."[57] By assigning the caste system to the farthest reaches of history, Mill establishes India as a place where nothing changes. The antiquity of Indian culture becomes a sign of barbarity and lack of development, whereas for Europeans the connection with the classical past showed just how firm were the foundations on which its progress was based.

The Brahmans, as the highest caste, are for Mill the epitome of a undeveloped society. He notes that, according to Julius Caesar, a similar priesthood existed in ancient Britain: "The Druids among the ancient Britons, as there was a striking similarity in many of the doctrines which they taught, also possessed many similar privileges and distinctions to those of the Brahmens." Here it is the Hindus who become the ancient Britons, whereas the moderns take on the role of dispassionate, superior observer. Like Caesar, it is Mill who has come to look at India (albeit from afar), seen its barbaric state, and then conquered it allusively.[58] It was the growth of reason, fostered by classics, that enabled the ancients to escape from their former prehistoric state: "Our ancestors were barbarous when the Druids exercised over them an unlimited authority. The soothsayers and priests among the Greeks and Romans lost their influence as knowledge increased."[59] Without that increase in rationality, the simple folk were left victim to the deceit of the priesthood, who would use begging as "no inconsiderable source of priestly power." In a footnote he adds, "The mendacity of the priests seems to have been a general instrument of priestly imposture. It was so among the Romans; and no unproductive one." He adds that Cicero "proposes to restrain the begging trade of the priests."[60] The fundamental division of India into a static and rigid hierarchy establishes it as a country where internal social fusion is impossible, and, therefore, so must be any external fusion with the ruling British. Not only that, but by portraying India as an inherently heterogeneous society, Mill creates an image of a place that positively needs government by outsiders to overcome its inbuilt domestic schisms.

At root it is the lack of civilization that Mill finds so damning about Indian society. In part this relates to what he sees as the low level of material progress. He believes material improvement is important because it acts as an indicator of wider social achievements. He notes how humans progress from wearing animal skins to weaving, which traces human progress "upwards from the lowest barbarism,"[61] adding that this is noticed also by Plato: "It is curious to observe how Plato traces this progress" when he is "endeavouring to account for the origin of society."[62] In other words, this seems to be a universal trait of humanity, which makes it a reliable gauge of advancement in civilization in general. Mill considers dyeing to be "an early art": "The purple, so highly admired by the ancients, they represented as the invention of Hercules, thus tracing back its origins even to the fabulous times." He attributes the discovery of weaving to the city of Arachne, "celebrated by the Greeks and Romans, as the place where weaving was first invented, and where it was carried to the highest perfection."[63] In comparison with that classical perfection, Indian society has lagged behind despite the popularity of weaving there: "That ingenuity is in its infancy among the Hindus," which is revealed in "the rudeness still observable in the instruments of this their favourite art." But Mill does not reject the quality of all oriental textiles. In fact he remarks, "We learn from Plato, that, when any fine production of the loom among the Greeks was represented as of the most exquisite fineness and beauty, it was compared to those of the Persians";[64] also that Pliny mentions Babylonian coverings costing eighty thousand sesterces. Nor does he claim that all the products of barbarian looms are of poor quality: "When the Goths first broke into the Roman empire, they possessed fringed carpets and linen garments of so fine a quality, as greatly surpassed the Greeks and Romans, and have been thought worthy of minute description by Eunapius and Zosimus."[65] It is something peculiarly indicative of the backwardness of Indian civilization that their celebrated weaving, printing, and dyeing of their cloth should still be of such low quality.

Mill finds the same lack of development in the fine arts. Quoting Major James Rennell, an important geographer and administrator in British India, he informs us that "the imitative or fine arts were not carried to the height not even of the Egyptians, much less of the Greeks and Romans, by the Hindus; that like the Chinese they made great progress in some of the useful arts, but scarcely any in those of taste."[66] He is taken aback that Indian music should be, in his opinion, of a base level because he believes this to be one of the easier fine arts: "It is anomalous and somewhat surprising that the music of the Hindus should be so devoid of all excellence"; for "it was in the earliest stage of civilisation, that Orpheus is fabled to have possessed the power of working miracles by his lyre."[67] Wilson feels compelled to defend Indian architecture against Mill's bigoted attack, stating that "the Hindus did not 'heap up stones' without a reason," and "although they depart, in the variety, and sometimes grotesqueness of their details, from the stately simplicity of the Grecian art, yet their rules of proportion are very much the same."[68] The problem for Mill was that they had "reduced architecture to a science." And even here Mill finds them wanting, this time for failing to invent glass windows: "In few climates is glass in windows more conducive to comfort than that of Hindustan, yet the Hindus had never learnt to afford this accommodation to themselves." As Wilson notes in their defense, "the use of glass for windows, is a proof of civilization, that neither Greek nor Roman refinement presents."[69] Mill attacks Indian literature too: "Yet Sir William Jones could say the *Ramayan* is an epic poem which 'in unity of action, magnificence of imagery, and elegance of style, far surpasses the learned and elaborate work of Nonnus.'" This opinion he dismisses: "We strongly suspect that Sir William Jones never read the poem; or more of it than scraps," an opinion that, given Jones's record, seems more than somewhat unlikely.[70]

Mill sees a base level of civilization as being evident in the literary style of the Hindus. It is a style, he says, that shows "all the vices which characterise the style of rude nations, and particularly those of Asia": such oriental stylistic failings he lists as: "inflation: metaphors perpetual, and there the mood violent and strained, often the most unnatural and ridiculous; obscenity; tautology; repetition; verbosity; confusion; incoherence." He rejects completely the opinions of Jones and his ilk about Sanskrit, which they have "celebrated as the mark of a refined and elegant people." Mill states, " 'It is more copious,' we are told, 'than the Latin.' It has several words to express the same thing. The sun has more than thirty names, the moon more than twenty." This for Mill is symptomatic of exactly what makes it an uncivilized language. For him, the highest merit of language "would consist in having one name for every thing which required a name, and no more than one. Redundancy is a defect in language, not less than deficiency." This is a utilitarian philosophy that saw words as wasteful verbiage unless they acted in a clear and simple functional manner. He sees, by contrast, Greek and Latin as possessing the perfect grammar because it supposedly met these criteria. Regardless of the dubious accuracy of that claim, Mill's strategy is clear: to fix important Hindu texts as the florid and overblown outpourings of a barbaric people who therefore have no claim to any higher level of culture.[71]

Mill suspects that what little cultural progress the Indians have made has been the result of Greek influence. As he says of the Arabs, "Their best writers are the translators or copiers of the Greeks."[72] He recalls that Gibbon describes how he has "long harboured a suspicion that *all* the Scythian, and *some*, perhaps *much*, of the Indian science, was derived from the Greeks of Bactriana." Mill also notes,

"A confirmation of this idea, by no means trifling, was found in China, by Macartney and his suite, who discovered the mathematical instruments deposited in the cities of Pekin, and Nankeen, not constructed for the latitude of those places, but for the 37th parallel, the position of Balk or Bactria."[73] But Mill rejects such an outlandish claim. In fact he disparages those who are so credulous as to believe anything so preposterous on account of their desire to find classical influence in everything they admire: "As evidence of the fond credulity with which the state of society among the Hindus was for a time regarded, I ought to mention the statement of Sir W. Jones, who gravely, and with an air of belief, informs us, that he had heard of a philosopher 'whose works were said to contain a system of the universe, founded on the principle of attraction and the central position of the sun.' This reminds the instructed reader of the disposition which has been manifest by some of the admirers of the Greek and Roman literature, and of these by one at least who had not a weak and credulous mind, to trace the discoveries of modern philosophy to the pages of the classics."[74] He adds another example of this practice: "Considerable currency was obtained by a very learned work of a clergyman of the Church of England, Mr. Dutens, who undertook to prove that all the discoveries which the moderns have made in the arts and sciences, may be found distinctly broached in the writings of the ancients."[75] Mill can see through this as being the kind of claim to cultural elitism that the Brahmans themselves practiced: "It is a well-known artifice of the Brahmens, with whose pretensions and interests it would be altogether inconsistent to allow there was any knowledge with which they were not acquainted, or which was not contained in some of their books."[76] Yet Mill is himself guilty of such practices, of seeing the Greek at every corner of the subcontinent: "It is worthy of remark, that the philosopher, of whom Sir William heard, and whose works contained such important discoveries, was called Yavan Acharya, that is Gentile or Greek."[77]

Science is, for the utilitarian Mill, a particularly important subject to measure a country's progress up the scale of civilization. This is Mill's clear description of the relationship between barbarity and utility: "Exactly in proportion as *Utility* is the object of every pursuit, may we regard a nation as civilized. Exactly in proportion as its ingenuity is wasted on contemptible and mischievous objects, though it may be, in itself, an ingenuity of no ordinary kind, the nation may safely be denominated barbarous."[78] A society's practical achievements and focus are to be measured by the state of its science: "According to this rule, the astronomical and mathematical sciences afford conclusive evidence against the Hindus. They have been cultivated exclusively for the purposes of astrology; one of the most irrational of all imaginable pursuits; one of those which most infallibly denote a nation barbarous; and one of those which it is the most sure to renounce, in proportion as knowledge and civilization are attained."[79] The Hindus are stuck in a quagmire of timeless superstition. Even those orientals who have managed to learn from the Greeks barely seem able, or interested enough, to grasp what they have read. Quoting a Mr. Scott Waring, he says, "The science of the Persians is, I believe, extremely confined. They have translations of Euclid, Ptolemy, the works of Plato, Aristotle, Pythagoras, and some other of the Grecian philosophers, which few of them read, and fewer understand."[80]

Mill turns to history to explain why India is in so retrograde a state as he finds it. One of the problems is that the oriental nations simply do not seem to have any awareness of the past. Comparing Greek and native histories of Persia, he quotes John Richardson's claim that there is "not a vestige of the famous battles of Marathon, Thermopylae, Salamis, Plataea, or Mycale, nor of the mighty expedition of

Xerxes." Like Gibbon, he is incredulous that "so little has been preserved of Eastern history before Mahomet, that the modern Persians are totally ignorant of the victory of Sapor, an event so glorious to their nation." And like Gibbon, too, he can only conclude that "the art and genius of history has ever been unknown to the Asiatics."[81] It is simply inconceivable to Mill that these events from the Greek past, which were so important to their history and self-identity, might be seen as irrelevant and minor border skirmishes by the dominant Persian power. For him, it is a sure sign that the modern Persians lack any self-respect or historical awareness that their ancient defeat of the Romans should be forgotten. Here are a people without self-knowledge, who have no historians because they themselves never change.

Some saw the Mughal invasion of India as having the sort of regressive impact on Indian society that the barbarian invasions had on the Roman Empire. But Mill refuses to accept this comparison. He sees it as rash to liken the Mughal conquest of India with the "overwhelming" of the Roman Empire by the northern nations that has "suggested so gratuitous a supposition as that of the degradation of the Hindus from an improved to a barbarous state of society by the calamities of conquest." The consequences of the barbarian invasions on the Roman world were far more significant: the Romans, he says, were "swept from the face of the earth" and reduced to "bondsmen and slaves"; their institutions were replaced, their language changed, and the provinces were already reduced to barbarity by the "detestable government, that the invaders had really not so much to accomplish to reduce them to the same level with themselves." Mill sees the scale of the destruction of this civilization as "abundantly seen in the state of the Greeks of the eastern empire; who, upon their very first subjugation to the Turks, exhibited a condition not greatly different from that in which they grovel at the present day." More comparable, to Mill, would be the conquest of China by a similar tribe of Tartars: "There is no reason to think that the one was a conquest of a more destructive nature than the other." This was nothing more than a change of barbaric faces at the top of an already barbaric society.[82] And in any case, the Muslim conquerors of India "were not perfectly barbarous when they advanced upon the countries of the West"; they had their own alphabet "in no degree corresponding with the troublesome characters of the Chinese, but as ingenious and simple as that of the Romans."[83]

But what history does tell Mill is that the Indians are simply not fit to govern themselves. Even their ancient sovereigns, such references as there are to them, "most of them declare the misgovernment and cruelty of the individuals to whom they relate." And he quotes Captain Francis Wilford, who contributed several articles on Indian history to the journal set up by William Jones, *Asiatic Researches*: "According to Plutarch, in his life of Alexander, Chandra-Gupta had been at that prince's camp, and had been heard to say afterward, that Alexander would have found no difficulty in the conquest of Prachi, or the country of the Prasians, had he attempted it, as the king was despised, and hated, too, on account of his cruelty."[84] Nor does it seem that the Indians have ever really wanted to rule themselves. The Hindus, says Mill, "have always allowed themselves to be conquered in detail, just as the tribes of Gauls and Germans by the Romans." But the Gauls "cost Julius Caesar himself five years to subdue"; and so great was the European spirit that Gaul "several times carried fire and sword to the gates of Rome." "The Gauls," he concludes, "must have known much more of the art of war than the Hindus."[85] Also, "that in war, the Hindus have always been greatly inferior to the warlike nations of Europe, during the middle ages . . . it seems hardly necessary to assert."[86] Not only did the Hindus roll over easily, but, unlike subjugated European peoples, they learnt nothing from their masters: "the barbarians from Germany and Scythia quickly learned the discipline of the Roman armies, and turned their own arts against the legions." And the reason for this was straightforward. Mill believed that "the Hindus have never been able, without European officers, to avail themselves of European discipline."[87] The Indians actively need the British to organize them and fill them with some martial spirit. With no interest in politics, they need the British to provide them with a just and fair government that would otherwise wallow in despotism. And they need the British to give them a sense of history: to insert a timeline into the static mass of the unprogressive Indian past so that they might finally attain a higher level of civilization.

What we see in Mill's history is an early sign of a drift toward a harder British line toward their Indian territorial possessions. Instead of the sympathetic approach of Hastings and Jones, who sought, at least at some level, to bring European and Indian cultures closer together in understanding, Mill reflects a shift in British attitudes. India is coming to be seen as irrevocably different from the West, a culture that is, as it has always been, fundamentally different from the European mold. After the events of 1857, the British were to respond to the near loss of India by trying to make British rule seem both fairer and more permanent.[88] As the flip side to that revised image of the British arose a new, more overtly orientalist, in the Saidian sense, view of Indian culture. India became a place where nothing ever changed despite the political fact of growing political nationalism. An innate disorder and lack of social cohesion meant that India positively required the British to stay to keep the peace. The British created a myth that they understood the true nature of India and governed it in its own best interests. Such a view meant that high barriers needed to be erected between the British and the Indians in order to maintain such a mythological distance, and such barriers were found in the permanent excluders of race and color. Indians could never be assimilated because they were racially different. One Victorian writer, T. Roger Smith, likens the separateness of the British to that of the Romans in their empire, who were visually different to their subjects in everything they did: "Were the British occupation of India to terminate tomorrow, the visible tokens would survive in our canals, and our railways, our ports, and our public buildings, or, at least, the remains of them for centuries to come." For the Romans "unquestionably not only cut their roads and pitched their camps in Roman fashion, but put up Roman buildings wherever they had occasion to build; . . . the Roman governor of a province in Gaul or Britain continued to be as intensely Roman in his exile as the English collector remains British to the backbone in the heart of India."[89]

The problem with all this was, of course, that it was myth. But it was a myth that gathered strength from the retelling. By the late Victorian and Edwardian periods, Britain was employing classical buildings to reaffirm Britain's ties to the continent and to the Roman tradition. Thomas Metcalf observes that, "To build the Foreign Office in a classical mode, as a 'majestic palace, regular and lofty, imposing to the age,' was to assert Britain's predominance in the larger world order."[90] Likewise Scott's India Office building was built in the classical manner but was ornamented with sculptures of the Indian tribes—an Afghan, a Goorka, a Malay, among others—the "social categories identified by the British as significant for their rule of the subcontinent." The Colonial Office had as its centerpiece a huge statue of Britannia in Roman garb, surrounded by classical figures representing Knowledge, Enlightenment, and Power. Works such as these made a clear statement of intention to stay. They sought both to assert the power of British rule and to make it seem as long-lasting and grand as the marble from which they were hewn. This late imperial classical revival can be seen, therefore, as an assertion of imperial authority at a time when British power was coming under threat from other nations in Europe, in particular Germany, and from rising nationalist feeling within India itself. The huge domes and endless classical columns built in New Delhi in the 1920s were in this respect "a device to mask a growing insecurity by shouting forth an assertive magnificence."[91]

Not all Britons held such xenophobic views. Thomas Trautmann has shown that some British writers were also engaged in an ideological promotion of an alleged affection between the ruler and the ruled—a kind of political "rhetoric of love"—that portrayed the relationship between the British and the Indians in far softer tones.[92] Similarly, the Aryan ideal was both powerful and troubling as it placed the British Empire in a grand narrative of universal history but also raised anxieties about how an imperialist relationship of inequality could be maintained over subjects who were in some sense kin.[93] Some, like Charles Trevelyan, saw the need for the British to Romanize the Indian elite in order to raise them up to a higher level of civilization, closer to that already achieved by the British.[94]

Nor did all Indians, of course, accept Mill's hostile assertions. Classics itself became a site of resistance to the attempt to mark the permanence of British rule. Colonial India was, like the rest of the British Empire, not exempt from teaching the ancient Western classics in its classrooms and universities. For example, Greek and Latin were compulsory subjects in the First Examination in Arts offered at the University of Calcutta from the second half of the nineteenth century.[95] But the classics of Indian literature were also used by some to assert the self-worth of the subordinate culture. Some Hindus found in the Vedas and the epics a history of their Arya ancestors. By extolling the virtue and superiority of the ancient Aryas, "Hindu ideologues were able to contest claims of inherent racial superiority."[96]

These Indian classics were flung by nationalist Indians "in the face of the British imperialists to refute their claim that they were ruling India so as to civilize the country."[97] But not all use of classics had an overtly aggressive nature. Some Indian writers were careful to tread a path that allowed them to express some limited dissent from the official view while staying well within the borders of what would be considered acceptable.

One such writer was Bholanauth Chunder, who published his *Travels of a Hindoo to Various Parts of Bengal and Upper India* in 1869.[98] Chunder was a Bengali educated at the Western-style Hindu College, which was designed to turn out the sort of young men who would be useful as minor officials in the imperial administration. On the face of it, Chunder fully bought into the colonial structure. He describes himself as "one who is indebted for his education to the paternal government of the British in India," and indeed his book is dedicated to the viceroy and governor-general of India, Sir John Laird Mair Lawrence, Baronet, whom he describes as one of the "illustrious statesmen from whose eminent talents and wisdom the country has reaped many signal benefits." As one of the rare few Indians who had read the Western classics, his work has a generous sprinkling of classical quotes and references to lend it a liberal, Western feel. For example, when about to set off on his journey, he recalls, "the hour, therefore, of our embarkation was as propitious as could be wished. Both Neptune and Aeolus seemed to look down with complacency upon our undertaking. . . . Thanks to their kind old godships!"[99] He quotes Caesar and compares his task to Xenophon's Ten Thousand. It has the relaxed, urbane air of the educated traveling English gentlemen it is aping.

But such a sophisticated, relaxed feel hides a determined attempt to use classical comparison to reassert the value of Indian history. He makes it clear that in his view the battle of Plassey was not some minor colonial skirmish but a major turning point in global history: the battle "may appear as distinguished by no valorous deed or memorable exploit, but in the importance of its political or moral consequences, its name shall stand on the page of history as equal to those of Marathon, Cannae, Pharsalia, and Waterloo—the greatest battles in the annals of war."[100] Perhaps to counter Mill's charge that the Hindus were an unwarlike people, he narrates their own tradition of the name of the river Adjai, which "means the *unconquerable,*" and hence "many a Hindoo mother, like Thetis, formerly dipped their children in its waters to make them invulnerable."[101] In another passage, he seeks to raise up Indian culture by favorable comparison with Rome. In a five-hundred-year-old water tank at Pundooah, known as the Peer-pukur, he sees a tame alligator that answers the call of a fakir on the embankment: "This beats Pliny's elephants dancing the rope-dance." Chunder footnotes how animal training may well have spread west from India: "Very probably it was from the Indians that the Romans borrowed many of their games in the Circus and Amphitheatre."[102] And if the Indians are superstitious, it is, as far as Chunder can see, no more than went on in ancient Rome: "Shiva, with his matted locks, besmeared body, and half-closed eyes, well personifies the man who drinks a glass too much. The toper-god may be thought to represent the Indian Bacchus. His *phallic* emblem is undoubtedly from the Romans, whose ladies used to wear it round their necks as a charm against sterility."[103]

Chunder laments the British treatment of his fellow Indians. By contrast, he notes that "the imperial Romans behaved not toward the Greeks as conquerors to the conquered, but as pupils to their masters." The British should look to their favored ancient authorities to learn how to deal properly with India: "In the same manner that Cicero and Atticus went to Athens to study eloquence at its source, did Lycurgus and Pythagoras travel to India to learn law and philosophy at their sources."[104] Likewise, "the behaviour of the great Caesar towards the Athenians should teach the Anglo-Saxon to 'forgive the living for the sake of the dead.'" He rejects the negative image of Indian culture created by Mill: "It was cruel in Mill to labour only to prove the Hindoos a nation of idolaters, forgers, and perjurers."[105] And he defends the "Oriental mind" as having "furnished the world with codes and jurisprudence, that Lycurgus and Solon adopted for their guide. It has produced songs and poetry scarcely inferior to the effusions of Homer." In these respects, he believes that the oriental mind can claim "an equality, if not a superiority, to the European mind." What he does concede, however, is that "it is decidedly wanting in the knowledge of the construction of a civil polity. It has never known, not attempted to know, any other form of government than despotism." Which includes, of course, the British system of government. For if Mill is such a utilitarian, says Chunder, the rulers of India "should learn to govern for the good, not of the fewest, but the greatest number."[106]

7

Empires Ancient and Modern

The British Empire and classics were inextricably intertwined. In part this was a matter of chance. Upper-class schools had traditionally focused on teaching traditional subjects like Latin and Greek, and so when those boys went off to conquer and administer the world it was not surprising that they took with them the accumulated learning that had been drilled into them. But the connection between Britain and antiquity went far deeper than the merely accidental. Classics retained its position at the heart of the school curriculum despite the huge growth in Britain's global role because it seemed well suited to meeting many of the demands that empire made on its educated classes. As Richard Hingley says, "a close knowledge of the fundamental works of the classics was generally felt to be adequate to qualify a public schoolboy for a university or an administrative career."[1] Classics helped the British understand their role in governing the hundreds of different cultures over which they acquired dominion. The shared experience of learning, and knowledge of, the classics enabled the imperial administrative elite to maintain a group solidarity that excluded the many inferior classes beneath them. As such, references to the ancient world helped establish a context of inequality within which contact with the subordinates of the British Empire were both made and theorized. Classics was not, therefore, an ivory tower discipline. It was, as Victoria Larson has argued, "intimately connected with both access to and validation of imperial power during this period."[2] It was connected with access because, as we have seen, in institutions such as the Indian Civil Service, a classical education could bring advancement. The ICS exams remained heavily weighted toward classics through to the end of Britain's imperial century.[3] This actually represented in many ways an improvement on the previous situation where patronage links had given ambitious young men the opportunities they sought in colonial positions of authority. After the Indian rebellion, those hopefuls at least had to show they had the brains to translate Virgil and compose pithy iambic verses of Greek poetry. But classics was not just about power relations. For many of these individuals, their education also led to an "intense individual commitment to the formative, and transformative power of classics."[4] It was how they understood and hoped to improve the world they found themselves governing. The various uses that classics was put to in the service of the British Empire created a far more Saidian, orientalist image of the East.

It is worth remembering that until the mid-nineteenth century, the very concept of empire was "confined to a small group of public men, whose classical and historical education was, undoubtedly, a factor which guided their minds to a fresh interpretation of an ancient political term."[5] This new kind of imperialism saw the relationship between the mother country and its colonies as having far tighter bonds than in the ancient model. Territorial expansion was seen as providing economic growth and increased political clout on the international stage. Above all, it came to be seen as part of a civilizing mission, which brought active benefits to the colonized. Empire, in other words, acquired a positive image. As the world's principal imperial power, Britain took a lead in developing the new kind of rhetoric that accompanied this image. The result was a new type of discourse that sought to justify colonization and imperialism and legitimate the Western powers' acquisition of non-European space for these purposes. The development of an orientalist discourse relating to the space of the Orient was part of this shift.

Imperial powers classified and codified the Orient the better to control and colonize it. Martin Bernal has pointed out how classics has provided "powerful support for the notion of Europe possessing a categorical superiority over all other continents, which in turn justifies imperialism or neo-colonialism as *missions civilisatrices*."[6] Ancient Greece provided Europe with a continuous and universal character that was "not merely the vanguard of world progress but is the essence of the world itself."[7] Imperialists established Britain as Rome's heir, locating Britain in a lineage that went directly back to the great civilizer. Previously, as Rosalind Ballaster notes, the Orient had existed only as a loose conceptual unity.[8] The nineteenth century saw a complete revision and reconstruction of this notion of the East as a place that lacked the essential elements of a civilized culture: it had failed to develop the work ethic, political rights, and institutions necessary to function as a progressive region. Its states were, therefore, failing states, and it was the moral duty of the Western powers to replace them with more modern and enlightened government. Moreover, as the inheritors of Rome and its Christian civilization, the European nations were seen as having the right both to rule over Muslims and to recover the Mediterranean lands that had been lost to the Arab invaders of the past.

Quoting the classics came easily to the educated British imperialist. Such references were directed primarily at other members of the upper echelons of British society, although public buildings in the classical style were partly aimed at impressing a far wider audience with British power and authority. School texts and popular novels also helped to communicate the idea of an imperial mission to Britons who were not members of the aristocracy.[9] Apart from a brief period of Hellenophilia in the first half of the nineteenth century, it is fair to say that Rome was always the more significant referent for British imperialists.[10] Indeed, as the century passed, more and more emphasis was placed on the analogy between Britain and ancient Rome. Rome provided both an imperial language that could adequately express the reality of British hegemony and a political model that could be used as a point of comparison. This kind of comparative study also came naturally to an elite brought up on the study of languages and cultures that were distant in both space and time.

Of course, one of the main points of comparing the two empires was to validate the British imperial enterprise and provide it with venerable precedents. The Roman precedent gave a sense of permanence to the whole imperial project and served to convince the British of "the rightfulness of imperialistic endeavor and of their role in it."[11] Roman colonization was seen as having helped the ancient Britons, and therefore the later British could argue that it would help those that they colonized. Just as the British had needed Romanization to fulfill their potential, so did the peoples that now came under British rule.[12] References to classics emphasized that Western society had ancient roots and was here to stay. The Roman model also acted as a useful guide in the practical problems of ruling so many diverse peoples across a vast expanse of geography. As competition grew between the European imperial powers, the study of empire itself took on a greater importance. Honing techniques for governing inferiors became a vital matter, if the empire was to continue to grow and thrive. For this reason many of the allusions "clustered around problematic areas of race and identity, in which allusions to Rome are more anxious than reinforcing."[13] For classics did not just reflect British power; it also reflected the doubts and insecurities that such power engendered. It was this, perhaps, that made antiquity so useful a tool for the British to think with. Rome could inspire a thousand different analogies and contrasts and generate a myriad moral tales. As Hingley observes, "part of the value of the image of Rome for the British may well have lain in its flexibility and complexity."[14] The various quotes employed by British imperialist writers, therefore, were generated by contemporary needs. It was not a matter of handing down wisdom from one generation to the next, but of helping those governing the largest empire the world had ever known cope with the problems this raised. These administrators who wielded such great power were well aware of that fact. They knew their place in history and, given that historical outlook, they turned naturally to the past to be their guide.

Lord Cromer was one such man. Consul-general of Egypt, leader of the Men's League for Opposing Woman Suffrage, and president of the Classical Association for the year 1909–1910, Cromer's commanding presence "seemed to radiate the essential spirit of imperial rule."[15] Having spent a lifetime in the service of the empire, Cromer had no illusions about what the East was really like: "Englishmen who have resided for long in the East, and who have thus been brought into close contact with the realities of oriental life, are prone to scoff at the ignorance and impracticable idealism displayed at times by sentimentalists and political doctrinaires."[16] A hard-nosed promoter of British interests, Cromer had, however, something of a soft spot for the classics. In an essay entitled "The Future of the Classics," he elucidated what role he saw the study of antiquity as having: the purpose of education is no less than to teach people to think, and this is best achieved by studying "the most thoughtful nation which the world has ever known. That nation is Greece."[17] His favoring of Greece over Rome might appear surprising, were it not for the fact that so many classical Athenian writers, such as Plato, Aristotle, and Thucydides, were skeptical about the merits of the Athenian democratic experiment. Their antidemocratic leanings and hostility to the masses made them appealing to the English aristocracy, who had seen so much social reform in Britain during the nineteenth century. Cromer had taught himself Latin and Greek, and untranslated quotations in his works "asserted his arrival among the classical cognoscenti."[18] It is easy to see why a man like Cromer would have approved of the paternalism of Plato's guardians of the republic, governing those incapable of governing themselves to society's benefit as a whole. Greek philosophical tracts such as this could easily be read as providing a manual on controlling and regulating the volatile masses of subject imperial peoples.

Cromer's feelings of natural affinity with the classical past greatly surpassed his empathy for the modern world. Quoting a German scholar who said that in dealing with the study of the classics, "the history of the past can be understood by no man who cannot transport himself into the souls of men passed away," Cromer concurs fulsomely: "For a modern Englishmen, however, it is far easier to realise the Greek or Roman past than the Chinese present. When we read the dialogue between Hector and Andromache we can at once make a mental bound over three thousand years. We feel that we are in some measure breathing the same social atmosphere as Homer, and that we are in the presence of a moral code which contains the embryo of our existing social system." By contrast, Cromer is unable to fathom "modern Chinese ethics": "As we read the pitiful record of murder, lust, intrigue and rapine . . . we cannot but feel that here we are dealing with a society separated from us by an abyss which it requires an almost superhuman effort of the imagination to bridge."[19] But Cromer's love of Homer was not of the kind that saw the earlier romantic movement turn away from the overly refined and derivative Roman arts in favor of the primitive, original, and sincere work of Homer. The Edwardians' love of Homer reflected the tastes of an imperial society that glorified its founders and leaders as heroes in the mold of Achilles and Hector. Empire builders like Clive and Kitchener, in this Homeric view, thrived on the thrill of battle, conducted themselves honorably and dutifully, and cared nothing for the wealth that their exploits had won them.[20]

Cromer's love of antiquity did not, however, simply inspire him in some vague and unidentifiable way. Cromer sought to learn from the empires of the past in a systematic fashion. And Rome provided the richest vein of profitable comparisons. In his essay "Rome and Municipal Government," he describes how "Rome can never cease to be of more than academic interest to the statesmen and politicians of Imperial England. Rome bequeathed to us much that is of inestimable value, both in the way of precept and example."[21] By contrast, the empires of Greece had little value—not because of their relatively modest size, but because of what Cromer saw as a lack of racial capacity for the demands of empire: "The undisciplined and idealistic Greek, with his intense individuality, was far less suitable to carry an Imperial policy into execution than the austere and practical Roman, who not only made the law, but obeyed it, and who was surrounded from his cradle to his grave with associations calculated to foster Imperial tendencies." In fact, he has one particular Roman in mind as the archetypal Roman imperialist—Virgil, who was "an enthusiastic Imperialist" and "probably a true representative of the Roman public of his day."[22] The fruition of this comparative study of the Roman world was his *Ancient and Modern Imperialism*, in which Cromer drew parallels from the classical past on a range of military and administrative issues that also faced the British Empire at the time.

The Roman Empire helped Cromer work out what Britain should be doing with its empire. Hingley notes that writers such as Cromer "used images of the Roman empire to help them define the identity and imperial destiny of Britain."[23] On the frontispiece of his book, Cromer chose to quote Euripides's *Suppliant Women*, naturally in the original Greek, with a translation for the lesser educated: "Dost see how thy country, when reproached for wanting in deliberation, looks sternly at those who assail her? For she grows great in the midst of toils."[24] Britain's imperial project will entail great effort, sacrifice, and external criticism. But for Cromer, the character of Britain's rule was also like that espoused by Aethra: though some "states, whose policy is dark and cautious, have their sight darkened by their carefulness," the British, like Theseus, should "have no fears for thee, starting as thou dost with right upon thy side." Looking back on his time as consul-general of Egypt, he muses that little has altered since ancient times: "I think I may say that long acquaintance with the government and administration of a country which was at different times under the sway of the Macedonian and the Roman does to some extent bridge over the centuries, and tends to bring forcibly to the mind that . . . the world has not so very much changed in 2,000 years." He recalls the terror that the thought of European justice could inspire in the corrupt Egyptian official: "Whenever, for instance, I read that graphic account in the Acts of the Apostles of how the Chief Captain, after he had scourged St. Paul, was afraid when his very intelligent subordinate whispered to him that his victim was a citizen of Rome, I think I see before me the anxious Governor of some Egyptian province in the pre-reforming days, who has found out that he has unwittingly flogged the subject of a foreign Power, and trembles at the impending wrath of his diplomatic or consular representative."[25] This was what British power meant to Cromer—the ability to force the weak to accept its righteousness, to enforce a higher standard of justice, and to spread the benefits of British influence throughout the world. It was leaders such as General Gordon who represented the highest embodiment of British imperial ideals. He is portrayed as nothing less than a martyr for the cause: "No Christian martyr tied to the stake or thrown to the wild beasts of Ancient Rome, ever faced death with more unconcern than General Gordon. His faith was sublime."[26] It was, for Cromer, a black-and-white battle between the forces of good and evil, with Gordon's death in Khartoum being "the final scene, in which the civilised Christian faced barbarous and triumphant fanaticism."[27]

Cromer is keen to play down the overbearing nature of Britain's power. Unlike Rome, who was "without a rival," Britain was just one of several competing imperial powers.[28] The British, he argues, were also reluctant imperialists. He likens the acquisition of empire to the Roman experience in Gaul, where it was "the acute dissensions amongst the neighbouring tribes," which "materially contributed in the case of Rome, as it did in the case of the British in India . . . towards the execution of an Imperial policy." In other words, it was only because of the ineptitude and internecine squabbling between tribes that Britain and Rome were dragged in to an imperial role. "Instances abound," says Cromer. "One Gallic tribe constantly asked for Roman assistance to crush another. Adherbal made an eloquent appeal to the Roman Senate for help against Jugurtha."[29] But once involved, Britain's military might was, like the Romans, unstoppable: "A Roman Centurion of the Tenth Legion, when taken prisoner, boldly stated that with ten of his men he would beat 500 of the enemy. With a mere handful of troops, Clive won the Battle of Plassy and founded the Indian Empire." The bedrock on which this strength lay was not technological but a matter of character: "There is, in fact, a good deal of similarity between the Roman and British character." It is a character that is best revealed under pressure:

"Both nations appear to the best advantage in critical times. Polybius said that the Romans were most to be feared when their danger was greatest." And this capacity to overcome adversity struck fear into the heart of their enemies: "I well remember being struck by the slight effect produced in Egypt by our early reverses during the recent South African War. All were convinced that we were the inheritors of that proud motto which laid down as a principle of policy that Rome should never make peace save as a victor."[30] Yet British power also rested on brains. They could, like the Romans, outwit the locals to divert their energies into supporting the British cause. As Cromer says, quoting Sir John Seeley, "the nations of India have been conquered by an army of which, on the average, about a fifth were English." In this respect "the methods employed by the British, both in India and Egypt, bear a striking similarity to that adopted by the Romans. Both nations have been largely aided by auxiliaries drawn from the countries which they conquered." Even if the reasons for using this strategy differed—the Romans being "driven to resort to this expedient owing to the paucity of their own numbers compared to the extent of their dominions, and to the unpopularity of foreign service amongst their own troops," whereas "Economy and convenience led the British . . . to follow their example on a large scale"—the end result was that many of the world's peoples were harnessed as willing agents in their own subjugation.[31]

The fact that so large a part of the globe was colored pink was a matter of great pride to the British, which was itself magnified by comparison with so influential an empire as that of the Romans. Lord Bryce, in his work *The Ancient Roman Empire and the British Empire in India,* argued, "There is nothing in history more remarkable than the way in which two small nations created and learnt how to administer two vast dominions."[32] But Bryce has no illusions as to the nature of British rule: "India is ruled despotically by the English."

The reason for this is partly expedience, partly the inherent incapacity of the Indians for self-rule: the English rule India so, not just because they "found her so ruled, but because they conceive that no other sort of government would suit a vast population of different races and tongues." He finds justification for this anti-democratic stance in antiquity. As in the Roman Empire, no free institutions were set up for the country as a whole but the English have "permitted such self-government as they found to subsist. It subsists only in the very rudimentary but very useful form of the Village Council."[33] For "the government of India by the English resembles that of her provinces by Rome in being virtually despotic. In both cases, whatever may have been done for the people, nothing was or is done by the people."[34] Bryce is well aware of the financial benefits that accrued to England from such an arrangement in her imperial territories. Rome's attitude to its conquests was, in Cromer's view, starkly financial: the Romans "exacted heavy tributes from their dependencies. They regarded the provinces solely from the point of view of the revenue which could be obtained from them."[35] He views the position of the Raj likewise: "Although the methods adopted by the British in India differed widely from those of the Romans, the principle . . . was much the same. For all practical purposes it may be said that for some years India paid a tribute to Great Britain."[36]

But the flow of benefits between ruler and ruled was not simply one-way. The British, like the Romans before them, believed they had instilled order into the chaos they acquired. Law was established, not of the local kind, but good English law: "Had Englishmen never set foot in India, their law would have been, so far as we can tell, exactly what it is to-day." And it was all thanks to the colonial masters: "Neither have those natives of India who correspond to the provincial subjects of Rome borne any recognizable share in the work of Indian legal development. Some of them have, as text-writers or as judges, rendered good service in elucidating the ancient Hindu customs. But the work of throwing English law into the codified form in which it is now applied in India to Europeans and natives alike has been done entirely be Englishmen." The English are the active drivers of this progress—"the more advanced civilization has shown its dominant creative force."[37] The British have also taken the initiative in administrative reforms, which once again bears comparison with Rome. Cromer's view was that Rome did not administer her provinces in a "broad-minded spirit, consulting the general interest." But despite this lack of consultation, the emperor Augustus made "very great improvements," especially by establishing "an efficient Department of Accounts."[38] This was a vital matter in the management of the corrupt Orient: "The establishment of a proper system of accounts must necessarily precede the inception and execution of any sound financial policy; and the inauguration of a sound financial policy is the necessary and indispensable precursor of all moral and material progress in backward Oriental states."[39] Augustus also "put a stop to those frequent changes of officials which did an infinite amount of harm to the Roman, as they have in our day to the Ottoman, Empire."[40]

This was not to deny that the British had made mistakes. Cromer condemns the spirit that "animated the merchant rulers of India"; they do not "gratify our national pride."[41] The methods of these early officials of the East India Company "did not differ very materially from those employed by the corrupt and rapacious officials of Ancient Rome. An interval of 1,700 years had not altered human nature." In fact, Cromer thinks that the British view of the practices of the East India Company during the latter part of the eighteenth century "could, without exaggeration, echo the cry of the Roman satirist . . .

> *Quae reverentia legum,*
> *Quis metus aut pudor est unquam properantis avari?*
> [what respect for laws, what fear, what sense of shame is to be found in a miser hurrying to be rich?]

But unlike the Romans, the British had learned from their errors, even if such a lesson had been compelled upon them. For it was not until the "convulsion of 1857" that "the principle which lies at the root of all sound administration" was "forced upon the rulers of India"; that "administration and commercial exploitation should not be entrusted to the same hands."[42] The consequence of such reform was that British government acquired a moral aspect that outdid Rome, where only "a few faint traces of the modern spirit of humanitarianism are to be found in Roman historical methods."[43] The Romans did, for example, temporarily exempt people from paying tribute when natural disaster struck; but for Cromer this is not enough: "The modern Imperialist will not accept the decrees of Nature. He struggles manfully, and at enormous cost, to resist them."[44] He is convinced that "the policy of preserving and prolonging human life—even useless human life—is noble."[45] But he believes that this benevolence has created problems in India. British rule has been so beneficial that the population level has risen markedly, and with it so has poverty: "But of this I am well convinced: that whatever impoverishment has taken place is much due to good than to bad government. It is largely attributable to a beneficent intention to deliver the people of India from war, pestilence, and famine." So if Britain has not always been completely successful in its administration in India, it has at least reformed itself and through its moral character brought many improvements to native life. This was far more than could be said of Rome or, indeed, of what British rule had replaced: "No such intention ever animated the Imperialists of Ancient Rome, or, in more modern times, the indigenous rulers of Asiatic States."

This moral stance, in Cromer's view, raised the British Empire above the level of ancient empires. After all, any despot could aim simply to conquer and thereby increase his territories: even "the boastful and incompetent Xerxes aimed at universal empire."[46] Cromer sees that empire is a heavy burden that should not be taken on lightly. Some of the wisest Romans had "struggled as honestly and manfully to check the appetite for self-aggrandizement as ever Mr. Gladstone and Lord Grenville strove to shake off the Egyptian burthen in 1882."[47] But civilizing the uncivilized and barbaric through imperialism had become the moral duty and responsibility of the cultured nations. Orientals displayed the full range of uncivilized behaviors and so needed to be improved. This role of civilizer was one that Rome had filled within its borders and so also made comparison between the two regimes profitable. In the same way that Rome had had to deal with backward and recalcitrant provincials and try and drag them up by their bootstraps into the civilized world, so Britain had to do the same with its colonial subjects. Britain was, in this way, represented as the receiver of the cultural baton from Rome. And just as "Rome enabled the British to achieve salvation" through its introduction of Christianity, so now the British would do the same for the nations under its care. The British Empire, in other words, was nothing less than the vehicle for the deliverance of the divine plan for the world.[48]

But civilizing meant a closing of the cultural gap that British imperialists believed existed between them and those they ruled. The problem was twofold: If the natives were to become civilized, then it was not clear on what moral basis British rule would rest; or if, once civilized, lesser peoples were to be assimilated, then the resultant loss of differentiation would itself create a diluting effect on the British people. As Catharine Edwards comments, "Roman models were used to articulate anxieties about the dilution of British identity as a consequence of empire."[49] One solution was simply to deny that any closure was possible or likely in anything but a generational time frame. Sir Charles Lucas, who published his *Greater Rome and Greater Britain* in 1912, felt, on the basis of the Roman experience, that assimilation would only have at most a supporting part to play in maintaining the cohesion of the empire: "The Roman Empire was held by force, supplemented by assimilation, the nucleus of which assimilation was in the Roman colonies."[50] As first head of the Dominions Department of the Colonial Office, Lucas was in a position to speak with some authority on the matter. What differentiated the Roman and British Empires, in his view, was the "great gulf" between the "sphere of rule and the sphere of settlement." Though many British settlers had gone to places such as North America and the Antipodes, India—"perhaps the most advanced of the British dependencies"—"never has been and never will be made British by settlement." Lucas felt that India "perhaps of all parts of the British Empire is most nearly akin to a Roman province." But possessing a culture wholly alien to Britain, it could never hope to achieve self-government: "If it were to be placed in the category of self-governing peoples, it would be placed in a category to which it does not naturally belong, and it would be endowed with entirely alien institutions." In Lucas's opinion, such unity as did exist in India, "is the result, as the Roman Empire was, of all the diverse elements being controlled by one alien rule," which would itself disappear if self-government were granted.[51]

Cromer saw Roman-style assimilation as an impossibility. Noting that India had been conquered and held by a small English force, he believes this "of necessity" leads to one of two consequences: "either the conquered race is ultimately placed on an equal—or even, possibly, on a superior—footing to its conquerors" or "the subject race acquiesces in its subjection, and loyally co-operates with its alien rulers." The fact that "the first of these two consequences ensued to Rome" meant that eventually even emperors could come from Spain. Likewise, "Terence was a Carthaginian slave." But this has not been the case in Great Britain's empire: the "Indian connection, although it has widely influenced British policy, has not in any degree influenced the composition of the legislative and executive machine."[52] Instead, to a large degree the British rulers have simply left well alone: "Save in dealing with some exceptionally barbarous practice, such as Sati, we have followed the example of Rome in respecting local customs."[53] How did Cromer account for this lack of British success in assimilation? "The comparative success of the Romans is easily explained. Their task was far more easy than that of any modern Imperial nation."[54] The problem confronting the British, by contrast, was extreme: five-sixths of the population of India were Hindus, one-sixth Muslims "who have adopted that portion of the Hindoo caste system which elevates association in the act of eating and drinking to the dignity of a religious practice. Thus a very formidable barrier to unrestrained intercourse exists in India."[55] The Romans did not face religious barriers of this kind, and any they did face were "easily surmounted" because the "easy-going polytheism and pantheism of the ancient world readily adapted itself to changed circumstances."

Language seemed to pose an insurmountable obstacle to assimilation. This was in contrast to Rome, where, Cromer believed, there were "practically only two languages in use in the ancient world—Greek and Latin."[56] Cromer was extremely pessimistic that English would ever be sufficiently widespread in India to be a useful cohesive: there is not the least probability "that the foreign will eventually supplant the vernacular languages. In India only 90 men and 10 women in every 10,000 of each sex read and write English."[57] He notes, however, that the number of upper-class Indians with knowledge of English had increased, "which is an unmixed evil—that there is less necessity than heretofore for the British officials to acquire proficiency in the vernacular languages." The result, as he somewhat paradoxically sees it, is "a most unfortunate tendency to widen still further the breach between the rulers and the ruled."[58] Cromer also draws a stark contrast between the natives' attitude toward their conquerors' language. Unlike the Romans, whose conquered races eagerly desired to learn Latin, "modern Imperialist nations have to deal with national sentiments which often cluster round the idea that the extrusion of the vernacular language should be stoutly resisted." He see this happening in Egypt, where "the curious anomaly is presented that the Nationalist party put forward the perfectly reasonable demand that superior education should, so far as is possible, be imparted in Arabic, while at the same time the whole weight of British influence has had to be brought to bear in order to prevent English being taught in the elementary schools." Cromer recognized that a matter as sensitive as the mother tongue was not an area where British power could avail itself: "The British Government would have been very unwise had they attempted to resist the teaching of Dutch in South Africa. As they have not done so, the language will not improbably in course of time die a natural death."[59] The situation in Rome, however, was completely different. A Gaul or Spaniard who learned Latin was motivated by manifest self-interest so that he could "rise to high positions in the service of Rome." Cromer accepts that "the native of India is even now complaining in shrill tones, and, in some cases, not without a certain amount of reason, that the opportunities accorded to him for rising are insufficient." But when he turns to comparing the original motives for learning the language to the use it is put, the analogy with the Roman Empire ceases:

> Rather may it be said that there is a remarkable contrast; for the knowledge of Latin did not serve as a solvent. On the contrary, it knit the subject race to its conquerors, and if it eventually helped to invert the parts which had heretofore been played, the result was due to a variety of causes, and not to any wish to subvert that Empire in which the Romanized provincial took no less pride than the true Roman. Can the same be said of any of the Asiatic or African races who, being the subjects of modern European Powers, have learnt the language of their rulers? I fear not. The bond of a common, if on one side acquired, language is, in fact, much too brittle to resist such powerful dissolvent forces as differences of religion and colour, which are constantly acting in the direction of disunion.[60]

In fact, Cromer sees the teaching of English and its literature as a potent threat, because it "may easily be perverted from a disquisition on the advantages of steady progress achieved by a law-abiding nation into one which eulogizes disrespect for authority, and urges on the governed the sacred duty of throwing off the yoke of unpalatable Governors."[61]

But if there was one factor that prevented any chance of assimilation, it was race. Lucas was of the view that "the greatest difficulty in the British Empire is probably the colour question."[62] The British saw themselves as naturally imbued with the ability and need to govern their own affairs. For this reason, primarily Anglo-Saxon settled countries were given self-rule when nonwhite populations were not: as Lucas says, "the Self-Governing Dominions have become self-governing, because self-government is inherent in the British race."[63]

Conversely, the Roman Empire is seen as having had no liberal tradition, "because its history is a history of taking away, not enlarging freedom."[64] This was despite the fact that the British Empire had to overcome the issue of race before any political rights could be granted, for, as Cromer put it, "antipathy based on colour also bars the way. The Romans had no such difficulty to encounter."[65] Lucas believed that if the Romans had "extended their rule into tropical Africa or Farther Asia, we might have heard more of the colour question in their Empire." As it is, British writers manage to discern a kind of protoracism in the Romans' views of the Orient: Lucas thought that "though they took little account of different shades of colour, they practically drew upon the West for the government of the East on much the same principle that we look to our own white race for the administration of the tropics."[66] Similarly, he says that although the Romans "were not called upon to deal with large numbers of coloured races. . . . There was no doubt strong race feeling among the Romans for the West as against the East."[67]

The British saw the Roman Empire in racial terms to help justify their own racial prejudices. The educated English elite often identified themselves with the ancient Romans. Lucas felt that both the Romans and the British alike had "an innate capacity for ruling, which grew by use," and that India has been "an unequalled school wherein to learn the lessons of responsibility and administration."[68] But he saw racial attitudes as being the fundamental difference between the Roman and the Briton: for in the British Empire "the tie of class runs counter to the tie of citizenship." So he felt that "to the labour man in Australasia it is of little or no account that an incoming coloured workman is a British subject, if he comes from India. He is a coloured man, not a white man, and a more dangerous competitor in the wage market than a white labourer, because his conditions of life and terms of work are not the white man's conditions and terms." This class divide was, for Lucas, the great split in British society, "as against the great fundamental class distinction in the Roman Empire between freeman and slaves, which was not based on race."[69]

Given their inherent quality, racial distinctions were seen as being discernible throughout history. George Rawlinson, in *The Five Great Monarchies of the Ancient Eastern World*, noted, "The general physical character of the ancient Arian race is best gathered from the sculptures of the Achaemenian kings, which exhibit to us a very noble variety of the human species—a form tall, graceful, and stately; a physiognomy handsome and pleasing." So pleasing in fact that it was "often somewhat resembling the Greek."[70] He elaborates in a footnote in reference to the work of a Dr. Prichard: "The outline of the countenance is here *not strictly* Grecian, for it is peculiar; but it is noble and dignified; and if the expression is not full of life and genius, it is intellectual and indicative of reflection. The shape of the head is entirely Indo-European, and has nothing that recalls the Tartar or Mongolian."[71] The moral characteristics of the Persians seem to be similarly inbuilt: Persians have moral qualities of "courage, energy, and a regard for truth" but their faults are "an addiction to self-indulgence and luxury; a passionate *abandon* to the feeling of the hour." The result is that in "joy and in sorrow, they were alike immoderate; in the one transported beyond all reasonable bounds . . . in the other proportionately depressed, and quite unrestrained in the expression of their anxiety or misery." This was something that had been obvious as long ago as Aeschylus: "Aeschylus' tragedy of the Persae, is, in this respect, true to nature. . . . The Persian was a stranger to the dignified reserve which has commonly been affected by the more civilised among Western nations."[72] Centuries of despotism have only made such degraded tendencies even more ingrained: "The modern Persian is a very degenerate representative of the ancient Arian stock. Slight and supple in person, with quick, glancing eyes, delicate features, and a vivacious manner, he lacks the dignity and strength, the calm repose and simple grace of the race from which he is sprung. Fourteen centuries of subjection to despotic sway have left their stamp upon his countenance and his frame, which . . . have been sadly weakened and lowered by so long a term of subservience."[73]

Such deep-seated and fundamental racial difference was too great for even the skillful rule of the British to overcome. Cromer quotes a Roman example to illustrate the ease with which assimilation could be facilitated back then: a Phoenician named Musac had a son who took the Roman name Saturninus and married a Roman lady called Flavia Fortunata. In the next generation, says Cromer, they named a son Flavius Fortunatus and "the Romanization was complete." But he goes on: "Such cases are now of extremely rare occurrence in countries where races of different colour and religion are brought in contact with each other." He believes it is natural that this should be the case, for "the European woman will generally resent union with the Eastern man, who is polygamous, whilst the seclusion of women in the East offers an almost insuperable obstacle to the counter-case of the European man being attracted by the Eastern woman."[74] The matter of racial intermarriage was of sufficient interest to Cromer that he included an appendix on its frequency between the "dominant races" and the "indigenous inhabitants of Asia and Africa." One factor for the infrequency of these unions may have been the active interference of colonial officials like Cromer, who recalls, "A very few cases of such marriages were brought to my notice during my tenure of office in Egypt. They generally led to such unhappy consequences that I endeavoured—and often with success—to prevent them."[75]

Cromer's conclusion is that racial difference disbarred the Indian from ever reaching parity with the British ruler. In a review of Ardosser Sorabjee N. Wadia's *Reflections on the Problems of India*, a work he considered "well worthy of study" by those interested in the "sundry and manifold developments of opinion elicited by the contact between East and West," Cromer comments on the vast gap between East and West that no amount of education can overcome: "Mr Wadia is so far Westernized that he is a master of the English language and is thoroughly versed in European literature and ratiocination. At the same time he is Eastern to the core in his profound distrust and dislike of European materialism."[76] Part of Wadia's program, to which Cromer thinks "he rightly attaches great importance," is "the removal of all invidious distinctions which humiliate Indians in their own eyes and in those of others." Cromer responds that it is "impossible to insist too strongly on the fact that the main barrier which separates the East from the West is not political but social. It is on this rock that the fair hopes of ardent reformers are especially liable to split." For no matter how much Indian nationalists might hope for political change, they "are apt to expect from political changes greater results than any political change can accomplish. The colour bar cannot be removed by any Act of Parliament, by eloquence, however fervid, or by argument, however cogent." He quotes Virgil:

> *Quid tam, si fuscus Amyntas?*
> *Et nigrae violae sunt et vaccinia nigra.*
> [So what if Amyntas is black? Both violets and hyacinths are black too]

But his racial pessimism cannot accept such indifference: "though nineteen centuries have elapsed since these words were written, the world has as yet not accepted the principle that the tincture of the human skin is a matter as indifferent as that of the colour of flowers. Time alone can solve this question, if, indeed, it be in any way capable of solution. It is not merely useless, but perhaps even hurtful, to discuss it. In the meanwhile, it may be noted that difference of colour remains the most formidable obstacle to intermarriage, and that without the possibility of intermarriage there can be no true sentiment of social quality."[77] Rather, it is, somewhat conveniently, best for the British alone to remain in power. They are the race most suited to rule, to rule over peoples genetically incapable of managing their own political affairs.

But Cromer does not expect any gratitude for this British effort. Any thanks that governed peoples feel for the British soon dissipates after their arrival on the ground: "It is, indeed, one of the inevitable incidents of the execution of an Imperial policy that, as a political force, the gratitude shown to the foreigner who relieves oppression is of a very ephemeral character. We have learnt this lesson both in India and in Egypt." This was a lesson the Romans had also learned: when Rome "was invited to become the champion of Hellenic freedom in Asia Minor, and when the invitation had been accepted, and help effectively given, it was soon found, in the words of Mommsen, that 'the most detestable form of Macedonian rule was less fraught with evil for Greece than a free constitution springing from the noblest intentions of honourable foreigners.'"[78] Lucas thinks the Indians do not realize how lucky they are to have the British in control: "The natives of India only know British rule. They would probably appreciate it more fully, had they been able to compare it with other alien white rule."[79] Once again, Cromer believes race will ever keep the two peoples apart and make gratitude impossible. Referring to a statement by Lord Lawrence that "the people of India can never forget that we are an alien race in respect of colour, religion, habits, and sympathies," Cromer is in full agreement: "This really sums up all there is to be said on the subject." Moreover, he sees it as being a universally applicable law of human interaction: "*Mutatis mutandis*,

Lord Lawrence's dictum may be applied to Egypt, Algeria, Tunis, Annam, the Asiatic provinces of Russia, and, in fact, to every country where the Western governs the Eastern." And it is a law that has applied throughout history, too: "History in this matter repeats itself. Gregorovius speaking of the rule of Theodosius in Italy, says: 'The unhappy king now learnt by experience that not even the wisest or most human of Princes, if he be an alien in race, in custom, and religion, can ever win the hearts of the people.'"[80]

If antiquity helped the British to formulate their theories concerning the character and purpose of their imperialist enterprise, it also helped to establish a clearer picture of what they saw as "Orientals." These caricatures functioned as the building blocks of an imperial discourse, giving writers the materials with which to create an essentialist image of the East. The strategic importance of the Ottoman Empire meant that it came under the close scrutiny of Western powers, especially as its relative military weakness signaled that opportunities for imperialist expansion could be imminent. Turkey, "the sick man of Europe," seemed to epitomize the problem with the oriental character: weak, corrupt, and unfit to govern. It cried out for European intervention. Cromer saw Istanbul as "an outpost of Asia planted in Europe."[81] Reviewing Sir Edwin Pears's *Forty Years in Constantinople, 1873–1915*, Cromer notes that when Sir Edwin first arrived there in 1873, he "soon discovered that the government was honeycombed with corruption." It was like "Rome in the time of Sallust." The Turk destroyed civilization, introducing in its place a barbarity that only now was beginning to be overcome: for when Constantinople was taken by the Turk, it "ceased to be the principal seat of learning in Europe, or, indeed, a seat of learning at all. The representatives of Greek intellect fled from the uncongenial atmosphere which surrounded them. They were scattered over the face of Europe and became the heralds of the Renaissance. All that was good in Byzantium departed." By contrast what was left characterized barbarity: "All that was evil—its cruelty, intrigue, and deceit—remained. . . . The humanizing element, which might perhaps in the end have brought the Turks within the comity of civilized nations, disappeared. The barbarian element gained the upper hand." This was a clash of civilizations that Cromer sees as having lasted for four and a half centuries. But the end is in sight: "The curtain has now apparently risen on the final act of the drama. Verily, as Homer says, Ate is slow at first, but in spite of her limping gait, she in the end generally reaches her goal." Fate has finally, relentlessly, reached its inevitable destination: the end of the Ottoman Empire and its replacement with Western virtues.

But it is Cromer's account of his experience in Egypt that gives his most detailed observations concerning the Eastern, Muslim subordinate. His *Modern Egypt* is not, however, simply a set of travel anecdotes. Cromer's twenty-four years as consul-general, from 1883 to 1907, placed him in a unique position to both see and shape Egyptian life. The attitudes he reveals were the attitudes that were foisted on the Egyptian people and that they had to live with. Unsurprisingly, they are strongly pro-British and deeply distrustful of all things local.[82]

Cromer sees the British involvement in Egypt as morally justified on account of the degradation of the previous Ottoman regime, which, in its spirit of cruelty, had not changed since ancient times: "The drastic nature of those methods, and more especially the punishments which the rulers of Egypt were in the habit of awarding during the first half of the last century, and even at a later period, did not indeed, differ very materially from those of their Pharaonic predecessors." Cromer then cites an example of this random, brutal justice from Herodotus: "King Amasis . . . established by law that every Egyptian should appear once a year before the governor of his canton, and show his means of living; or, failing to do so, and to prove that he got an honest livelihood, should be put to death."[83] Similarly, Cromer's account of the great ruler of Egypt, Mehmet Ali, emphasizes that dealing with such a regime was akin to living under the bad emperors of Rome. One Turkish admiral, of "noted courage," had gone over to Mehmet Ali's side, who later, probably wishing to ingratiate himself with the sultan in Istanbul, sent an agent to the admiral ordering him to kill himself: "A short conversation, which it would be difficult to rival in pathos and dramatic effect, ensued. The agent, after the usual Oriental compliments, merely said, 'Life, O Admiral, is uncertain. We must all be prepared to meet our death at any moment.' The admiral at once took the hint. He knew what those fatal words meant. The tenets of his religion had taught him not to resist the decrees of fate. Like many a Stoic philosopher of Ancient Rome, he had probably at times reflected that a self-inflicted death was, as a last resource, a sure refuge from earthly tyranny and injustice, however galling."[84] And with that he drank the poisoned coffee—an admiral, in Cromer's portrayal, hardwired by his religion to passively accept the dictates of fate.

The final independent ruler of Egypt, Ismail Pasha, for Cromer combined traditional oriental despotism with new levels of incompetence. Cromer mocks his attempts at reform by comparing them with Augustus's power grab: he was one of the "great high-priests of a policy having for its object a transfer of power from the people to their ruler." "But," he continues, "so far as my historical knowledge goes, the clumsy experiment made by Ismail Pasha was of a somewhat novel character": he "endeavoured to call free institutions temporarily into existence as an instrument through whose agency he might regain his personal power, which was threatened by foreign interference."[85] As Cromer comments, "This was perilous work for a despotic ruler."[86] For even those "who were not conversant with Eastern affairs might not unnaturally think that when an Oriental

Gracchus complained of sedition his arguments were not to be accepted without some reserve."[87] He is portrayed as financially corrupt; Cromer notes that "there is certainly a somewhat close analogy between Verres and Ismail Pasha." But it takes the intervention of the just British to bring him to book: "the Egyptian Verres was at last, therefore, obliged to render an account of his stewardship to a body of men who were determined to arrive at the truth."[88] The British, therefore, restore justice and good order to Egypt. It is a move that Cromer, in line with "the Horatian maxim," thinks should be applied to other parts of the Ottoman dominions: "Might not the principle of deposition by reason of misgovernment be applied elsewhere?"[89] For in the end Cromer is convinced that British imperial policy is not merely driven by self-interest but is also founded on morality and duty. Summing up his account of the British occupation of Egypt, he states: "A great nation cannot throw off the responsibilities of which its past history and its position in the world have imposed upon it. English history affords other examples of the Government and people of England drifting by accident into doing what was not only right but was also most in accordance with British interests." And he quotes, in Greek, the original advice that Demosthenes gave to his fellow Athenians to this effect. "In spite of some mistakes of detail," Cromer concludes, "it was on this sound principle that, broadly speaking, the British Government acted in dealing with Egyptian affairs in 1882."[90]

Once instated as consul-general, Cromer had dealings with all aspects of Egyptian affairs. He established a view of Egyptian private life that mirrored his image of a despotic public life. He believes that the toleration of slavery is "another fatal blot in Islam."[91] But it is an area where his administration was able to improve matters: "Often during the long period when my countrymen and myself were engaged in what at one time seemed the hopeless task of evolving order out of the Egyptian chaos, have I repeated to myself those fine lines of the Latin poet which Pitt quoted when he dealt the first blow to the infamous traffic in slaves." He quotes Virgil's *Georgics*:

> *Nosque ubi primus equis Oriens afflavit anhelis,*
> *Illic sera rubens accendit lumina Vesper.*
> [when the rising Sun first breathes with panting steeds on us,
> there glowing Vesper is kindling his evening rays]

"Was the prophecy of the English statesman, I asked myself, about to be fulfilled? Is it destined that, under the guiding hand of England, the rays of true civilisation shall at last pierce into the oldest and most interesting corner of the dark African continent, and lighten with their sunshine even the mud hut of the Egyptian fellah?"[92]

Cromer frequently uses the Roman past to condemn the Islamic present. Islam was associated with the Egyptian nationalist reaction against the involvement of the British Empire and so became a target of Cromer's attacks. His sense of moral superiority was reinforced by what he saw as Islam's degrading treatment of women, this despite his opposition to female suffrage in Britain. He is adamantly opposed to multiple marriage: "Monogamy fosters family life, polygamy destroys it."[93] In a neatly circular argument, Cromer sees the Islamic acceptance of polygamy as a sure sign of an Islamic lack of civilized standards, evidence for which he finds wherever he sees multiple marriage. His concern for Muslim women is based on what he discerns as their lack of bargaining power over their spouses: "In the West, a wife, whose personal attractions have disappeared under the hand of time, can often, in default of other influences, maintain her hold over her husband's affections through the children which she has borne to him." He quotes Claudian's lines to this effect. By contrast, he believes the hold that the discarded or neglected Muslim wife might maintain on grounds such as these "is weakened by the presence of younger and more attractive rivals, who have perhaps borne other children to her husband."[94] But he does see "one feature in connection with family life in the East, where the Oriental contrasts very favourably with the European."[95] There is "greater outward respect" for parents and the aged in general. But this is not something that Islam can be praised for introducing: Egyptians, he says, have been like this from time immemorial, and he quotes Herodotus describing how young Egyptian men "when they meet their elders in the streets, give way to them and step aside; and if an elder man comes in where young men are present, these latter rise from their seats."

Cromer sees the common Egyptian as inherently devious and anti-authoritarian. "From time immemorial," he says, the fellah's "main end in life has been to find some means for evading the extortionate demands of the tax-gatherer." He quotes the historian Mommsen: "The Romans assure us that the Egyptians were proud of the scourge-marks received for perpetrating frauds in taxation." Egypt is a place where nothing changes: "As it was in the days of Augustus, so was it in the days of Ismail."[96] The Egyptian would go to any lengths to avoid his militarily duties, but the favorite modern method was "not to cut off a finger" as in Roman times but to sacrifice an eye.[97] But such immutability has not prevented the British from introducing moral progress into the lives of these people. It is part of their civilizing mission. Discussing the education of colonial subjects, Cromer recalls that "many years ago, Lord Macaulay asked a pertinent question in connection with the system under which India should be governed." His question was, "Are we to keep the people of India ignorant in order that we may keep them submissive?" His reply was "an indignant negative." "Governments, like men," he said, "may buy existence too dear." *Propter vitam vivendi perdere causas* (for the sake of living to lose what makes life worth living) was, Cromer agreed with Juvenal, "a despicable policy both in individuals and in States."[98] That is why, says Cromer, England has first raised up the fellah. But if he were to fall back into his former state and thereby undo Cromer's work, then he would, like the Homeric hero, declare, in the original Greek, "May the earth swallow me up." But he hastens to add, "I not merely hope, but strongly believe that no such disappointment of my political hopes is, in the smallest degree, probable."[99] In his concluding paragraph on education, he makes clear the qualities that British education should inculcate in the average Egyptian: "What the Egyptian man most requires is the acquisition of all those qualities comprised in the expressive Greek term 'aidos' [written in Greek script]—poorly translated by the English word 'self-respect.'" But Cromer believes this is only possible if "like the Christian European, he becomes monogamous, and thus learns to honour the one woman whom he will also have sworn to love and to cherish until the hand of death parts him from his life-long helpmate."[100]

When Cromer looks to the future for Egypt, he realizes that this is a strange question for an Englishman to ask: "It is probable that few Englishmen ever ask themselves seriously the question of *Quo Vadis* in connection with either Indian or Egyptian affairs. Even fewer are tempted to hazard any confident answer to this crucial question."[101] His quote on the title page to Part 7, *The Future of Egypt*, is taken from the close of Juvenal's tenth satire:

> *Nullum numen abest, si sit prudentia; nos te,*
> *Nos facimus, Fortuna, Deam coeloque locamus.*
> [You would not be a goddess, Fortune, if we had wisdom; it is we that make you a goddess and place you in heaven][102]

Cromer was not a man to leave the future passively to fate. That was the kind of oriental attitude he believed had held Egypt in its repressive and regressive grip for millennia. And in his final paragraph he expresses his earnest hope that the country with which he has been associated for so long "in the future, as in the recent past . . . will continue to be governed in the interests of the Egyptians," saying, "I commend to my own countrymen the advice which was given to Rome by one of the later Latin poets":

> *Quod regnas minus est quam quod regnare mereris* [103]
> [It is less important that you rule than that you deserve to rule]

Not that Cromer did have any doubts about Britain deserving to rule. Any changes that are to occur in the future must accept that as a given: "The foundation-stone of Indian reform must be the steadfast maintenance of British supremacy."[104] Of course, the comparison with Rome also raised the uncomfortable fact of its demise. Cromer is aware of this possibility but pushes it far off into the future: "Nations wax and wane. It may be that at some future and far distant time we shall be justified, to use a metaphor of perhaps the greatest of the Latin poets, in handing over the torch of progress in India to those whom we have ourselves civilized."[105] But for the time being, racial differences prevent any substantial reform from taking place, because it would endanger what progress had already been achieved in India: "Until human nature entirely changes, and until racial and religious passions disappear from the face of the earth, the relinquishment of that torch would almost certainly lead to its extinction."

The historian and novelist Charles Kingsley, in his 1875 work *The Roman and the Teuton*, compared the fourth-century Roman Empire to the Chinese and Ottoman Empires to prove the superiority of the British Empire. His picture of the later Roman Empire is bleak: "The Roman Empire, toward the latter part of the fourth century, was in much the same condition as the Chinese or the Turkish Empire in our own days. Private morality (as Juvenal and Persius will tell you) had vanished long before. Public morality had, of course, vanished likewise. The only powers really recognized were force and cunning. The only aim was personal enjoyment. The only God was the Divus Caesar, the imperial demigod, whose illimitable brute force gave him illimitable powers of self-enjoyment, and made him thus the paragon and ideal of humanity, whom all envied, flattered, hated, and obeyed." He continues to describe the "sink of corruption" that was the imperial palace, the senate's role in judicial murders, the consuming hierarchy of extortion that was the official bureaucracy. He is vitriolic about the cruelty of emperors but saves his greatest bile for the institution of Roman slavery: "the atrocities of the Romans toward their slaves . . . notably drew down on them the just wrath and revenge of those Teutonic nations, from which so many of their slaves were taken." The atrocities committed were so severe that "Roman domestic slavery is not to be described by the pen of an Englishman." "And yet," he is astonished to say, "they called themselves Christians." In fact, the state of affairs at Rome and later in Constantinople was "altogether fantastic, abnormal, utterly unlike anything that we have seen, or can imagine to ourselves without great effort." To illustrate just how far the English state would have to sink in order to be comparable to ancient Rome, he adopts a passage taken from a Mr. Sheppard's *The Fall of Rome and the Rise of New Nationalities*, in which the problems of Rome are transferred to 1861 England.

> An entire revolution has taken place in our principles, manners, and form of government. Parliaments, meetings, and all the

> ordinary expressions of the national will, are no longer in existence. A free press has shared their fate. There is no accredited organ of public opinion; indeed there is no public opinion to record. Lords and Commons have been swept away, though a number of the richest old gentlemen in London meet daily at Westminster to receive orders from Buckingham Palace. But at the palace itself has broken out one of those sanguinary conspiracies which have of late become unceasing. The last heir of the house of Brunswick is lying dead with a dagger in his heart, and everything is in frightful confusion. The armed force of the capital are of course "masters of the situation," and the Guards, after a tumultuous meeting at Windsor or Knightsbridge, have sold the throne to Baron Rothschild, for a handsome donation of £25 a-piece.[106]

Since "Mr. Disraeli lost his head a few days ago" and Lord Palmerston lies "in the Tower under sentence of death," England lies exposed to "every foe whom her aggressive and colonizing genius has provoked": "The red man of the West, the Caffre, the Sikh, and the Sepoy, Chinese braves, and fierce orientals of all sorts, are hovering on her frontiers in 'numbers numberless,' as the flakes of snow in the northern winter. They are not the impotent enemy which we know, but vigorous races, supplied from inexhaustible founts of population, and animated by an insatiate appetite for the gold and silver, purple and fine linen, rich meats and intoxicating drinks of our effete civilization. And we can no longer oppose them with those victorious legions which have fought and conquered in all regions of the world. The men of Waterloo and Inkermann are no more. We are compelled to recruit our armies from those very tribes before whose swords we are receding!" Kingsley has no doubt that readers will scoff, but "*Every single statement*," he asserts, "may be paralleled by the circumstances and events of the decadence of the Roman Empire." The British Empire is shown to be far superior to the decadent Rome of the later empire. But there is another lesson for the English here: that empires do indeed wax and wane, and both their future and their empire's future rested on their claim to higher morality.

The Roman Empire provided a rich source of moral lessons for British who were anxious about the future of the empire. At a time of great social change and increased international competition, particularly form Germany, reaching for such traditional images as decline and fall was doubtless reassuring. As Hingley says, "Thinkers often articulate images of tradition in order to establish identity in the face of the actual or potential loss of a cherished past and at times of rapid change."[107] Lord Cromer did in fact give much thought to the possibility of future British decline, by considering the Roman parallel. In his essay "The Government of Subject Races," he begins by quoting Claudian, "the poet of the Roman decadence," and his "dogmatic assertion that no limit could be assigned to the duration of Roman sway. *Nec terminus unquam Romanae ditionis erit.*" As Cromer observes, "At the time this hazardous prophecy was made, the huge overgrown Roman Empire was tottering to its fall." The question he asks, therefore, is, "Does a similar fate await the British Empire?"[108]

He begins by considering the causes of Rome's fall and finds six: the foundation of Constantinople, Christianity, slavery, the pauperization of the Roman proletariat, the destruction of the middle class by fiscal oppression, and barbarous finance.[109] The first he finds irrelevant, and in the case of the second he finds Christianity to be a "powerful ally" in dealing with "subject races who are ignorant or irreceptive of its precepts."[110] Moreover, "it is an ally without whose assistance continued success is unattainable." Above all, Christianity is no longer the explosive force it was in Rome when it disrupted its institutions. He is assertive in his view that the British Empire must retain its moral character and not simply be a matter of trade: instead, the British trader "must be taught patience at the hands of the statesman and the moralist."[111] On the question of the pauperization of the proletariat, he describes this as "the *Panem et Circenses* policy."[112] Cromer is concerned that rising international competition is eroding Britain's trade base, "for the loss of trade involves as its ultimate result the pauperisation of the proletariat, the adoption of reckless expedients based on the *Panem et Circenses* policy to fill the mouths and quell the voices of the multitude, and finally the suicide of that Empire which is the offspring of trade."[113] He does not see Roman-style channeling of money from the provinces to the imperial treasury as a real risk to the British Empire: "The lesson taught by the loss of the American colonies has sunk deeply into the public mind."[114] In fact the opposite may provide "some little danger": that too much will be spent by Britain on outlying dependencies with the result that the British people might become "restive" and "might therefore be disposed to cast off too hastily the mantle of Imperialism."[115]

Cromer fears the overcentralization of the Roman Empire. But he believes that the fate of Rome, caused by these special factors, can be averted by close adherence to two important principles: "local revenues should be expended locally" and "over-centralisation should above all things be avoided."[116] He notes that both Rome and Britain levied unfair land taxes,[117] but considers that the danger to Britain comes not from barbarous taxes but rather from "ultra-scientific finance."[118] The Englishman must not be constrained "to bow down in that temple of Logic, the existence of which the Oriental is disposed altogether to ignore." The comparison with Rome, Cromer concludes, is encouraging: "To every danger which threatens there is a safeguard."[119] Above all, what will maintain Britain's preeminent position is the kind of good government the Romans rejected: "Rome did not habitually act on the recognition of any very strong moral obligation binding on the Imperial government in its treatment of subject races," whereas the "British Government is altogether different. Its intentions are admirable," and much of its fiscal legislation "has been perfectly justifiable and even beneficial."[120] "There was truth," he remarks, "in the commonplace remark made by a subject of ancient Rome, himself a slave and presumably of Oriental extraction, that bad government will bring the mightiest empire to ruin."[121] Cromer is confident this can be avoided: "If we make a good use of our power, we may face the future without fear that we shall be overtaken by the Nemesis which attended Roman misrule. If the reverse is the case, the British Empire will deserve to fall, and of a surety it will ultimately fall."[122] Within fifty years of Cromer writing these words, the British had left India.

8

Colonial Adventures

British colonial texts created an image of the East that left it open to exploration and exploitation. This imperialist discourse represented Britain as knowledgeable, powerful, and politically stable in contrast to the perceived ignorance, weakness, and instability of the East. The Orient seemed to be crying out for British intervention to ensure that it was well governed and able to progress. The administrators and writers we examined in the last chapter were not, however, the only Britons to embark on trips to the East. Many individuals went there in search of adventure, excitement, and fame back home. The resultant travel literature, which blossomed in the colonial period, reflected a far more subtle range of views concerning the Orient than did the imperial theories of a Cromer. For the dominating relationship with the East that imperialists found highly rewarding left some other English writers cold. To be sure, the genre of travel writing can be seen as another expression of the same colonial obsession with foreign land and empire. Travelers could also see Eastern regions as something to be overpowered and exploited. Some texts were even written with the backing of European governments keen to promote national imperialist ambitions in their readers and collect information on how to deal with tribal and local customs. But travel writing also expressed these concerns in a form that reflected domestic social developments—the move toward greater personal freedom in combination with the questioning of traditional political and religious authority.

Travel writing in the nineteenth century became far more focused on the biographical nature of the narrative than on serving any overtly didactic purpose. As a genre, of course, travel writing was nothing new; we have seen some of the early texts of British travelers to the East. The eighteenth century had also generated a large corpus of travel literature, but "it remained a genre that offered instruction of anecdotal quality only. Neoclassical taste dictated to a large extent what the eighteenth-century traveller could say."[1] Authors observed more generic conceptions of description, often searching for the picturesque rather than the autobiographical to illustrate their accounts. What is most noticeable in the genre in the imperial age is that the traveler becomes the hero of the piece, with the scenery a mere "backdrop for his progress."[2] As Rana Kabbani puts it, "The *moi haissable* of classical sensibility was appropriately revamped to accommodate a Victorian glorification of individuals." The standard traveler was now a survivor, an adventurer, a white Anglo-Saxon male who overcame the sobering array of difficulties in front of him yet still managed to stay civilized throughout. The traveler also becomes far more of an individual. He is a representative of his home culture and its virtues but also separate and removed from its constraints. Implicitly he is rich, explicitly an exile wandering abroad to discover new attributes both in the foreigners he encounters and in himself in order to educate and entertain his readership back home.

Often traveling lightly so as not to be encumbered with the material trappings of home, the traveler nevertheless could not leave his mental baggage behind. Most travelers seem to have arrived in the East with a clear preconceived idea of what they would find. Their heads were filled with the classical stories and texts they had read since early childhood. The ancient sources made the people of Arabia, for example, already known to the travelers who went there. Charles Doughty recalls the ill-fated campaign of the Roman general Gallus, dispatched by the emperor Augustus, into the Arabian Peninsula. The Roman general found the inhabitants of the land to be "a people unwarlike, half of them helping their living by merchandise, and half of them by robbing," adding in parentheses "such they are now." For this is presented as a place of timeless stability: " 'The nomads living in tents of hair-cloth are troublesome borderers,' says Pliny, (as they are to-day!)." It is a place where the local guides were not to be trusted even back in Roman times: "those Italians looking upon that dire waste of nature in Arabia, and grudging because they must carry water upon camels, laid all to the perfidy of their guides." Writers such as these drew on a wide range of classical figures and references to help them represent and understand the Orient. It was a process of mediation, whereby they translated the East into a familiar past in order to familiarize it to their audience back home. This route to cultural knowledge relied heavily on passing through the classical past. But it was also a way to maintain a safe distance between the domestic and the strangely foreign. Using antiquity as a mirror for the present both established a basis of similarity between the two cultures and made it clear that fundamental differences existed too. For the modern European could never be entirely comfortable with the peculiar philosophies and practices of a pagan past.

The geography was also already familiar terrain. Doughty finds the description of the Arabian desert by Strabo ("writing from the mouth of Gallus himself, who was his friend and Prefect of Egypt") so accurate that it cannot be bettered: "It is a sandy waste, with only few palms and pits of water: the thorn (acacia) and the tamarisk grow there; the wandering Arabs lodge in tents and are camel graziers."[3] At other times, the classical screen through which the physical world was seen recalled lines of ancient verse. Burton, on entering the creek of Marsá Damghah, which he found "more like a lake" and "gloriously blue," could not help "calling to mind, after dinner, the old school lines—

> *Est in secessu longo locus; insula portum*
> *Efficit objectu laterum; quibus omnis ab alto*
> *Frangitur, inque sinus scindit sese unda reductos.*

> [There is a place in a long inlet: an island forms a port by the projection of its sides by which every wave from the deep is broken and it splits itself into a bay set back]

All that was missing, he says, was the dark grove, the "atrum nemus," of the original. "Where, however," he asks, "shall we find such luxuries in arid Arabia?"[4] Or looking at a coral reef in the Red Sea, Burton muses: "you might have heard, without astonishment, old Proteus calling his flocks with the writhed conch; and Aphrodite seated in her shell would have been only a fit and proper climax for its loveliness."[5] Not that there are specific parallels being drawn here. It is more that when waxing lyrical and moving into a higher register of pleasure at the sight of some beauty spot, the writer feels moved to adopt a classical tone to fully express the degree of his delight.

Many writers share the classical belief in the power of climate and geography to affect the manners of a people. On the first page of his introduction to *An Account of the Manners and Customs of the Modern*

Egyptians, Edward Lane remarks, "It is generally observed that many of the most remarkable peculiarities in the manners, customs, and character of a nation are attributable to the physical peculiarities of the country"; they affect the country's moral and social state.[6] Even the anthropologist Sir James Frazer was to become convinced of the relationship between oriental religion and geography: "I have paid more attention than formerly to the natural features of the countries in which they arose, because I am more than ever persuaded that religion, like all other institutions, has been profoundly influenced by physical environment."[7] Not surprisingly, this could easily become an oblique way to attribute to the Arabs character traits that reflected the harshness and hostility of the desert environment. Burton, for example, was of the opinion that "the Arabs, who suffer greatly from melancholia, are kind to people afflicted with this complaint. . . . Probably it is the effect of over-working the brain, in a hot dry atmosphere."[8]

For Burton, it is the tribes of Asia, tribes who have been toughened by their environment and their simple life as pastoral nomads, who act as the scourge to the soft cultures of civilization: "It is curious that these pastoral races, which supply poetry with namby-pampy Colinades, figure as the great tragedians of history. The Scythians, the Huns, the Arabs, and the Tartars were all shepherds. They first armed themselves with clubs to defend their flocks from wild beasts. They then learned warfare, and improved means of destruction by petty quarrels about pastures, and, finally, united by the commanding genius of some skin-clad Caesar or Napoleon, they fell like avalanches upon those valleys of the world—Mesopotamia, India, and Egypt—whose enervate races offered them at once temptations to attack, and certainty of success."[9] Much European travel writing shares a familiar hostility to the Orient. It is a place of strange habits. Indeed, the pagan familiarity of many religious practices is a recurrent theme. When Burton was in Mecca, disguised as a Muslim pilgrim, he recalls how, at night, he and his fellow pilgrims "threw ourselves upon our rugs, but not to sleep"—not to sleep because "close by, to our bane, was a prayerful old gentleman, who began his devotions at a late hour and concluded them not before dawn." The endless drone of this devotee reminds Burton of his undergraduate neighbor when he was at Trinity College, Oxford, "who would spout Aeschylus at two A.M. Sometimes the chant would grow drowsy, and my ears would hear a dull retreating sound; presently, as if in self-reproach, it would rise to a sharp treble, and proceed at a rate perfectly appalling."[10]

The peculiar yet recognizable oddness of oriental religious practices as they appeared to these travelers is reflected in their spotting a close link between what they saw as modern and ancient superstitions. In his account of the Egyptian Copts' wedding ceremonies, Lane describes a curious custom that takes place in their prenuptial feasts, "which reminds us of the *alites* or *praepetes* of the Romans." Two pigeons, with bells attached to them, are made giddy by being whirled about. They are then placed in sugar balls, placed before the guests, who break the balls open and birds fly about ringing their bells: and "if they do not fly immediately, some person usually makes them rise, as the spectators would draw an evil omen from their not flying."[11] Burton thought that the Orient had always had a pernicious superstitious influence on the West and finds that the sevenfold perambulation of the Kaaba enacted as part of the Muslim Hajj "was adopted by the Greeks and Romans, whose Ambarvalia and Amburbalia appear to be eastern superstitions, introduced . . . into their pantheism."[12]

Many see the oriental as typically cowardly. Doughty describes how one of his group, Abdullah, tells him of his time in prison. Some of the prisoners had undergone extraordinary physical tribulations in order to effect an escape: he told "with wonder of some offenders who cast by night into the city prison, had wound and wrung their limbs quite out of the gyves and escaped; and one of them, because his foot could not pass the fetter, had cut away the heel, and was fled with his fellows!" But Doughty has seen this before in the classical past and is not impressed: "The like is mentioned by Herodotus, of a Greek prisoner who never afterward showed himself to be of a worthy or manly nature:- for will not a rat as desperately deliver herself, leaving even her limb in the trap?"[13]

The ability of Arabia to ensnare the greedy Westerner seems to be closely connected with the traditional propensity of the Arab for deceit. Doughty recounts how the Roman army sent by the emperor Augustus under Gallus was "to make a prey of the chimerical riches of Arabia Felix." Instead, the army of eleven thousand strong "marched painfully over the waterless wastes for six months! wilfully misled, as they supposed, by the Nabateans of Petra, their allies." When they managed to bring the Arabs to battle, the natural oriental cowardice in battle resurfaced: the Romans "met with a great multitude of the barbarous people assembled against them, at a brookside. In the battle there fell *many thousands* of the Arabs! and of the Romans and allies two soldiers." The Arabians did not know how to fight, fighting like "men unwont to handle weapons, with slings, swords and lances and two-edged hatchets." On their long retreat, most of the Romans "perished of misery in the long and terrible way of the wilderness," even though "only seven Romans had fallen in battle!" Poor General Gallus was disgraced for this high-profile disaster. "Surely," Doughty protests, "the knightly Roman poet deserved better . . . because he had not fulfilled the dreams of Caesar's avarice! Gallus had returned with a "European man's disdain of the thievish and unwarlike inhabitants!" It was, after all, Augustus who had fallen for the Arabs' tall tales of unimaginable riches, just as many Europeans have since been "deceived by the Arabs' loquacity" and "have in every age a fantastic opinion of this unknown calamitous country."[14] Later in the life of the Eastern Roman Empire, when the Byzantines were hard-pressed by the Muslims, Doughty uses this as a yardstick for Roman military health: "But what may be thought of the rottenness of the Roman power at that time? when her legionaries clad in iron, could not sustain the furious running-on of weak-bodied and half-armed dissolute Arabians, in their ragged shirts!" After all, the only thing that had changed was that the Arabs had been "banded (which alone can band Semites!) by the (new) passion of religion, and their robber-like greediness of the spoil!"[15]

But if the Romans had declined from their ancient vigor, so too had the Arabs. The contemporary Arab inhabitants of the Middle East seemed, in their base state, to spoil the idyllic beauty of the classical ruins that provided the backdrops for their everyday lives. The painter David Roberts, who produced idealized scenes of classical ruins, bemoaned: "Splendid cities, once teeming with a busy population and embellished with temples and edifices, the wonder of the world, now deserted and lonely, or reduced by mismanagement and the barbarism of the Muslim creed to a state as savage as wild animals by which they are surrounded. Often have I gazed on them till my heart actually sickened within me."[16] The Arab attitude to architecture, especially classical architecture, seemed to encapsulate everything that appeared barbaric about them. Just as their own internal strife reduced their modern towns to a state of ruinous disrepair, they further reduced the remains of the far greater classical civilization they had replaced. Doughty's excitement at finding the ruins of hewn monuments, "Greekish palatial frontispices of two storeys now much decayed by the weather," is tempered by the fact that "pompous portals" lead into nothing but "inconsiderable solid halls without ornament" that are now the "nightstalls of the nomad flocks" and are "blackened with the herdsmen's fires."[17] The Cambridge don Edward Clarke, when returning from the Cyanean islands in 1859, landed on the Argyronian Cape to examine the "Bed of Hercules" mentioned by Dionysus Byzantius. "We there found the capital of a very ancient column of the Ionic order, not less than two feet and a half in diameter. It had been hollowed, and now serves as a basin, near the residence of the *dervish*." His account of how the rock came to be there manages to blend views of the Turk as superstitious, stupid, lazy and destructively barbaric: The dervish, he says, "relates the idle superstitions of the country, concerning the mountain, and the giant supposed to be there buried: It is therefore evident, that a temple of considerable magnitude once stood in this situation; as a slight knowledge of the country suffices to induce the belief that the inhabitants would never have been at the pains to carry this piece of antiquity there, whatever remains they may have removed by rolling them down the mountain."[18]

The East seemed to many to possess an inferior level of civilization to the West, a fact that was presented as being self-evident even to many Arabs. Doughty, when lodging at el-Ally with two Damascene tradesmen, recalls how he went at their request to pass an evening with them. "One of them, Abu Rashîd, had trafficked to Egypt, and could tell marvels of great cities lighted with gas, of waterworks and railroads, all made he affirmed by the Engleys whom he praised as the most ingenious and upright of the Frank nations." As a consequence, "this year he would send his son, he told us, to the English schools in Syria:- the new technic instruction." "By which only they think they fall short of the European," adds Doughty, amused that this man should think that it is only education that separates Easterner from Westerner. He also notes that this "is all the present appetite of such up-waked Mohammedan Arabs," as if to underline just how hopelessly, and perhaps stupidly, optimistic they are about achieving European-style progress. That hopelessness is revealed clearly in the manner in which this Arab tradesman took "a solemn volume in hand, bound in red leather, in which he studied religion and philosophy," and then "read forth where mention was made of the Platonical sect." For Doughty, the contrast is stark: "The barbarous Arabic authors, without knowledge of the tongues or times, discourse with disdainful ineptitude of the noblest human spirits which lived almost a thousand years before their beginning."[19] Given such attitudes it is not surprising that many travelers concurred with contemporary imperialist thinking with regard to what should be done with these uncivilized natives.

For many travelers the Turks seemed to epitomize the worst of the Orient. But if Western writers had once feared the Turks, this fear had now turned to condescension and contempt. The Turks seemed to retain their grip on their empire purely as a result of political machinations among the Western powers. As such it lacked any of the moral purpose that the British felt characterized their own imperial project. The military and political weakness of the Ottoman Empire during the nineteenth century therefore gave the European imperial powers a clear lesson in the fate that awaited them if they lost their sense of their civilizing mission. This lack of inner moral strength seemed to be reflected in the poor quality of governance the Turks exercised in the territories under their control. Lane, who lived in Egypt in the guise of a Turk for several years, recounts, "Most of the governors of provinces and districts carry their oppression far beyond the limits to which they are authorized." It was a system that relied on brutality, where the village sheikh was often beaten for failing to produce sufficient tax for the village and often did not even pay himself "until he has been well thrashed." The brutalizing effects of this regime left both physical and mental marks: physical in that the local peasants were "proud of the stripes they receive for withholding their contributions," and mental, in their refusal to show any weakness, which made them "boast of the number of blows which were inflicted upon them before they would give up their money." But for Lane there was nothing new in this behavior. It is how Egyptians have always acted in the face of bad government: "Ammianus Marcellinus gives precisely the same character to the Egyptians of his time."[20]

In fact, Lane seems to accept that some decline had taken place in the quality of the country's administration. He notes that the Christian Copts hated their Byzantine rulers so much that "they gladly received the Arab invaders of their country, and united with them to expel the Greeks." But the short-sightedness of this action meant that although "their revenge was gratified," they were "made to bow their necks to a heavier yoke."[21] Doughty certainly seems to find that Turkish rule equaled the basest level achieved under the Roman emperors. Describing Mohammed Aly, surveyor of the kellas between Tebûk and el-Medina—an "amiable bloody ruffian" and former soldier who boasted of hanging three men and torturing others by feeding them only two biscuits a day and everyday "caused to be ground a measure of meal in a handmill (which is of intolerable weight) upon their breasts"—Doughty lists the physical features that seemed to embody the moral corruption of the individual. He had a "diseased senile body," which was "full of ulcers," and had a "licentious military tongue"; his mind was "now in the shipwreck of a good understanding, with the bestial insane instincts and the like compunctions of a spent humanity." In summary, Doughty declares, "it seemed the jade might have been (if great had been his chance) another Tiberius senex," the corrupted, corrupting successor to the emperor Augustus.[22] It was all an abject lesson in how not to run an empire.

Like the Persian Empire of antiquity, the Ottoman seemed to stand in opposition to English values of liberty and democracy. Some chose to help Greece achieve independence and so reject the domination of the Turks. As David Roessel shows so well, Greece was thought to be needing to throw off the oriental traits it was seen to have acquired under the Turks. A feminized Greece needed to be rescued from the male Turkish occupier and become a man again.[23] As such, the Greek war of independence was seen in a "Herodotean framework of the heroics of the Persian Wars to the exclusion of the rest of Greek history."[24] Even if the Turks' only real crime was to stand in the way of European expansion, their military and moral weakness seemed to cry out for the hand of the Westerner to correct it. Comparing contemporary Constantinople with the Byzantine metropolis of eight hundred years earlier, Burton notes that, like Carthage, "fate has marked upon the Ottoman Empire in Europe 'delenda est': we are now witnessing the efforts of human energy and ingenuity to avert or to evade the fiat."[25] Clarke concludes in the final paragraph to his long work: "Never was there a people in possession of such advantages, who either knew or cared so little for their enjoyment. Under a wise government the inhabitants of Constantinople might obtain the riches of all the empires of the earth. Situated as they are, it cannot be long before other nations, depriving them of such important sources of wealth, will convert to better purposes the advantages they have so long neglected."[26]

But if travelers shared some of the more orientalist assumptions of their imperialist compatriots, that did not mean they saw no value in Eastern cultures. The very fact of their travel underscores just how inherently interesting and valuable a place the Orient was to explore. Lane highlights the fact that the Arabs kept alive the flame of classical learning and that "how science was cherished by the Arabs when all the nations of Europe were involved in the grossest ignorance . . .

is well known."[27] Frazer sought to express the commonality of religious experience of pagans, Christians, and Muslims by examining the similarities among their practices. Noting that Arabs and Christians resort to the hot springs of Callirrhoe in Moab in April and May, he describes how they both "propitiate the spirit or genius of the place by sacrificing a sheep or goat at the spring and allowing its red blood to tinge the water." He thinks that such acts "may help us to understand the worship which at similar spots Greek men and women used to render to the hero Hercules. As the ideal of manly strength he may have been deemed the father of many of his worshippers, and Greek wives may have gone on pilgrimage to his steaming waters in order to obtain the wish of their hearts."[28] Burton defends "Easterns" against those who accuse them of want of gallantry by comparing the "genuine politeness" and "kindness of heart" of travelers helping a lady and her children, one of whom was sick and "appeared to be dying, and was not strong enough to wail." "Contrast this trait of character," he proclaims, "with the savage scenes of civilisation that take place among the 'Overlands' at Cairo and Suez. No foreigner could be present for the first time without bearing away the lasting impression that the sons of Great Britain are model barbarians." Burton adds that on one occasion he had to intervene personally to "prevent a party of ladies being thrust into an old and bad transit-van; the ruder sex having stationed itself at some distance from the starting-place in order to seize upon the best."[29]

Above all, the Arabs were seen as free. Theirs was a world that came to epitomize for many travelers of the late nineteenth and early twentieth centuries the kind of pure and simple culture Europeans had left behind. They found the basic material for a positive view of the Arabs in ancient sources, which reflected "the attitude of a highly developed civilization towards savage peoples who seemed to possess the simple virtues which were vanishing at home."[30] These references enabled them to create a far more sympathetic view of Arab virtues. But the resurrection of the positive aspects of the Arab image was never simply an end in itself. In the contemporary situation, to love freedom was to hate the Turk. Arabia was under Ottoman domination at the time, and many Western writers championed the cause of Arab resistance to this despotic empire in the same way that they had in Greece earlier in the century. Again they turned to the classical past for precedent. The fact that Arabia had never been conquered by such formidable foes as Alexander the Great and the mighty Romans helped to reveal the racial valor of the Bedouin, who now became exemplars of freedom from both external and internal domination. The creation of a positive Arab image was also intimately linked with the new spirit of individualism that was influencing contemporary Western thinking. The desert itself seemed to generate the space for individual expression to flourish away from the constraints of social norms. It became nothing less than the best place to go to find your true self. And the Bedouin nomads became the people to reeducate the British in the simple values they had lost.

Many travelers tended to focus on the lack of change in Bedouin society. Says Kathryn Tidrick, "The idea of social immobility was fascinating to Europeans whose society was in the process of rapid change. Believers in progress deplored it and conservatives admired it, but all found it remarkable that such a society should exist."[31] The Arabs are presented as lovers of traditional honor. Burton describes how the English were willing to fight for liberty, the Spaniards for religion, the Irish for "the fun of fighting"; but "gain and revenge draw the Arab's sword." For the Arab to become desperate, he must have "the all-powerful stimulants of honour and fanaticism. Frenzied by the insults of his women, or by the fear of being branded as a coward, he is capable of any mad deed."[32] Doughty also rescues the Arabs from the slurs that have historically been levied against them; he argues that although the Arabs "may be styled a nation of robbers, whose principal occupation is plunder, the constant subject of their thought," that did not mean that people could "attach to this practice the same notions of criminality that we entertain respecting highwaymen, house-breakers, and thieves in Europe." By the end of the nineteenth century this reputation of the Bedouin as being both honorable and independent meant that for many British writers their manners reminded them of their own: the kind of unsycophantic, plain-speaking self-assurance found in the English gentleman. As Tidrick observes, "It was with the realization that the Arabs, unlike other Orientals, were gentlemen that literate Englishmen began to feel a sense of affinity with them."[33] For those looking to escape the perils of modern-day progress, such a realization made the desert a powerfully attractive place. Arabia became a museum case brimming over with the relics and curiosities of their glorious past. Like the Greeks did to Rome, the Arabs could educate their more powerful Western neighbors in the truly civilized arts.

But it was not just political freedom that the East could represent. The Orient became a place synonymous with sexual fantasy and freedom. Lane describes the celebrated dancing girls of Egypt's Ghawázee tribe who "perform unveiled in the public streets, even to amuse the rabble." They begin their dancing, which has "little of elegance," with a "degree of decorum," but soon, "by more animated looks, by a more rapid collision of their castanets of brass, and by increased energy in every motion, they exhibit a spectacle exactly agreeing with the descriptions which Martial and Juvenal have given of the performances of the female dancers of Gades."[34] Like these ancient artists, the Egyptian dancers "extinguish the least spark of modesty," and are even "plentifully supplied with brandy or some other intoxicating liquor." The end result is so shocking that "the scenes which ensue cannot be described."

If there was one writer who did more than any other to establish the myth of the Orient as a place of erotic fantasy, it was Richard Burton. The East became a place that could satisfy the yearnings denied by the Victorian British home. As Holly Edwards says, during the nineteenth century's cult of pure womanhood, with its ideals of chastity, piety, and quietude, the Orient served as "a safety valve for gender friction by providing imagery for male wish fulfilment and idealization."[35] But it took a hero of Burton's quality to adopt the detailed disguises that were necessary to penetrate these mysteries of the Orient. He reaches the parts of the East that other travelers could not, even, in Latin for decency's sake, discussing practices such as female circumcision and the size of Arab and African penises as evidence for the racial origin of the Egyptians.[36] Such treatment of their womenfolk, whether in the form of the present-day Orient or the classical past, was for Burton a sure sign of barbarity. Arguing that Muslims, Christians, and pagans will all hold up examples of female perfection, he notes, however, that "when the barbarian becomes a semi-barbarian, as are the most polished Orientals, or as were the classical authors of Greece and Rome, then women fall from their proper place in society." Then they become "mere articles of luxury, and sink into the lowest moral condition." It is only in the next stage, civilization, that they rise again to be "highly accomplished, and not a little frivolous."[37]

Polygamy seemed especially threatening to Burton as it represented a viable and, to the Western male fantasist, attractive alternative to monogamy and the nuclear family. When discussing the arrival of Islam into India, Burton sees it as a continuation of superstitious belief carried down from ancient pagan times: "Moslem divines . . . ascribe to Mohammed miraculous authority over animals, vegetables, and minerals, as well as over men, angels, and jinnis." "It is probably one of the many remains of ancient paganism pulled down and afterwards used to build up the edifice of Al-Islam."[38] Moreover, Islam seems to him to combine the traditional Indian backwardness in religion with the barbarity of their sexual mores. He notes that mosque janitors—*battalin*—are generally married, "some of them indulging in three or four wives—which would have aroused Juvenal's bile."[39] It is incomprehensible for Burton to see any form of religious behavior existing outside of Christian monogamy—it would be a practice so obviously perverse that Juvenal would have been unable not to satirize it. But the present state of affairs was at least an improvement of the previous situation where the principal of a mosque was a "neuter."[40] This too was in Burton's view a continuation of ancient barbaric practice: "The Persians, in remote times, as we learn from Herodotus, were waited upon by eunuchs, and some attribute to them the invention." But for Burton, a eunuch was simply "an abomination."

In Western oriental art of the period we find perhaps the clearest visual expression of the stereotypical image of Eastern women. These highly popular pictures contrasted the luxury and vibrancy of the Orient with the rigidities of European classicism. It is, in many ways, the classicist who is the absent observer of their work, watching their lavish scenes of harems, wanton cruelty, eunuchs and odalisques, slavery and timeless political chaos, and wondering where the constraints of harmony and order have gone. Such paintings created a fantasy world onto which to project suppressed sexual desires. By constructing a stereotypical female other, it liberated the male self from the narrow bonds of European attitudes. Like the neoclassical artists before them, who portrayed nudity by "placing it in a removed mythological setting" to render it safe, so orientalist painters located sensuality in a far-off world, surrounded by soft and luxurious material objects and furnishings.[41]

But if this view represented the desert as a place for men, this was at odds with Western social developments that saw attitudes toward women change. Once not seen as tough enough to travel, women travelers became far more commonplace as the century progressed. If the East offered men the opportunity for freedom and some kind of sexual liberation, it also allowed these women travelers freedom of thought and comparative independence from men and the constraints of domestic expectations of female behavior.[42] Even the ability to discard the conventions of dress and "go native" allowed a greater degree of liberation than would be available back home. One particular advantage these women had over their male counterparts was that they were able to go inside harems. The demand for accounts of such experiences meant that they frequently became one of the great selling points of such female literature, which was something of an irony given that they went in search of greater freedom only to find it in an institution considered by many male fantasists to be little better than sexual slavery. But what the travel texts of these women travelers do show is that *Western*, always a general term, was acquiring many more apparent internal divisions. The "West" no longer simply meant masculine.

Some of these female-authored travel texts reveal a hint of the same sexual tourism that characterized much male work. Lady Duff Gordon, journeying through Egypt in the 1860s, recalls, "At Aswan I dined on the shores with the 'blameless Ethiopians', merchants from Sudan, black as ink and handsome as the Greek Bacchus."[43] Likewise, Gertrude Bell described one of her muleteers, Habīb, as "a young man of twenty-two or twenty-three, dark, upright and broad-shouldered, with a profile that a Greek might have envied."[44] But it was not just their idea of male aesthetics that showed classical influence. Egypt constantly brought Herodotus to mind, affecting Duff Gordon's whole way of looking at the country: "Nothing is more striking to me than the way in which one is constantly reminded of Herodotus. The Christianity and the Islam of this country are full of the ancient worship, and the sacred animals have all taken service with Muslim saints."[45] She saw Egyptian culture as a multilayered palimpsest "in which the Bible is written over Herodotus, and the Koran over that."

Bell certainly shared Western male writers' interest in classical architecture, delighting in finding at Kastal a fortified Roman camp standing on a mound: "The masonry is unusually good, the walls of great thickness; with such defences stretching to his furthest borders, the citizen of Rome might sleep secure o'nights."[46] But like male authors, she is saddened by the steady corrosion that modern life was effecting on these ruins. The land around the fort was cultivated by families of fellahin since her visit five years before, and "now under the broken vaults the young corn was springing in the levels below the walls, circumstances which should no doubt warm the heart of the lover of humanity, but which will send a cold chill through the breast of the archaeologist." Wistfully she notes that she found "other signs of encroaching civilization." It is as if the Orient could be for Bell, too, a place of escape from the harsh realities of the present, that same present that had given her the freedom to travel in the first place. Bell expresses her enthusiasm for the multiculturalism of the Hellenistic period. At Kala'at el Mudīk of the Seleucids, she finds this "an epitome of the marvellous fusion between Greece and Asia that came of Alexander's conquests." For here was a "Greek king, whose capital lay on the Tigris, founding a city on the Orontes and calling it after his Persian wife." And how the style of these "Greek-tinged towns of Syria," brought harmoniously together colonnades and classic forms with "a spirit of Oriental lavishness" that was "holding out hands to Athens and to Babylon."[47] Bell sees the Orient as forever affecting the West positively, tempering the soberness of Greek classicism with "the spirit of Oriental magnificence which never breathed without effect on the imagination of the West."[48]

Although the Orient was a place of potential sexual liberation for many male writers of the period, most female authors avoided such matters, preferring to concentrate on domestic details such as furnishings, dress, and diet. Bell, whose interests were "manly" in most respects, notes that she was unable to buy a sheep in the mountains during the winter. How was it, she asks, that all the books she had with her had not hinted at such a fact? She answers, "The writers of these works seemed to have been more concerned with Roman remains than with such weighty matters as roasts and stews."[49] But one female writer whose focus was certainly trained on such weighty matters was Lady Hester Stanhope, who traveled to Palmyra, where no European woman has visited since Roman times, and "sought the remains of Zenobia's greatness." Writing to a Mr. H. W. Wynn in 1813, she recounts "with a certain satisfaction" her triumphal coronation in that once great city: "Without joking, I have been crowned Queen of the Desert under the triumphal arch at Palmyra! . . . I shall soon have as many names as Apollo. I am the sun, the star, the pearl, the lion, the light from Heaven, and the Queen, which all sounds well in its way." There had been nothing meek about this aristocratic British woman's arrival at Palmyra: she had entered "lance in hand, in her Oriental dress, followed by thirty camels, which had brought into the desert all that was choicest of European luxuries."[50] The experience of travel made it impossible for women like Stanhope ever to return to England. As she grew old and increasingly indebted, she was constantly at odds with the English Consul at Beirut, fearing lest some plot was being hatched by the British authorities to get her home. Writing to Lord Strangford in 1824, she likens herself to the aged Horace and declares, "I shall trim my vines, and contemplate the beauties of Nature in this solitary spot, until the veil of ignorance is withdrawn from the eyes of all judging men; but I will not allow anybody to interfere with me, and I hope your Lordship will not allow it either."[51]

As well as being a place of some freedom from domestic sexual and gender constraints, the Orient was a site of emotional liberation for many writers. With the author becoming an integral part of the interest of the landscape, the desert bloomed with their expressive outpourings. Free from the social pressures to conform at home, they were able to explore their inner selves and generate new identities. Many British travelers to Arabia—men like Doughty, Burton, and Lawrence—were in particular awkward personalities, ill at ease in Britain, but paradoxically they sought domestic fame by means of their travel accounts.[52] These works had far more focus on the subjective and the emotional attitudes they encountered, but despite this new angle the authors still found many resources in antiquity on which to draw.

The adventurer Charles Doughty revealed a passionate desire to strip away the unnecessary complications of modern life and return to what he saw as the pure but harsh virtues he found intact among the Bedouin. He was a primitivist, always looking to dig down to the "ultimate substratum" that underlay all aspects of his life, a kind of modern ascetic seeking to reduce life to its bare essentials.[53] Doughty uses archaic and Latinate language to help locate the Arabs and their pure lifestyle in the past. He uses classical references to help elevate the geographical attractions of the desert and glorify the physical rigors through which the terrain purifies the individual body. He was like Virgil, as Bevis describes, "who in the days of Empire, recalled his countrymen to their primitive virtues and manifest destiny by celebrating the exploits of *pius Aeneas*."[54] He saw in the nomads of the desert a society of individuals unfettered by the vices of modernity: "Hazardry, banquetting, and many running sores and hideous sinks of our great towns are unknown to them. The Arabs, not less frugal than Spartans, are happy in the Epicurean moderation of this religion."[55] He finds in the simple purity of the desert people the virtues that Britain needed to rediscover if its character was to be restored to its former vigor.

But not all travelers shared such sympathy for the native. Many shared the assumptions of British imperialism and superiority. Burton, for example, uses the classics to reinforce a far more vigorous expression of the current state of Britain's rude health. He feels the company of all Orientals is "antipathetical" to an Englishman, but believes that the worst is "an East-Indian." Like the fox in the fables, he is "fulsomely flattering at first, he gradually becomes easily friendly, disagreeably familiar, offensively rude, which ends by rousing the 'spirit of the British lion.'"[56] Burton believes that the British need to maintain a certain distance from their barbarian subjects if they are to maintain the necessary sense of authority: "I am convinced that the natives of India cannot respect a European who mixes with them familiarly, or especially who imitates their customs, manners, and dress." Instead what is required is "The tight pantaloons, the authoritative voice, the pococurante manner, and the broken Hindustani." It is these that "impose upon them," this is "the master's attitude," and "they bend to it like those Scythian slaves that faced the sword but fled from the horsewhip."[57] He sees the locals as uncivilized cowards. Discussing the battle of Bissel, "when Mohammed Ali of Egypt defeated Faisal son of Sa'ud the Wahhabi," many were found dead, tied by the legs with ropes. Burton explains, "This system of colligation dates from old times in Arabia." He notes also, "It seems to have been an ancient practice in the West as in the East: the Cimbri . . . were tied together with cords when attacked by Marius. Tactic truly worthy of savages to prepare for victory by expecting a defeat." For Burton saw the British citizen as the successor of the Roman. Complaining of the passport system—"we cannot but lament its inconvenience"—he is outraged that "mighty Britain . . . should charge five shillings to pay for the shadow of her protecting wing! That I cannot speak my modernised 'civis sum Romanus' without putting my hand into my pocket."[58]

Doughty's reverence for the traditional virtues of Muslim life meant that he accepted that they were in many ways unsuited to modern life. One young Turkish surgeon told him how he had seen inscriptions written in French and that he could read them plainly. They read, "'HIPPOCRATES!' And afterward another told me, he could read the inscription,—it was PHILIP OF MACEDON!—These were spirits, only good to be set to divinity studies: they wear the livery, but are aliens from the mind of Europe!"[59] But if Doughty's view of the backwardness of the East was based on a fundamental respect for their strengths, others saw the Orient as having had nothing but a decivilizing influence on the West. Frazer, describing the worship of the cult of Magna Mater, notes that in Greece "the bloody orgies of the Asiatic goddess and her consort appear to have found little favour. The barbarous and cruel character of the worship, with its frantic excesses, was doubtless repugnant to the good taste and humanity of the Greeks." Yet such characteristics "positively attracted the less refined Romans and barbarians of the West." This was the mechanism by which this and other "similar Oriental faiths" spread throughout the Roman Empire and "by saturating the European peoples with alien ideals of life gradually undermined the whole fabric of ancient civilization." As such, oriental religions were responsible for nothing less than the West's "relapse into barbarism." It was not until the end of Middle Ages that "the revival of Roman law, of the Aristotelian philosophy, of ancient art and literature . . . marked the return of Europe to native ideals of life and conduct, to saner, manlier views of the world." Only then was the "long halt in the march of civilization" over and the "tide of Oriental invasion had turned at least. It is ebbing still."[60]

Burton deployed the myth of racial difference to maintain an appropriately imperious distance from the locals. Likewise, Doughty saw the Arabs as a pure and unspoiled race, from which the English could learn. As Tidrick has shown, during the first half of the twentieth century these two beliefs coalesced into a view of the Arabs as a virtuous race with whom the English had a natural affinity.[61] Combined with the innate feeling of superiority English travelers possessed, this meant that they saw themselves as the Arabs' natural rulers. The British believed that they understood the intricacies of Arabian society and so their particular type of government was uniquely and perfectly suited to Arabian conditions. This also meant they believed that they were able to manipulate Arabian society for their own advantage.

No one individual brings together all these contradictory attitudes of British adventurers in the East better than T. E. Lawrence. In some ways his *Seven Pillars of Wisdom* can be seen as a justification for British imperial expansion within the Middle East. Lawrence, the heroic genius, leads the Arabs to national expression under the powerful guidance of the British hand. Relying on the trope of orientalism that the Arabs are inherently tribal and so naturally riven by internecine feuds, it establishes a narrative in which the Arabs positively require British leadership in order to progress politically. But like Doughty, Lawrence shared a feeling of close empathy with the proud, independent Arabs. He identified with the solitary romanticism of the nomad and admired his toughness and unfussy virtues. Any empire the British were to have over a people such as this would have to be placed on a more equal footing than an out-and-out imperialist like Burton could ever have countenanced. It was an ambivalence expressed by his famous native dress: pure white, local, androgynous yet macho.

Lawrence had been influenced by Homer as a boy, had later translated the *Odyssey*, and was offered by the war the chance to generate his own epic adventures.[62] His himself describes his "main springs of action" as a personal, pugnacious desire to win the war but also curiosity; he had read "Super flumina Babylonis" as a boy and it had left him "longing to feel myself the node of a national movement."[63] Literature stood high in Lawrence's estimation of what counted as civilization, and classical literature was at the pinnacle of that judgment. It was one of the great services Arab culture had performed, that, at a time when "Europe had fallen barbarous" and the "memory of Greek and Latin learning was fading from men's minds," the Arabs, by means of imitation, "performed a real service in preserving something of a classical past for a medieval future."[64]

Studying the classics was not simply an ivory tower activity for Lawrence. To be sure, at college he had "read the usual books (too many books)" and "worked at Hannibal's tactics, and the wars of Belisarius, like any other man at Oxford," but he had found it all useless in the actual theater of war.[65] When faced with the realities of fighting the Turk on the ground, he "sheered off episteme [written in the original Greek], the mathematical element, and plunged into the nature of the biological factor in command."[66] In his military theorizing, he realizes that the number of troops that have been deployed, what he calls the "felt" element, is not expressible in figures, but "had to be guessed at by the equivalent of Plato's doxa [in Greek], and the greatest commander of men was he whose intuitions most nearly happened." He then posits, "There had been men whose doxa so nearly approached perfection that by its road they reached the certainty of episteme. The Greeks might have called such genius for command noesis [in Greek] had they bothered to rationalize revolt."[67] He concludes his consideration of the theory of military rebellion by examining the "psychological element to building an apt shape." He turns to Xenophon and "stole, to name it, his word *diathetics*, which had been the art of Cyrus before he struck."[68] Throughout his work, Lawrence turns to classics when he is at crucial points or when generalizing from specifics. Here in the narrative he is recuperating after an illness and deliberating what course a necessary change in tactics should take. But despite his contemporary focus on the psychology of warfare, it is Plato who provides him with the tools with which to build a new military model.

Lawrence also looked to the classics when thinking about the impractical. When he examines the nature of the divine, he again turns to Plato for the means to articulate his sense of the impalpable nature of God: "There was no human effort, no fecundity in Nature: just the heaven above and the unspotted earth beneath. There unconsciously he came near God. God was to him not anthropomorphic, not tangible, not moral nor ethical, nor concerned with the world or with him, not natural: but the being achromatos [in Greek]."[69] This colorless, formless, but sophisticated notion of the divine is found also in Lawrence's account of Christ's Galilee. For Lawrence it was a place of "intellectual freedom" where Jesus chose to pass his ministry "not among the mud-huts of a Syrian village, but in polished streets among fora and pillared houses and rococo baths, products of an intense if very exotic provincial and corrupt Greek civilization." It was a place of multicultural urbanity where the people were "not Greek—at least not in the majority—but Levantines of sorts, aping a Greek culture." They did not simply reproduce "the correct banal Hellenism of the exhausted homeland, but a tropical rankness of idea, in which the rhythmical balance of Greek art and Greek ideality blossomed into novel shapes tawdry with the larded passionate colours of the East."[70] Here was the model for the British

Empire to follow. To allow the freshness of the Middle Eastern desert to breathe new life into the stale familiarities of British imperialism and thereby generate a new fusion of British and Arab cultures.

But in such a partnership, the Arabs would still play a junior role. For the Arabs were unable to resist physical temptation, but rather were passive to their senses. That "hedonistic streak among the Arabs which made them helpless slaves of carnal indulgence," was, in Lawrence's view, the result of life in Arabia, "where superfluities lacked" and "the temptation of necessary food lay always on men." Every morsel could become a pleasure, and "luxuries might be as plain as running water or a shady tree," whose misuse often turned "into lusts." Like the men of Tarsus in Apollonius, they sit on their river "like geese, drunken with its white water!"[71] And in any case, the British are simply superior at bearing the burden of empire. Like Lawrence, the British ruler could endure "more than Palomides' pains, not merely to seem better than myself, but to make others better."[72] And though capable of riding fourteen hundred miles by camel in four weeks, and not sparing himself anything to advance the war, when Lawrence gets the chance to return to civilization he talked like Chrysostom to bring it about, refusing "to spend a single superfluous night with my familiar vermin. I wanted a bath, and something with ice in it to drink: to change these clothes, all sticking to my saddle sores in filthiness: to eat something more tractable than green date and camel sinew."[73] For Lawrence could both appreciate the value of these luxuries and earn them in a way that the Arabs could not.

On the plain near Tafileh, in the winter, Lawrence found the way was too slippery, except on the ancient paving of the Roman road. Here was the "last footprint of Imperial Rome which had once, so much more preciously, played the Turk to the desert dwellers."[74] This was the fate that awaited any empire that failed to maintain the vigor of its rule, however much more civilized than the Turk. And when sitting among the ruins of Roman frontier towns, "thinking hard about the Amman demolition" and "puzzled as to what expedient would be quickest and best," Lawrence finds that "the puzzle of these ruins added to my care." What troubles him is that there "seemed evidence of bluntness of mind in these Roman frontier cities, Um el Jemal, Um el Surab, Umtaiye. Such incongruous buildings, in what was then and now a desert cockpit, accused their builders of insensitiveness; almost of a vulgar assertion of man's right (Roman right) to live unchanged in all his estate. Italianate buildings—only to be paid for by taxing more docile provinces—on these fringes of the world disclosed a prosaic blindness to the transience of politics."[75] That was the fate that awaited the British Empire if it simply imposed its way of doings things onto those below and failed to accommodate the unique sensitivities of the region they controlled. For as Lawrence understood, politics changed and, no matter how well they governed, if they failed to take advantage of their special understanding of the Arabs, then the British, like the Romans before them, could easily end up the incongruous remains of a half-forgotten world.

PART III

Afterwords

9

Screen Classics

The postwar world saw the end of Britain's empire and the start of American supremacy. It also saw a fall in the popularity of classics in schools. Studying Latin, Greek, and ancient history seemed less suited to the technological demands of the modern, globalized economy. Yet the fact that classics is no longer central to the educational syllabus has not meant that ancient sources have played a marginal role in helping the wider anglophone world shape its understanding of the East. Film and political discourse, in particular, have continued to refer to the ancient past to help establish vivid images of the West's relationship with the East. Classics has adapted to the less literary landscape by providing, instead of the direct quotations of ancient authors, the material for a range of visual references and political analogies. Both British and American examples reflect the shift in Western leadership from Britain to America, and as we will see in the final chapter, images of the Orient and the classical past have combined to help both countries understand new political realities and their relationship with the increasingly important East.

The decline in the teaching of classics since World War II has undoubtedly led to a reduction in the role of ancient sources in the shaping of oriental imagery in travel writing and history. Television and film have, however, both continued to make use of well-known classical stories, such as the affair between Antony and Cleopatra or the story of Alexander the Great, to create images of the East. These are often strongly orientalist. The Orient is shown as a hackneyed backdrop—an ossified society where nothing changes, peopled by caricatures addicted to exoticism, eroticism, and decadence, fit only to be oppressed by sadistic despots. Paradoxically, the end of empire has coincided with the use of classics to help portray some far less nuanced images of the East. In part, of course, this is the result of film being a more popular medium. Popular images of Islam going right back to the *Chansons de Geste* have always tended to be more broad-brush in their approach. It is also the product of a conservative Hollywood approach to the portrayal of foreigners and the past, happy to rely on stock images to provide the backdrops for plots more focused on the domestic concerns of their audiences. But far more subtle uses of the ancient past, such as in the film adaptation of *The English Patient*, show how film has also been able to contradict these more orientalist constructions by using the classical past to generate a set of complex and contradictory messages.

Count Lászlo de Almásy, burned beyond recognition after being shot down in his biplane in the Egyptian desert, and tagged by the hospital orderlies simply, and incorrectly, as the "English patient," kept one possession with him throughout his ordeals: his copy of Herodotus. This leather-bound translation, stuffed full of his own mementoes of his travels, acted for this fictional explorer-cum-mapmaker as his guidebook to Egypt and, for the viewers, to his own identity. It is Herodotus, the Father of History, who provides the key to unlocking the secrets of the Hungarian aristocrat's past. Made in

1996 from Michael Ondaatje's novel and winner of nine Academy Awards, the film is set at the end of the colonial era and looks back nostalgically to the era of intrepid adventurers. The book sold over a million copies, but Anthony Minghella's film adaptation was even more successful, grossing over $230 million. Made for an audience who for the most part would not know who Herodotus was, it shows how important classics has remained in helping new media establish images of the East. The huge success of the film also played an important role in disseminating such classically inspired images.[1]

Postwar cinematic representations of the East have been dominated by two negative images of the East: as a place of political otherness and as a place of sexual otherness. No films show the political difference between East and West better than the story of the battle of Thermopylae as told in *The 300 Spartans* of 1961 and the 2006 graphic novel version of the same story, 300. The first was closely bound up with the Cold War. The opening voice-over, in serious and authoritative tones and read out against a backdrop of the Parthenon, booms: "Greece: that hard and timeless land where even the stones speak of man's courage, of his endurance, and his glory." We know immediately whose side we are on. "This is the story of a turning point in history, of a blazing day when three hundred Greek warriors fought here to hold with their lives their freedom and ours." The contrast with the Persians could not be more extreme. Before the action starts, a block of text appears on screen: "In the year 480 B.C., King Xerxes of Persia set in motion his enormous slave empire to crush the small group of independent Greek states—the only stronghold of freedom still remaining in the then known world." And in what follows, the Persian exhibits all the signs of a classic, oriental despot. Early in the film Xerxes looks upon a captured Spartan spy who is brought before him. His guard decribes the Spartan as a man on whom "our best torture is wasted. . . . He's worn out two of my men without uttering a sound." Xerxes is incredulous that the Greeks are even contemplating resisting him: "Your country is divided," he tells the Spartan, "You have no single ruler. How can you defy me, the master of the whole world?" The Spartan's response respectfully spells out the political polarity that characterizes their two systems of government: "That's not for you to understand, Sir, for you are the master of slavery and you know nothing of freedom."

The Athenian orator Themistocles, in Churchillian tones, warns of what lies ahead and the necessity for the free Greeks to unite against their common enemy: "The whole of Asia is descending upon us—many times more than there are Greeks. These men are fierce, savage, bloodthirsty, numberless, but that is not the reason we should fear them. That is not the source of their power. Their power lies in their unity!" Thankfully, Greek leadership is at hand in the form of the Spartan king, Leonidas, with American accent and all. It is Sparta that will lead the free world to fight this barbarian horde. Taking his coalition of willing Greeks to Thermopylae, he rebuilds the ancient wall that stands there: "From this wall we do not retreat," he affirms. In what can clearly be read as an ideological response to the Berlin Wall and the Iron Curtain that divided Eastern from Western Europe, the film also establishes important gender differences. "Sparta," we are told, "gives her women more freedom than any state." By contrast, Xerxes orders his commanders, "Give your men this one night then destroy all the soldiers' women. There are enough women in Sparta and Athens and I want my men to be eager to get at them." What started as a military conflict is now recast as an attempt at nothing less than an attempt at massive gang rape. But the Persians are repelled, and the significance of the battle for the modern West is restated in the closing spiel: "But it was more than a victory for Greece; it was a shining example to free people throughout the world of what a few brave men can accomplish once they refuse to submit to tyranny."

Not much had changed by 2006. The film *300* refines such stereotypical negative images of the Orient into a quintessence of evil. The Persian army is animalized: "A beast approaches," we are warned; it is "the monster that is Xerxes' army." When the Persians appear, it is to the accompaniment of whip cracks and the groaning wails of the damned. The Persian soldiers are dark, black, faceless, dressed in Arab-style headscarves. Xerxes's personal bodyguards are "the deadliest fighting force in all of Asia," who have "served the dark will of Persian kings for five hundred years" and have "eyes as dark as night, teeth filed to fangs" and are "soulless." They look like a cross between Teenage Mutant Ninja Turtles and the Iranian Revolutionary Guard. Lacking any individuality, a slip of one of their masks reveals an ogre-like figure lurking beneath. And when even this terrible force fails, the Persians "turned to their magic," throwing explosive grenades at the Greek lines. Xerxes himself is represented as an eight-feet-tall giant, wearing makeup, and covered with bondage-style chains and body piercings. He is a crazy man who thinks himself a god: "It's not the lash they fear but my divine power," he utters as he places his huge hands homoerotically on Leonidas's shoulders. An air of sexual deviancy and excess surrounds him and his entourage. A deformed woman shares a lesbian kiss. Numerous seminaked women gyrate over the outcast Spartan hunchback and traitor, Ephialtes. It is an alternative demimonde with which Xerxes entices Ephialtes: "Every pleasure your fellow Greeks and your false gods have denied you, I will grant you." And all Ephialtes can do in the face of such overwhelming temptation is yield: "Yes, I want it all—wealth, women, and one more thing—I want a uniform."

The 1945 British film *Caesar and Cleopatra* emphasized how politically backward the Orient was in comparison with the experienced colonial powers. Based on George Bernard Shaw's play, it was the most expensive film ever made in Britain at the time. It quickly establishes Egypt as a place of darkness, a world of superstition where the royal household come running out screaming because "the sacred white cat has been stolen!" Into this world walks Julius Caesar, carrying a torch aflame, lighting up the gloom as he walks through the palace halls. The very fact that Cleopatra and her young brother, Ptolemy, are vying for political control only emphasizes how undeveloped this political system is by Western standards. But Caesar, "impressed by her spirit and intelligence and seduced by her charm," determines to make her queen. And as he tells Cleopatra, if Caesar thinks her "worthy to rule, he will set you on the throne by his side and make you the real ruler of Egypt." The Cleopatra we meet is not a fearsome seductress, but a young, innocent sixteen-year-old: "You're a silly little girl," Caesar says to her. Cleopatra and Ptolemy are portrayed as whining and squabbling children, and, laughably, married. Ptolemy sticks out his tongue at his sister-wife. Cleopatra is not allowed to wear makeup by her nurse, Ftatateeta. She hates baths: "A bath?" she cries. "But I had a bath yesterday!" The boy-king Ptolemy is nothing but a schoolboy forgetting his lines, needing to be given prompts by his courtiers and then placed by Caesar on the Chair of State. This is still a pre-Suez world where European powers thought nothing of acting as kingmakers, deciding who could and who could not act as co-regent alongside them.

The problem is that however much potential the young Cleopatra might have, she also seems to have an inbuilt capacity for the typical oriental vices of despotism: "When I'm old enough," she fantasizes, "I shall do just what I like. I shall be able to poison the slaves and see them wriggle and pretend to Ftatateeta, my nurse, that she is to be put into the fiery furnace." As she grows more confident in her regal powers, she cries, "I must beat somebody—I will beat him," and attacks a nearby slave. This is what the Orient does to its native rulers: it makes them brutal, cruel, and irrational. And an oriental despot in turn produces a lazy people, given to flattery instead of hard work. Cleopatra herself sleeps while Caesar works through the night. "My father was king of Egypt and he never worked!" complains Cleopatra. "And he lost his throne," replies Caesar. The viewer is constantly aligned with Caesar, aware of the duties of overseas imperial office. The courtier Pothinus is amazed that Caesar bothers to involve himself in Egyptian domestic matters: "Is it possible that Caesar, the conqueror of the world, can find time to occupy himself with such a trifle as our taxes?" But as Caesar and the British audience know, "taxes are the chief business of a conqueror of the world." They are what pay for the whole imperial project. And when reproached for his execution of the king of the Gauls and for the cutting off of enemy soldiers' right hands to prevent them from fighting again, Caesar excuses these acts as a "wise severity."

When the crowd starts shouting "Egypt for the Egyptians!," the Roman commander Rufio is forced to remind them, "There's a Roman army of occupation here." But Roman rule was more than a question of military force. It is portrayed as rational and above all moral, something for which the locals should be grateful and certainly not be looking to change. "You will always be my king. My nice, kind, wise, good old king," says Cleopatra to Caesar appreciatively. Caesar's rule is government "without punishment, without revenge, without judgment," for "that is the right way, the great way, the only possible way in the end." Of course, the film holds out the hope that the British can train the local (in this case, white and by origin Greek and European) elite to govern alongside them, but the process cannot be rushed. "You think you know more than I do already," complains Caesar to Cleopatra at one point when she is getting ahead of herself. "No. That would be very silly of me," she meekly demurs. Learning how to rule is something that will need the Orient to change its very character and will take time, a long time. As one of her handmaidens complains to Cleopatra: "He makes you so terribly prosy and serious, so learned and philosophical." And even then she cannot help succumbing to her tendency for murder and intrigue. In fact, this Cleopatra is seen as longing for the protection of a European man. Caesar says, "I will send you a man . . . but bright and fresh and strong and young. Hoping in the morning, fighting in the day, and reveling in the evening," and when Cleopatra hears that it is to be Mark Antony, she shrieks girlishly with delight and hugs Caesar like a father. "So now are you satisfied?" he asks, before kissing her paternally on the forehead. Understandably, Cleopatra weeps as Caesar sails away from Egypt.

The film constructs a colonialist image of the politics of the East, which seeks to resist the growing nationalist clamor of the time. It is also the product of a Western male gaze, which is structured to lead to the inevitable conclusion of the justness and benevolence of British rule. We all know what happened to Cleopatra in the end, after all. The Western male right to rule is based on reason, lack of sentiment, and hard work. But the film is not just about the arrogance of the colonial. The Irishman Shaw was keen to distance himself from British imperialism. Caesar is an old man, looking back on his life's work and wondering if it has all been worth it. Rome, he says, is "only a madman's dream." Caesar is forced to admit to a life of emotions and feelings, even if, in the end, he is too old to give them expression.

Julius Caesar's affair with Cleopatra has been "played most frequently as a teasing prelude to a markedly more sensuous affair with

Mark Antony."[2] Cinematic representations of this affair are probably the most widely known bearers of the stereotype of the Orient as a place of sexual license and fantasy. These "bad-girl" Cleopatras, as Lucy Hughes-Hallett calls them, present a woman who is the opposite of the traditional virtuous Western wife—a woman of the world who is nasty, predatory, and sexually adventurous, a "sensualist celebrating the mortal sins of the flesh."[3] She symbolizes the struggle between such traditional female roles and the desire for women in the twentieth century to pursue their own independence and ambitions.

The 1963 Elizabeth Taylor Cleopatra offered a total rejection of old-fashioned modesty, frugality, and restraint. This approach was mirrored in the production of the film itself, which went massively over budget and was famous for both its profligacy and the real-life affair between Taylor and her male co-star, Richard Burton. Taylor's Cleopatra is a modern woman, not the asexual juvenile of 1945. She is knowledgeable, sensuous, and ambitious, a sophisticate who dismisses "the notion of sexual sin as being outmoded, oppressive and absurd."[4] She overhears Julius Caesar being briefed about her by his advisers. She is "reputed to be extremely intelligent and sharp of wit . . . she speaks seven languages perfectly." In attaining her objectives she "has been known to employ torture, poison and even her own sexual talents, which are said to be considerable." In fact, she chooses her lovers "in the manner of a man." She is aggressive toward Caesar when his men inadvertently destroy the great library of Pharos: "How dare you and the rest of your barbarians destroy my library!" She refuses to be summoned by Mark Antony and instead makes him kneel before her. It is an image that was to some extent recycled in the 2008 HBO *Rome* series, where Cleopatra appears as a drug-addicted, self-absorbed, and violent seductress. This Cleopatra's sexual habits are likewise extraordinary. Her attendant summons the Roman soldier Vorenus:

> "Majesty commands that you enter her."
>
> "I do not understand."
>
> "You have coitus with her."
>
> "It is not in our custom. Roman men are not used by women in this way."

He nearly succumbs before he recalls his wife and his duties and escapes with the cry: "I am not a slave to be commanded."

Both the 1963 film and the *Rome* television series peddle stereotypes about the Orient. Both share a visual infatuation with Egypt's material abundance, emphasized in shots of great monuments, lavish feasts, rich tapestries and furnishings, and ornate jewelry and dress. Both emphasize its mysticism and irrationality. In *Rome*, Jocasta manages to combine the two, complaining that Her Majesty doesn't like Roman hairstyles on her women: "Quite irrational about it, if you ask me." Similarly, the court is dominated by the machinations of a verbose, effeminate eunuch chamberlain. Cruelty is commonplace and refined. A morbidly obese slave brings in Pompey's head in a jar as a gift for Caesar: "We were going to make him a body with moving arms and legs and do a mime show with real animals and everything," explains the young Ptolemy. Ptolemy himself has regressed from being a petulant teenager in the 1963 film to being a foul-mouthed spoilt brat who hates his sister, Cleopatra: "Do not speak of her," he commands Caesar, "I piss on her, I shit on her!" And it is a place where nothing much happens: "Things move ever so slow around here," explains Jocasta. "It's the heat."

The East is reduced in such visions to a desert, a symbol of its backwardness, the "essential unchanging decor of the history of the

Orient."[5] The desert becomes a place of heat and passion, recklessness and primordial, uncensored emotions. It is a place that needs to be brought to life by the European intruder, who alone can fertilize its virgin land and make it fecund. The geographical conquest of the land is "naturalised as sexual possession of a woman's body."[6] For such images of the Orient were not simply a product of imperial conquest; they were also a way of expressing repressed desire. Cleopatra's Egypt became synonymous with sensuousness, idleness, and casual sex, in direct contrast to Rome's respectability, duty, and marriage. The relationships that the Orient is presented as offering are "a fantasy structure that evades proper Western courtship customs by offering visions of rape and polygamy."[7] And the relationship between the West and the East becomes stereotyped as one of sexual dominance. These fantastical imaginings are in many ways represented by the veil. As Sarah Graham-Brown argues, "No single item of clothing has had more influence on the Western image of Middle Eastern women than the veil."[8] The desire to penetrate behind the veil itself helped to establish the colonial identity, even if the veil also acted as an obstacle to colonial visual control.

The journey into the desert became for the Westerner, therefore, a journey into the self. Films helped map out the Orient for Western purposes by locating it as a place for sexual self-discovery. But such temptations brought with them risks. Like Mark Antony did, it was possible to yield too much to the allure of the East and turn native. In *Rome*, after wallowing in "a world of numbing debauchery," he becomes womanish, wearing makeup, and takes drugs and spends his time sleeping. He indulges in cruel games, hunting with arrows a slave dressed as a stag: "Venison for dinner then?" he jokes after the kill. Octavian's herald on the streets of Rome makes it clear how degraded he has become: "Mark Antony has coupled himself to the sorceress Cleopatra. . . . He worships dogs and reptiles, he blackens his eyes with soot, like a prostitute, he dances and plays the cymbals in vile Nilotic rites." And even he becomes aware of his fallen state after his defeat at Actium: "Look around us," he says to Cleopatra, "whores, hermaphrodites and lickspittles—this is our army now." The incorruptible, true Roman, Vorenus, has nothing but disdain for what his leader has become but remains loyal to the end. Antony is left to die, the embodiment of the danger for the West of getting too close to the Orient and taking on its ways.

The dangers of close involvement with the Orient are also evident in the film versions of Alexander's life. Both the 1956 *Alexander the Great* and the 2004 *Alexander* repeat many of the standard tropes of a stereotypical representation of the East. Aristotle speaks authoritatively in 1956 against the Persian peril. "The Persian way of life has the seed of death and fear in it," he warns, "the Greek, of life and courage. The gods of the Greeks are made in the image of men, not men with birds' heads and bulls with lions' heads but men who can be understood and felt." He was still at it in 2004: "It is true that the oriental races are known for their barbarity and their slavish devotion to their senses." Darius the despot is a static figure, seemingly stuck to his chariot. Alexander, by contrast, is the energetic young ruler buzzing with new ideas. Babylon is portrayed as a mistress whose conquest is almost sexual. When the 2004 Alexander arrives in India, he finds a land of internecine fanaticism, "a land without a centre, kings who conspired against one another, a labyrinth of tribes urged on by zealots and philosophers to die by the thousands for their strange gods." The local water is putrid, the culture characterized by exotic dancing, heavy drinking, debauchery, and homosexuality.

For this Alexander, his campaign is nothing less than a civilizing mission. It is a war of liberation: "to free the people of the world; such would be beyond the glory of Achilles." Alexander is commendably multicultural but, as Aristotle had earlier warned him, "the East has a way of swallowing men and their dreams." Later Aristotle feels compelled to write to Alexander to express his concern about his project of cultural fusion between East and West: "I confess a certain disappointment especially on the reports of your taking on eastern ways. Beware how these manners inflame the senses with pride." And sure enough, instead of achieving his aim, Alexander falls into the oriental trap and turns into a corrupt, drunken tyrant, dressed in fancy clothes.[9]

Alexander's legend has endured not simply because of his military achievements, but because of the deep chord it has struck through centuries of East–West antagonism. To many, Alexander is at his most fascinating not charging Porus's elephant on Bucephalus but agonizing in Babylon among a crowd of cupbearers and concubines. Orientalism and the sexually charged fantasy of an unattainable East–West syncretism have only obscured further portrayals that were already distorted from the start, and have little to do with the few reasonably ascertained deeds of the Macedonian conqueror.[10] But the orientalism of the 2004 *Alexander* is often blurred and contradicted in the film, which makes a simple imperialist reading difficult. Alexander is keen to respect the ancient Persian culture; and what disturbs him most is his friend's "contempt for a world far older than ours." Yet in the end, the pragmatic view of Ptolemy prevails. For as the aged Ptolemy recounts, it was only the dreamer, idealist Alexander who ever believed in such cultural harmony. "What did we have to look forward to?" he asks. "To give away our wealth to Asian sycophants we despised? Mixing the races? Harmony? Pah! How he talked of these things . . . I never believed in his dream. None of us did."

Film is often well aware of the silliness of its over-the-top portrayals of oriental luxury and decadence. Hughes-Hallett notes that,

"The vast majority of modern Cleopatras have a comical ambivalence."[11] Taylor, in her 1963 portrayal, mocks the stories that are told about her famous asses' milk baths: "We must not disappoint the mighty Caesar," she says, climbing into a tub to await his arrival. "The Romans tell fabulous tales of my bath and handmaidens . . . and my morals." But no film has sent up the excessive consumption and luxuriousness of Hollywood epic more than *Carry on Cleo*.[12] As Nicholas Cull has argued, the film can be seen as a discussion of the declined British Empire and the future of a postcolonial Britain as a satellite state of the new American empire. In its mocking way, the film subverts American values and Britain's subservience to them. Such delicate issues are joked about and so made safe. In this carnivalesque world, Cleopatra becomes nothing more than a bimbo: childlike, lisping, giggling, stupid, vain, sultry, and sulky. But she is still very much an object of a naughty-but-nice sexual fantasy. As Hughes-Hallett observes, the bimbo Cleopatra is "a luscious young woman whose silliness in no way detracts from her sexual allure." In fact, dumbness makes her more attractive. Yet she is also "a woman whom men can encounter without fear," because her sexuality is canceled by her infantilism.[13] And as for the Arabs, Seneca tells Mark Antony that they are "intense lovers." "Of course," he replies, "they do everything in tents!"

If laughter made women and Arabs seem both inferior and safe in *Carry on Cleo*, other postwar representations have sought to show that they are aware of their orientalist strategies and to undercut them. *Rome*, in particular, tries to put forward a more balanced picture. When the down-to-earth soldier Pullo claims he's not scared of a god with a dog's head, the more serious Vorenus checks him: "Their gods are old and powerful. Egypt was a great nation long before Rome." But Pullo is having none of it: "Was it?" he replies.

"Made up for it now then, haven't they?" Later he describes Cleopatra as "that gypo princess," but is again pulled up by his more politically correct colleague: "Her father's people rode with Alexander. You can't speak of her like that!" Likewise, when Mark Antony calls Cleopatra a whore, she is quick to defend herself as a woman who is simply doing her best by her family and country: "If I must prostitute myself for the good of my country and my family I will." And when he accuses her of "playing the Queen," she reacts strongly: "Playing the Queen? I am the Queen," before throwing him on his back and jumping on top of him. But no matter what efforts are made to apologize for the stereotypical images used in the series, *Rome* ultimately falls back on caricatures of oriental otherness, in this case the violent, sexual struggle that ensues.

At first sight *The English Patient* also fails to escape the pull of these orientalist tropes. The focus of the blurb on the back cover of the DVD is that as the count slowly regains his memory, "a passionate and consuming love affair with a married woman is unveiled." In the film, great emphasis is placed on his copy of Herodotus. Repeated shots of it visualize the authority of the classics. Herodotus is presented as the authentic guide to Egypt, a world that implicitly has not changed in the intervening centuries. It is a land of temptations and love affairs. The reserved and thoroughly English-like Almásy loses control in the face of these oriental temptations. But that is what Egypt does to a Westerner if he is not careful. As his friend Madox says to him, while flirting with a young man, Kamal, sitting on top of his truck as he drives through the desert, "How do you explain to someone who has never been here feelings which seem quite normal?" Within seconds, Madox has lost control of the vehicle, recklessly pursuing Kamal, who has fallen off into a sand dune. The desert becomes a place for sexual adventure. The landscape itself is anthropomorphized, with Almásy searching for a mountain in the shape of a woman's back. Mapmaking becomes the equivalent of lovemaking.

Herodotus is the key to understanding Almásy. Herodotus's account of the love triangle between Candaules, his wife, and Gyges becomes particularly important. Almásy is Gyges, and the effects of his love affair leave him burned both literally and metaphorically. Herodotus is not known primarily for his stories of love affairs, and by focusing on this example the film eroticizes the text itself in an oriental context. Katherine, the wife, reads out the story round a campfire to further heighten the erotic tension the text creates. The scholar Almásy, who writes books and lives his life through books, who emulates historians, is opened up by Katherine. But Almásy's copy of Herodotus is also his own scrapbook, a personal map of his adventures that parallels the maps he is drawing for the wartime Allies. The book itself is fetishized. Long, lingering shots focus on the turning of pages. The count's maps and scraps of personal information become nothing less than the modern equivalent of Herodotus. He too is creating a document that establishes his version of the Orient, and by making maps creates a new territory. And when he loses his memory after the plane crash, the book still retains his memories. Badly burned, Almásy is preserved like a book, his leathery skin resembling his hidebound Herodotus. An equivalence is established between the count and the book. Herodotus is an inherent part of his controlled identity; at least, the English version of the text is. But however much Almásy may love the Father of History, he is in Egypt to search for a lost, prehistoric world. The cave where he finds the paintings is a hidden world that predates Herodotus and was never found by him. The figures in these paintings are shown swimming and free. It is a motif that recurs throughout the film: the lovers share a bath, the wife distances herself from her husband by spending the whole time swimming and bathing. The freedom of love is pretextual, before the accounts written by Herodotus created a past.

The film tries to distance itself from orientalist fictions. When Madox explains to Almásy the impossibility of explaining to someone back home the homosexual feelings he experiences in the desert, Almásy at first bats his eyes disapprovingly, but then compassionately holds Madox's arm, saying: "I don't know, my friend, I don't know." The film is strongly anticolonial, even as it looks back with some nostalgia to the romanticism of this age when adventure could still be found. Almásy tries to get the Indian bomb expert, Singh, whom he calls "the boy," to read Kipling properly:

> *Singh:* "'Chapter 1: He sat, in defiance of municipal orders, astride the gun Zam-Zammah.' I can't read these words. I can't read them. They stick in my throat."
>
> *Almásy:* "Because you're reading it too fast."
>
> *Singh:* "Not at all."
>
> *Almásy:* "You have to read Kipling slowly. Your eye is too impatient. Think about the speed of his pen. What is it? 'He sat, comma, in defiance of municipal orders, comma . . . outside the wonder house as the natives call the Lahore museum.'"

Almásy understands the very grammar of imperialism. But so too does Singh, and he knows where it ends:

> "It is still there, the cannon outside the museum. It was made of metal cups and bowls taken from every household in the city as tax, then melted down. Then later they fired the cannon at my people . . . comma, the natives, full stop."

Almásy cannot see beyond the qualities of the text to the realities that underpinned its production: "What is it you really object to? The writer or what he's writing about?" Singh spells it out to him: he objects to "the message I read everywhere in your book, however slowly I read it, that the best thing for India is to be ruled by the British."

But Singh sees in Almásy and his fellow bomb disposal expert, Hardy, "everything that's good about England." He explains that Hardy "never once . . . He didn't ask me if I could spin the ball at cricket or the Kama Sutra." It is an anti-orientalist spirit that represents the best that England has to offer. Almásy finds it ironic that he finally came to be labeled as an "English patient" only after having been arrested by the British on suspicion of being a German spy: "Isn't that funny—after all that I became English. I couldn't even say what that was." Like his Herodotus, he has been translated into English and is unsure of what has been lost and gained in that process. The fact that both Almásy and Hardy die could be taken as a pessimistic message for the better qualities of Englishness. But Almásy, at least, will live on in his copy of Herodotus.

When Almásy's nurse agrees to put him out of his misery and kill him with an overdose, he asks her, "Read to me. Read me to sleep." The words that she reads are not Herodotus's, or his, but the dying words of his lover, Katherine. Almásy had left behind his copy with her as she lay injured in the Cave of the Swimmers, as close an equivalence as possible for his own self and their love affair. Waiting in vain for his return, she wrote in the failing light: "We are the real countries. Not the boundaries drawn on maps with the names of powerful men." She wants "an earth without maps." But Herodotus has come into the cave and there is no turning back. Writing has political consequences, and to make maps is a matter not simply of observing the landscape objectively but of getting involved in issues of territory. However hard they might try to get back to the innocence of the figures in the cave, they cannot escape the figurative texts that now map out their lives. Writing in Herodotus against Herodotus is a hopeless task.

The book is left on the table by Almásy's bed after his body has been removed. The nurse, heading off to find Singh in Florence to renew their relationship, comes back for it. She, from the new world, a Canadian professional who still plays hopscotch, is the opposite of the rich colonial wife, Katherine. Whereas Katherine was "charming and has read everything," even knowing the stories of Herodotus by heart, Hana the nurse cannot even pronounce Candaules's name. But she still needs and wants Herodotus for the journey ahead, a journey to a place where the new world will meet the Asian in the heart of the old. For no matter how old-world a book it is, Herodotus can still be a map for a postwar, postcolonial future. Indeed, Herodotus cannot be written out; there is no escape from history. For the new-world nurse picks up Herodotus, but her own hybrid French-Canadian identity has itself been shaped by the mapmaking, warfare, and colonialism of the past.

10

America Roma Nova

In varied ways, images of the Orient and the classical past have combined to play an important role in helping America establish its own identity. Hugely popular late nineteenth-century travel books, such as Bayard Taylor's *The Lands of the Saracen* and Mark Twain's *The Innocents Abroad*, used contrasting images of classical beauty and supposed modern oriental decline to highlight American industry and practicality. This hardheaded, egalitarian self-image implicitly contrasted with the hierarchies of the old European colonial powers. Since World War II, when global leadership transferred from Britain, classics has helped America come to terms with the nature and extent of that power and its limitations. The Vietnam Veterans Memorial was built in the context of traditional classical buildings such as the Lincoln Memorial and the Egyptian-style obelisk of the Washington Monument. Although in many ways she designed it as an anticlassical piece, the architect Maya Lin also sought to recreate the nonwhiteness of classical temples in a piece she wanted to be read as "an epic Greek poem." The fierce controversy surrounding the memorial showed how important classics continued to be in shaping postmodern, postclassical discussions of American involvement in the East. More recently, the fall of the Berlin Wall left America as the world's sole superpower and invited much comparison with the Roman Empire at its height. But the events of 9/11 and the subsequent wars in Iraq and Afghanistan have seen that image reversed, with comparison now focusing on the declining Roman Empire struggling to deal with the barbarians coming from the East.

According to the U.S. National Center for Education Statistics, in 2008, American academic institutions awarded just over 2,250,000 bachelor's, master's, and doctoral degrees. Of these, just 1,823 were collected by students of purely classical subjects. The fact that only 0.08 percent of the higher-education population have focused on studying antiquity might suggest that Americans have little interest in the classical past. It might be thought that classics would therefore have lost its role as the prism through which the English-speaking world often peers out at Islam and the East. This is far from the case. Many thousands study aspects of classical civilization as a part of their broader degree. And although it is obviously true that classics does not act as the cornerstone of the Western imagination, as it did, alongside the Bible, in former periods, the ancient world continues to play an important part in helping the world's superpower understand its position in the postmodern world. A peculiarly American discourse has evolved involving classics and the image of the East.

As American society grew richer and more consumer-oriented in the second half of the nineteenth century, readers grew hungry for a taste of foreign otherness. The boom in American travel literature reflects something of this quest for excitement.[1] The Orient seemed to resonate with an audience who desired something a bit more exotic than apple pie. One of the writers who popularized the foreign travel experience and published copiously on his own journeys was

Bayard Taylor. Taylor had a theatrical streak and would sometimes appear at readings dressed in Arab clothes and carrying a scimitar, a getup that reportedly left some women swooning.[2] Traveling on a shoestring budget, he provided his American audience with the vicarious thrill of the East in a way that made it seem all too possible that they too could be there. His account of his travels into the Middle East, *The Lands of the Saracen*, published in 1856, was one of the most popular travel books of the century.

As with most travel literature, Taylor writes from a position of assumed superiority of the reader's culture. That is not to say that he believes that America does not fall short in comparison with foreign lands in some ways. But if the United States could not compete with Europe and the Orient's antiquity, that did not mean it was in any way inferior. In fact, it is the visits to ancient monuments and ruins that bring out the highest praise, both to highlight the fall from such ideals that modern Europe and the East have experienced and also to underline the fact that it is now America that has picked up the torch of civilization. In his *Travels in Greece and Russia* of 1859, Taylor visits the Parthenon in Athens. Immediately he was "seized with an overpowering mixture of that purest and loftiest admiration which is almost the same thing as love."[3] Ancient Greece is spared the kind of hard-nosed skepticism he reserves for the modern world. Instead, in Greece he finds that "the soul of ancient Art and Poetry throbs in the splendid air, and pours its divinest light upon the landscape."[4] As with so many travel writers, the juxtaposition of this classical perfection with the shoddy realities of modern life in the Middle East elicits harsh criticism of the locals. Contemplating the ruins of Baalbek, Taylor expounds that he knows of "nothing so beautiful in all remains of ancient art" as the six surviving pillars of the temple. But the condition and treatment of the remains lead him to complain that of the four pillars of the superb portico that remain, "the Saracens have nearly ruined these by building a sort of watch-tower upon the architrave." They are, he concludes, an "unscrupulous race."[5]

Taylor uses classical figures to affirm orientalist tropes as a way of establishing an alternative American identity. In his *Dissertation on Bathing and Bodies*, Taylor begins by lumping together Orientals and Greeks alike into an image of Eastern sensualism: the bath is, he says, the "peculiar institution" of the East, "that sensuous elysium which cradled the dreams of Plato, the visions of Zoroaster, and the solemn meditations of Mahomet" and is "only to be found under an oriental sky."[6] But the decay from classical to modern is quickly reestablished: "I envy those old Greek bathers, into whose hands were delivered Pericles, and Alcibiades, and the perfect models of Phidias. They had daily before their eyes the highest types of Beauty which the world has ever produced." By contrast, oriental life is "too full of repose, and the Ottoman race has become too degenerate through indulgence, to exhibit many striking specimens of physical beauty." This physical degeneration he accepts is also seen in those of Anglo-Saxon descent: "Our Saxon race can supply the athlete, but not the Apollo."[7] But whereas the oriental is characterized as lazily languishing in the hot baths so dear to him, the American is a man of action, a competitor, who is always striving to improve his performance, even if he can never attain the graceful beauty of the classical past. Indeed, Taylor confirms that oriental repose forms a strong contrast to "the over-active life of the New World."[8] The difference between East and West is unbridgeable, Taylor suggests, because "Oriental races draw comfort and strength from other sources than we do." But he is also able to sympathize with the downtrodden Eastern peoples: "Alas, for the Orientals! They get but scanty justice, I fear, even from us: we praise the rulers who keep them abject and ignorant, and then revile the people because they are not manly and intelligent."[9] In revealing such empathy, Taylor distances himself from the European colonialists who treat the oriental subordinates so poorly and derogatorily. But he also highlights the problem of American foreign policy to this day: that the practical need to maintain order and stability is often at loggerheads with the requirements of justice.

But if there is one thing that characterizes Taylor's writing, it is his gently ironic mocking of the pretensions of the Old World. In chapter 13 of *Lands of the Saracen*, for example, he includes a dissertation on pipes and coffee, emphasizing how central tobacco was to oriental life. How did the ancients cope without such benefits, he asks: "How did Plato philosophize without the Pipe? How did gray Homer, sitting on the temple-steps in the Grecian twilights, drive from his heart the bitterness of beggary and blindness?" Tobacco would have softened the extremes of classical Greek culture and left an even better heritage to the world: "It is also our loss, that Tobacco was unknown to the Greeks. They would else have given us, in verse and in marble, another divinity in their glorious pantheon—a god less drowsy than Morpheus and Somnus, less riotous than Bacchus, less radiant than Apollo, but with something of the spirit of each."[10] Taylor went so far as to experiment with cannabis, detailing the effects that it had on him. Here we have the forerunner of the stereotyped modern American tourist: consuming and enjoying, taking in the sights of the Old World in a relaxed, partly reverential, partly mocking style.

It was Mark Twain, in his hugely successful *The Innocents Abroad, or The New Pilgrims' Progress*, who took this irreverent tone of voice to a higher plane.[11] Published in 1869 on a subscription basis, this was a book designed to have popular appeal: big, over six hundred pages, plenty of gold leaf on the jacket, and lots of illustrations. At a time when few in the United States had much knowledge of the East, it played an important role in bringing the Orient into the average American home. In it, Twain adopts the persona of the American everyman: skeptical, shrewd, businesslike, not too cultural, and occasionally naive—providing, in other words, an account of the developing American psyche.[12] Twain sends up the smug seekers of high culture, posing as a cultural boor from the frontier western states. The original cover captured the essence of this approach. It displayed a collage of Old World icons—the dome of St. Peter's in Rome, Vesuvius erupting, a mosque with minarets, the Parthenon, the Sphinx, a pyramid—over which are trampling a collection of figures. A camel carries a hookah-smoking tourist over the word *Abroad*, like Bayard Taylor enjoying the exotic physical experiences the East could offer. An elephant stomps on the word *Progress*, perhaps to emphasize that progress is not something that should be associated with the Orient. Another enjoys himself by sliding down the side of the pyramid, while two pilgrims carve Mark Twain's name on its face in the style of Pompeian graffiti in a symbolic New World attack on the hallowed icons of the old.

Twain did not stop at mocking the Holy Land or the way many American pilgrims suspended their usual hardheadedness when confronted with Palestine. His attitude displayed the usual ambivalence Americans applied to the civilization of Europe, refusing to be automatically impressed: "We examined modern and ancient statuary with a critical eye in Florence, Rome, or anywhere we found it, and praised it if we saw fit, and if we didn't we said we preferred the wooden Indians in front of the cigar stores of America. But the Holy Land brought out all our enthusiasm. We fell into raptures by the barren shores of Galilee. . . . After dismal, smileless Palestine, beautiful Egypt had few charms for us."[13] But for all Twain's mocking of the new, American-style grand tour, he too fell for its classical charms. Greece brought to the fore all his and his fellow travelers' natural enthusiasm: "No land we had yet seen had aroused such universal interest among the passengers." Their excitement at approaching Greece and Athens outshone the fine sunset and also highlighted how their idealism basked in the glow of classical ideals: "What cared we for outward visions, when Agamemnon, Achilles, and a thousand other heroes of the great Past were marching in ghostly procession through our fancies? What were sunsets to us, who were about to live and breathe and walk in actual Athens?"[14] In comparison with such an idealized outlook on the ancient past, the present could only seem massively disappointing. Traveling from Athens through the Greek islands, Twain complains that "we saw little but forbidding sea-walls and barren hills, sometimes surmounted by three or four graceful columns of some ancient temple, lonely and deserted—a fitting symbol of the desolation that has come upon all Greece in these latter ages." Indeed, he goes so far as to suppose that "ancient Greece and modern Greece compared, furnish the most extravagant contrast to be found in history."[15]

The decline of Greece is further evidenced when Twain and three companions, confined by quarantine to their boat, sneak ashore at night to visit the Parthenon, "in all its ruined magnificence."[16] Finding it locked, they are not to be deterred and rising American power and modern Eastern decline produce a powerful contrast with antiquity: "Xerxes took that mighty citadel four hundred and eighty years before Christ, when his five millions of soldiers and camp-followers followed him to Greece, and if we four Americans could have remained unmolested five minutes longer, we could have taken it too." The arrival of the Greek garrison of four did not impede the Americans—they turned simply to "bribery and corruption." What a contrast are the classical remains within: "the noblest ruins we had ever looked upon." Athens by moonlight reveals the skeptical frontier American's inner idealist: "Overhead the stately columns, majestic still in their ruin—under foot the dreaming city—in the distance the silver sea—not on the broad earth is there another picture half so beautiful."

Twain is particularly impressed by the practicalities of ancient building works: "What builders they were, these men of antiquity!" In order to bring home to his American audience the sheer size of the ancient remains at Baalbek, he has to think of modern comparisons. The stone foundations are built of blocks of stone "as large as an omnibus" and these structures are "traversed by tunnels of masonry through which a train of cars might pass." The massive arches of the ruins at Ephesus he finds later rest upon solid blocks of marble, some of which, he says astonished, "are as large as a Saratoga trunk, and some the size of a boarding-house sofa."[17] The local inhabitants present the usual sorry picture by comparison: "the miserable huts of a little crew of filthy Arabs are perched upon the broken masonry of antiquity."[18] And with mock hardheadedness he considers the lessons that the U.S. government could learn from the autocratic Xerxes's attitude toward bridge building. The first bridge across the Hellespont had been badly built and fell into the sea, and the king "thinking that to publicly rebuke the contractors might have a good effect on the next set, called them out before the army and had them beheaded. In the next ten minutes he let a new contract for the bridge. It has been observed by ancient writers that the second bridge was a very good bridge. . . . If our government would rebuke some of our shoddy contractors occasionally, it might work much good."[19] Here Twain ironically aligns himself with the Persian tyrant to criticize failings in the American government, emphasizing that for all its idealism America too could fall short of its own standards.

Twain also seeks to convey something of what he sees as Arab failings by implicitly conflating their treatment of the remains of antiquity with their horses, an agrarian image presumably aimed to appeal to his horse-loving rural American readership. He is assigned a new horse, which he decided to call "Baalbec," because, with most of his teeth gone, with one of his hind legs bent the wrong way, and being as blind as a bat, he is "such a magnificent ruin." He dismisses the much-vaunted Arab love for their horses as a fraud: they have "no love for their horses, no sentiment of pity for them, and no knowledge of how to treat them or care for them." He goes on: "These pirates never think of washing a horse's back. They do not shelter the horses in the tents either; they must stay out and take the weather as it comes. Look at poor cropped and dilapidated 'Baalbec,' and weep for the sentiment that has been wasted upon the Selims of romance!"[20] An equivalence is established between the horse and the ancient remains, which has the effect of creating an image of Arab carelessness and barbarity. It takes an American to know how to treat the vestiges of the classical world correctly and to tell an Arab how to treat horses properly.

Modern Asia is constructed as the antithesis of the classical past. Arriving in the city of Smyrna, "our first notable acquaintance in Asia," he finds it is "just like any other Oriental city. That is to say, its Moslem houses are heavy and dark, and as comfortless as so many tombs." Everywhere he sees "there is dirt, every where there are fleas," "every alley is thronged with people," "all manner of sounds assail the ear, and over them all rings out the muezzin's cry from some tall minaret, calling the faithful vagabonds to prayer." Over and above this tattiness, Twain is oppressed by what he calls "a combination of Mohamedan stenches," a smell so bad that "the smell of even a Chinese quarter" would be far pleasanter. "Such," he bemoans, is "Oriental luxury—such is Oriental splendor!"[21] But directly after leaving Smyrna, Twain traveled to nearby Ephesus on the train that linked the two, run by an English company. The contrast is sharp. Ephesus, "the proudest city of ancient times," "whose Temple of Diana was so noble in design, and so exquisite of workmanship."[22] Ephesus, a "world of precious relics, a wilderness of marred and mutilated gems." Reminded of the story of the seven sleepers, who slept for two hundred years in a cave, Twain notes that "so firm a faith had the ancients in this legend, that as late as eight or nine hundred years ago, learned travellers held it in superstitious fear." But although such ancient beliefs were pardonable, the modern inhabitants have not progressed at all: "Even at this day the ignorant denizens of the neighbouring country prefer not to sleep in it." Despite their love of Ephesus, Twain and his travel companions are unable to bring a single relic away with them. They had gathered fragments of sculptured marble and ornaments broken off from mosques but were forced to hand them over by a government officer who had an order from Constantinople "*to look out for our party*, and see that we carried nothing off." Most of the American party are outraged, particularly when it is discovered that the imperial order was enclosed in an envelope "bearing the seal of the British Embassy at Constantinople and therefore must have been inspired by the representative of the Queen." "This was bad," concludes Twain, "very bad." For if the order had come solely from the Ottomans, "it might have signified only Ottoman hatred of Christians, and a vulgar ignorance as to genteel methods of expressing it; but coming from the Christianized, educated, politic British Legation, it simply intimated that we were a sort of gentlemen and ladies who would bear watching!"[23]

Twain's *Innocents Abroad* reveals how a burgeoning American society was forging its own international sense of identity, which contrasted with the Old World both of Europe and of Asia. The constant disrespecting of these traditional societies is used as a way to assert American significance to a wider audience. Twain refuses to act deferentially to the old colonial powers. But the overrespecting of the classical past served not only to undermine the supposed civilized nature of the modern European and Asian empires but also to claim the ideals and heroes of antiquity for America. Yet Twain is always tonally complex. He can also look to ancient tyrants like Xerxes for guidance in modern government, with an irony that highlights American failings. Everyone is open to mockery and criticism, except perhaps the idealized heroes of antiquity. Here was a complicated, new type of travel literature that sought to bridge the divide between high and low culture, to combine a rough-and-ready humor with a serious, idealistic core of beliefs, and to use antiquity as a means to establish a clearer idea of America's new sense of its own identity.

The transfer of global imperium from the British Empire to America after World War II created a new relationship between America and the East. Some saw the new American dominance as merely the latest in a long line of empires that could be traced back to Rome. The historian Richard Van Alstyne, in his 1960 book *The American Empire*, stated, "the United States is by its very essence an imperial power. It is a creature of the classical Roman-British tradition. It was conceived as an empire; and its evolution from a weak State, strung out on a long exposed coastline in 1789, to a world State, with commitments that are truly Roman in their universality, has been a characteristically imperial type of growth."[24] But as the Romans had so often found, the East could prove a difficult opponent to defeat militarily. Vietnam demonstrated the limits of superpower status and presented a new kind of war to America: messy, widely unpopular, and unsuccessful. How was this debacle to be memorialized? Originally there was no federal plan to establish a national memorial for the conflict. But a small group of veterans set up the Vietnam Veterans Memorial Fund (VVMF), which staged an open and anonymous competition for a design to be built on a site close to the Washington Monument and the Lincoln Memorial. Both of these buildings had their roots in the classical past: the Lincoln Memorial, built in 1922, had been modeled on the Parthenon, and the Washington Monument harked back to the use of Egyptian obelisks in the imperial trophies of Roman architecture. The VVMF's only stipulation was that the new memorial should be apolitical about the Vietnam War itself.[25]

The form a war memorial takes reflects both the purpose of the war and the way in which it has been conducted. But it also reflects how a society chooses to remember and construct the past. As Marita Sturken argues, shifting discourses of history, personal memory, and cultural memory converge in such public commemoration, meaning that remembrance and memorialization can be contested. The fierce political debate that had surrounded the execution of the war itself probably meant that the VVMF's hope for an apolitical memorial design was always destined to be in vain. The competition was won by a twenty-one-year-old Yale undergraduate, Maya Ying Lin. Initially welcomed, perhaps because of its modesty, Lin's design caused an uproar. Tom Carhart, a member of VVMF and holder of two purple hearts, denounced it as "the most insulting and demeaning memorial to our experiences that was possible." It was, he said, a "black gash of shame." Lin was born and raised in America but came to be seen as an Asian outsider. What outraged the critics above all was that the planned memorial substituted the classical codes of heroism of traditional monuments, such as the Washington and the Lincoln buildings, for what they perceived as a passive Asian aesthetic, a dreadful irony given that the war had taken place in Indochina.

At first glance it is easy to interpret the memorial as functioning in polar opposition to the classically inspired monuments beside it. Its black stone sank into the earth, whereas the older monuments' white stone was meant to be seen from a distance. It has therefore a strongly antiphallic character. Lin had clearly aimed to establish a more female sensibility, saying in a later interview, "I didn't set out to conquer the earth, or overpower it, the way Western man usually does. I don't think I've made a passive piece, but neither is it a memorial to the idea of war." Instead, the individuality of the dead soldiers was emphasized by having their names carved at a level that made them both easily readable and touchable. Gone is the heroism of traditional classical monuments. But to its critics, it represented an architectural castration that mirrored the emasculation America had symbolically suffered in losing the war.[26]

Although it is certainly true that the Vietnam Veterans Memorial makes no direct reference to classical architecture, it would be wrong to see it as a completely unclassical or anticlassical piece. Pointing from its central axis toward the Washington and Lincoln memorials, it "references, absorbs, and reflects these classical forms."[27] In the polished black walls, the viewer sees both his or her own reflection alongside that of the Washington Monument's Egyptian obelisk superimposed on the names of the dead. The war is in this way linked with both the imperial wars and the republican ideals of the past. The image of the oriental obelisk reminds the visitor of the perils of overseas adventures but also of the political ideals that can render them so attractive in the first place. The emphasis on the carved names, listed not alphabetically but in chronological order of the soldiers' deaths, reflected Lin's wish that the memorial should read "like an epic Greek poem" and "return the vets to the time frame of the war."[28] The superficially unheroic stance of the memorial therefore comes to be seen as a way of reestablishing the heroic individualism of the victims. Like Hector and Achilles, the dead deserve their place in a chronicle that does not seek to repackage their death in pursuit of a political agenda, but rather lets their place in the narrative speak for itself. Even the black stone reflected some classical motivation, for as Lin said when asked why she had chosen it: "Classical Greek temples were never white. They were highly colored. At some point much later, someone decided that white signified classical architecture."[29] The choice of black stone did not simply, therefore, constitute a rejection of classical architecture but instead laid claim to a more accurate interpretation of classical art. It rejected the unimorality that had later been forced onto the classical world in favor of a construction representing multiple cultures. In this the memorial emphasizes the soldiers' range of ethnic backgrounds and also the impossibility of ever understanding so complex a war. The Vietnam Veterans Memorial therefore became a place where the very meaning of the classical was itself contested in order to express a more multicultural image of American identity.[30]

After the dramatic failure of foreign policy in Vietnam, American victory in the Cold War came as something of a shock. The fall of the Berlin Wall and the collapse of the Soviet empire left America as the world's only superpower. Moreover, the economic vigor of the high-tech boom of the 1990s made it seem as if the United States was simply unstoppable. It was at this time, as Murphy shows in his book *Are We Rome?*, that the comparison between the United States and the Roman Empire became widely used. "President and Emperor, America and Rome—the comparison is by now so familiar, so natural, that you just can't help yourself: it comes to mind unbidden." Rome became "the Empire that won't go away."[31] By the time the European edition of Murphy's book had been released, the question mark had been dropped and the title became simply *The New Rome.* There was no longer any doubt as to the validity of the comparison. Of course, America has always been looking over its shoulder back toward the ancient past. The founding fathers explicitly modeled their republic on that of Rome. Vaclav Smil has recently issued a counter-challenge to the Roman Empire comparison, entitled *Why America Is Not a New Rome*, concentrating on the fundamental realities of the comparison and criticizing its accuracy.[32] As he says, "Superficial (albeit often clever) comparisons may make for provocative remarks on talk shows and intriguing essays or interesting books, but a systematic deconstruction of these recently fashionable preoccupations shows them to be wide of the mark." But whatever parallels can be correctly drawn, it is undoubtedly true that the empire analogy has been used by a wide range of commentators from across the political spectrum. The image of the Roman Empire has become widespread in helping America to express its political and military supremacy and to cope with challenges to that dominance emanating from the East. For the benefit of the Roman Empire comparison is not so much in the practical help that such an analogy can provide, but in the help that it brings in thinking about power and the exercise of power, and articulating the fears that result from this. This is what makes the comparison resonate so well.

Even in the halcyon days of the 1990s, some felt a vague sense of unease about American dominance. Samuel Huntington's *The Clash of Civilizations* argued that culture rather than politics, ideology, or economics had become the fundamental source of conflict in the new global political structure. He looked to the Greeks to help him define what exactly constituted the component parts of civilization: "The key cultural elements which define a civilization were set forth in classic form by the Athenians when they reassured the Spartans that they would not betray them to the Persians." He quotes Herodotus, saying that "blood, language, religion, way of life, were what the Greeks had in common and what distinguished them from the Persians and other non-Greeks." Civilization is therefore defined in opposition to the East. Above all, Huntington argued, it is religion that most differentiates civilizations: "Of all the objective elements which define civilizations, however, the most important usually is religion, as the Athenians emphasized."[33]

The 9/11 attack on New York by Islamic extremists turned these theoretical concerns into a very real threat. Some saw in its "martyrdom," the World Trade Center transformed into a character in a classic tragedy, "its very size and the hubris of its builders led to its destruction."[34] But more common was to invoke the Roman Empire analogy as a call to arms. The commentator Charles Krauthammer argued, "People are coming out of the closet on the word 'empire' . . . The fact is, no country has been as dominant culturally, economically, technologically and militarily in the history of the world since the Roman empire." Similarly, Tom Wolfe stated that America had become "the mightiest power on earth, as omnipotent as . . . Rome under Julius Caesar." Krauthammer argued that America had to face up to the responsibilities that its new imperial role brought with it. Max Boot, in his article "The Case for American Empire," likewise argued that the United States had to respond to Islamic terrorism by embracing its imperial role. It was no use thinking that the attacks would stop if America became a kinder, gentler nation, eschewing quixotic missions abroad, becoming in Senator Pat Buchanan's phrase "a republic, not an empire." "In fact," Boot argued, "this analysis is exactly backward: The September 11 attack was a result of insufficient American involvement and ambition; the solution is to be more expansive in our goals and more assertive in their implementation." President Bush heeded this call, invading Iraq and then Afghanistan, and was subsequently pictured on the front of the *New York Review of Books* dressed in the garb of an armed Roman centurion.[35]

Once the initial successes had transformed into a series of military setbacks, the Roman Empire comparison helped Americans understand what was happening to them in the East. But instead of being used to bolster support for a more aggressive foreign policy, the image now expressed a sense of impending decline. The protracted fighting brought to mind Rome's endless confrontations with the barbarians. The challenge to American supremacy from the East recalled the eventual fall of the Roman Empire. The dean of Harvard's Kennedy School of Government, Joseph Nye, was of the view that "it is true that no nation since Rome has loomed so large above the others, but even Rome eventually collapsed."[36] 9/11 was compared to crushing defeats suffered by the Romans, first by Augustus's legions in the forests of Germany, an event that, it was suggested, marked a turning point in Rome's fortunes and the end of her efforts at imperial expansion, and second at the battle of Adrianople in 378 CE, after which the Goths were for the first time allowed to settle within the empire on their own terms. In his 2007 online article "Quo Vadimus?," D. Weigel explained: "Our confidence leads us to make the same kinds of military blunders as the Romans, and the only argument is whether Iraq is our Teutoburg forest or our Adrianople—if we've learned our lesson and will stop pushing outside our boundaries, or if we've used up all our get-out-of-jail cards and are primed for a fall."[37] Murphy suggested that Varus's defeat was of even greater significance: "The impact is hard to overstate. Imagine a combination of 9/11, Pearl Harbor, and Little Bighorn." But as with America and the terrorist attacks, "it was all the worse for coming at a moment saturated with feelings of omnipotence," just like before a triumph.[38] Murphy quotes an account concerning the mood in New York concerning the post 9/11 antiterrorism measures: "There was a strong feeling that federal agencies had let down New York City, and that the city should no longer count on the Feds for its protection." It was, he says, like how the Romans must have felt toward the end of the empire when faced with the barbarian hordes from the East: "Reading those words, you may get some feel for the worldview of a Roman magnate in distant Gaul in the fourth or fifth century, who sees that Rome is increasingly far and threats are increasingly near."[39]

Nye also put forward the view that it was internal decline, not just barbarian outsiders, that had brought Rome low and threatened to do likewise to America. "Rome," he says, "succumbed not to the rise of a new empire, but to internal decay and a death of a thousand cuts from various barbarian groups." Many commentators saw clear parallels between overconsumption in the United States, evidence for which was found in the budget and trade deficits, and the excesses and vices of Rome. The love of luxury that was thought to have softened Rome's martial spirit was having the same effect on America's military capacity. In fact, Nye did not see evidence of this internal rot occurring yet in the United States, but believed it was "harder to exclude the barbarians." He argued that the cheap, universal availability of technology and communications put massive destructive power into the hands of groups and individuals. "The paradox of American power in the 21st century," he concluded, "is that the largest power since Rome cannot achieve its objectives unilaterally in a global information age." Others turned to Rome to supply a cautionary tale of what such external threats can do to a country's inner workings, especially to the vulnerable democratic workings of a republic. The author Robert Harris, in a *New York Times* article in 2006, described how in 68 BCE the world's only military superpower was "dealt a profound psychological blow by a daring terrorist attack on its very heart," when Rome's port at Ostia was set on fire, the fleet destroyed, and two prominent senators kidnapped. "An event that was merely a footnote five years ago has now, in our post-9/11 world, assumed a fresh and ominous significance. For in the panicky aftermath of the attack, the Roman people made decisions that set them on the path to the destruction of their Constitution, their democracy and their liberty. One cannot help wondering if history is repeating itself."[40]

The lessons of Rome for American foreign policy in the Middle East were what seemed paramount to many. In a lecture entitled

"The Lessons of the Roman Empire for America Today," sponsored by the Heritage Foundation in 2005, the aptly named J. Rufus Fears expressed his concerns about current American actions in the East. Fears argued that the founding fathers of the United States "understood the profound lessons of Roman history for those who sought to fashion a new republic in a new world. Those lessons are even more compelling today. The Roman Empire of the second century AD and the United States of the twenty-first century are the only two absolute superpowers that have existed in history. From foreign policy in the Middle East to cultural diversity at home, the Roman Empire offers an enduring model of how to establish world peace and prosperity by combining freedom and empire."[41]

Fears holds the Roman Empire in the highest respect: for the "immense majesty of the Roman empire" brought peace and prosperity and social mobility, creativity, low taxes, religious unity, and values; in other words, an almost American dream. The decline and fall of this ancient utopia happened because Rome "failed to solve two critical issues of foreign policy: the Middle East and Central Europe." The Middle East in particular, he argues, has been "the graveyard of empires." Rome was drawn into the Middle East by "the problem of Iran—that vast empire, basically passive as long as it was left alone." It was Augustus, "perhaps the shrewdest statesmen ever to live," who came up with that holy grail of American military endeavors, "an exit strategy." But the spheres of influence he agreed to with Iran (Fears deliberately uses the modern name to highlight the comparison) meant that the Middle East became a "quagmire" instead of enjoying the benefits of Roman rule. The result was that it acted as a constant drain on Rome's resources and caused a loss of focus on the German threat.[42]

Fears argues that it was an outburst in religious zealousness in the third century that turned Iran from "passive to a powerfully offensive nation." The shock of dealing with the combined barbarian and Iranian threat left Rome in an utterly different form. Society, he says, became "rigid and formalised." The army deteriorated at the same time as the bureaucracy ballooned. And in Italy, "barbarian chieftains sat in the half-ruined palaces of the Caesars." In the end, the banners of Islam swept away the Eastern remnants of the Roman Empire. The comparison with Rome and the Middle East in antiquity therefore establishes a clear morality tale: the Romans understood that "freedom is not a universal value," and they were not afraid to take up the burden of imperial rule. Fears spells out the lesson for America: "So we must ask ourselves the question: are we willing to follow that path of empire? Do we have the reserves of moral courage that the Romans did to undertake that burden of empire? And what will be our legacy? For I am quite convinced that of all the people who passed through the Middle East, of all the people who have passed through history, there has been none so generous in spirit, so determined to leave the world a better place, and so imbued with the technology and the wealth and the opportunity to leave a legacy far more enduring and far better than that of the Romans." America must look to emulate Rome and impose its will in the world if it is to escape the fate of Rome. Political settlements that do not deliver freedom will just create another quagmire, which it is perhaps too late to avoid in any case.[43]

But as the wars in the East dragged on, other commentators became far less optimistic. Murphy's concern was that America had lost its moral high ground: "The Romans made a habit of publicly degrading the captured leaders of vanquished peoples, a practice now turning up unexpectedly in the American repertoire—recall the official video of Saddam Hussein's medical exam, broadcast worldwide."[44] He is not surprised that America, like the Romans, "presented a tempting target," because "to Christian writers, Rome was the Great Whore, just as to Islamists, America is the Great Satan. The Romans talked loudly of liberty—for themselves." And instead of delivering freedom, America is setting up puppet governments in the Roman style: the Romans sought "symbolic deference" from enemies and supplicants; the tombstone of a first-century governor proclaims proudly that he had brought barbarian leaders "to the riverbank that he protected" in order that they should "adore Roman standards." In 2004, as America looked for a suitable Iraqi to head a provisional government, the president laid down a single criterion: "It's important to have someone who's willing to stand up and thank the American people for their sacrifice in liberating Iraq."[45]

There was also much greater pessimism about the chance of military success, which again found precedent in the Romans' experiences in the Middle East. Murphy describes how "on numerous occasions proud Roman armies sallied across those parched Middle Eastern plains and into Mesopotamia; often, much smaller armies hobbled back. The target was generally Ctesiphon, the capital of the Parthian and Persian Empires, a few leagues south of modern Baghdad. Military transport planes supplying America's own Mesopotamian war rattle Ctesiphon's ruins every day as they fly into Rasheed Air Base."[46] In the end, Murphy can even imagine a "dystopian fantasy parallel" between the growing corporate influence of Asia upon America and Attila the Hun's invasion of the Roman Empire: "It's not hard," he argues, "to envision how a modern Asian catalyst could produce an analogous, Hun-like ripple effect." The Chinese force down the dollar and then with other Asians start to buy up more and more American companies, with the result that there would be "small-scale 'barbarian kingdoms' sprouting up from Tacoma to Marietta, Long Beach to New London, with American workers by the millions answering to foreign managers, and local governments looking eagerly for ways to establish a *modus vivendi*." In the distant future, Murphy suggests, such a scenario would see textbooks showing maps of America at its greatest extent, "with little crossed swords showing where, say, the Chinese were deterred at the gates of Maytag, or the United Arab Emirates were held off at the mouth of New

York Harbor. But mostly there would be sweeping arrows of corporate conquest." It would be the end of American culture, with the English spoken in Alabama being influenced by Korean and all the slang terms in Missouri for "efficiency" and "downsizing" being loanwords from Japanese.[47] This is, of course, a worst-case fantasy. But such exaggerations can tell us much about contemporary American fears: the fear of becoming bogged down in Middle Eastern quagmires; the fear of rising Asian superpowers; the fear of losing domestic vibrancy and vigor.

In this final chapter we have looked at three distinct and very different episodes in the history of America's conceptualization of Islam and the East. Each shows something of the unique way in which Americans have continued to use the ancient world to help them understand the Orient and, above all, themselves and their own complexity. Classics in the nineteenth century helped America develop its own sense of identity relative to the East and the European Old World. In the aftermath of the Vietnam War, classical influences helped generate a new form of memorialization that in many ways sought to reassess ancient architecture and distance itself from traditional readings of classical art. To this day, analogies between the ancient and modern worlds continue to inform American understanding of the East and the West's relationship with it. The classical world has been a plastic concept in all of this image creation, its malleability enabling it to act as a tool for Americans to fashion the East according to their own needs and anxieties. Its plasticity also reflects the wide spectrum of ideas that Islam and the East have generated in the American imagination, just as they have in the English imagination across the centuries. This capaciousness has perhaps been the defining characteristic of the use of classics: the seemingly unlimited ability to create meaning by means of reference and comparison. It is this that has allowed classics to shape ideas of the East within the English-speaking world.

Notes

1. *Classicizing Orientalisms*

1. *The Relation of a Journey Begun An. Dom. 1610. Foure Bookes: Containing a Description of the Turkish Empire, of Ægypt, of the Holy Land, of the Remote Parts of Italy, and Ilands Adioyning* (printed for W. Barrett, 1615), 51.

2. The two classic texts are the revised edition of Norman Daniel, *Islam and the West: The Making of an Image* (1960; Oxford: Oneworld, 1993); and Richard W. Southern, *Western Views of Islam in the Middle Ages* (Cambridge, MA: Harvard University Press, 1962). More recent is the impressive study on medieval views by John V. Tolan, *Saracens: Islam in the Medieval European Imagination* (New York: Columbia University Press, 2002). On British imperial texts, see the fascinating work by Javed Majeed, *Ungoverned Imaginings: James Mill's* The History of British India *and Orientalism* (Oxford: Clarendon Press, 1992).

3. In his foreword to David Wills, *The Mirror of Antiquity: 20th Century British Travellers in Greece* (Newcastle: Cambridge Scholars, 2007), x.

4. Donald Malcolm Reid, *Whose Pharaohs? Archaeology, Museums, and Egyptian National Identity from Napoleon to World War I* (Berkeley: University of California Press, 2002), 140. On the importance of classics in

English education, see Christopher Stray, *Classics Transformed: Schools, Universities, and Society in England, 1830–1960* (Oxford: Clarendon Press, 1998); and M. L. Clarke, *Classical Education in Britain, 1500–1900* (Cambridge: Cambridge University Press, 1959).

5. Kenneth Haynes, "Text, Theory, and Reception," in *Classics and the Uses of Reception*, ed. Charles Martindale and Richard F. Thomas (Oxford: Blackwell, 2006), 44–54, 44.

6. See Edith Hall, "Putting the Class into Classical Reception," in *A Companion to Classical Receptions*, ed. Lorna Hardwick and Christopher Stray (Oxford: Blackwell, 2008), 386–397.

7. Seth L. Schein, "'Our Debt to Greece and Rome': Canon, Class and Ideology," in Hardwick and Stray, *Companion to Classical Receptions*, 75–85, 76, quoting Aul. Gell. *NA* 19.8.15. Note that the text could possibly also mean a writer suitable to be read by a first-class (classicus) reader.

8. Hall, "Putting the Class," 387.

9. Richard Jenkyns, "United Kingdom," in *A Companion to the Classical Tradition*, ed. Craig W. Kallendorf (Oxford: Blackwell, 2007), 265–278, 273.

10. Robert Irwin, *For Lust of Knowing: The Orientalists and Their Enemies* (London: Allen Lane, 2006), 159.

11. Suzanne L. Marchand, *German Orientalism in the Age of Empire: Religion, Race, and Scholarship* (Cambridge: Cambridge University Press, 2009), 55.

12. Ibid., 53–101.

13. Reid, *Whose Pharaohs?*, 140.

14. Phiroze Vasunia, "Greek, Latin and the Indian Civil Service," *Cambridge Classical Journal* 51 (2005): 35–71.

15. Ibid., 67.

16. E. E. Kellett, *Literary Quotation and Allusion* (Cambridge: W. Heffer, 1933), 12, quoted in Ruth Finnegan, *Why Do We Quote? The Culture and History of Quotation* (Cambridge: OpenBook, 2011), 191.

17. Bernard Porter, *The Absent-Minded Imperialists: Empire, Society, and Culture in Britain* (Oxford: Oxford University Press, 2004), 62.

18. W. D. Rubinstein, "Education and the Social Origins of British Elites, 1880–1970," *Past & Present* 112 (1986): 163–207.

19. Jonathan Rose, *The Intellectual Life of the British Working Classes* (New Haven, CT: Yale University Press, 2001).

20. Hardwick and Stray, *Companion to Classical Receptions*, 1. On classical reception, see Martindale and Thomas, *Classics and the Uses of Reception;* and Anthony Grafton, Glenn W. Most, and Salvatore Settis, *The Classical Tradition* (Cambridge, MA: Belknap Press of Harvard University Press, 2010). For an introduction to reception theory, see Robert C. Holub, *Reception Theory: A Critical Introduction* (London: Routledge, 2003).

21. Charles Martindale, *Redeeming the Text: Latin Poetry and the Hermeneutics of Reception* (Cambridge: Cambridge University Press, 1993), 3.

22. See James I. Porter, "Reception Studies: Future Prospects," in Hardwick and Stray, *Companion to Classical Receptions*, 469–481.

23. Schein, "'Our Debt,'" 75.

24. Porter, "Reception Studies," 469.

25. Simon Goldhill, *Who Needs Greek? Contests in the Cultural History of Hellenism* (Cambridge: Cambridge University Press, 2002), 297.

26. Reid, *Whose Pharaohs?*, 143.

27. Edward W. Said, *Orientalism* (London: Routledge and Kegan Paul, 1978), 1.

28. For various examples, see Marchand, *German Orientalism*, xix n15.

29. Ibid., xxii.

30. Phiroze Vasunia, "Persia," in Grafton, Most, and Settis, *The Classical Tradition*, 701–703.

31. Edith Hall, *Inventing the Barbarian: Greek Self-Definition through Tragedy* (Oxford: Clarendon Press, 1989), 99.

32. See Steven W. Hirsch, *The Friendship of the Barbarians: Xenophon and the Persian Empire* (Hanover, NH: University Press of New England, 1985).

33. For example, Isocrates, *Paneg.* 150–158; *cf.* Plato *Rep.* 5.470B–C. But Plato was also aware of the oversimplification of the polarity; see *Statesman* 262D and *Theaetetus* 174–175.

34. Margaret C. Miller, *Athens and Persia in the Fifth Century BC: A Study in Cultural Receptivity* (Cambridge: Cambridge University Press, 1997).

35. See Thomas Harrison, ed., *Greeks and Barbarians* (Edinburgh: Edinburgh University Press, 2002).

36. G. Strohmaier, "Die Griechen waren keine Europäer," in *Hellas im Islam: Interdisziplinäre Studien zur Ikonographie, Wissenschaft und Religionsgeschichte*, Diskurse der Arabistik 6 (Wiesbaden: Harrassowitz Verlag, 2003). See also Edith Hall, "The Many Ages of Herodotus," *Times Literary Supplement*, June 25, 2008.

37. Martin Bernal, *Black Athena: The Afroasiatic Roots of Classical Civilization*, vol. 1 (London: Free Association Books, 1987).

38. Jonathan Burton, *Traffic and Turning: Islam and English Drama, 1579–1624* (Newark: University of Delaware Press, 2005), 11.

39. Lisa Lowe, *Critical Terrains: French and British Orientalisms* (Ithaca, NY: Cornell University Press, 1991), ix.

40. Hall, *Inventing the Barbarian*, 99n198. Hall argues, "Representations of the Turks right through until the seventeenth century owed much to the ancient European view of Asiatics, focusing on their tyranny and decadence." Hall, Bridges, and Rhodes also state that "one of the most important factors underlying the longevity of the Persian Wars traditions has been the identification of the ancient Greeks' struggle against Achaemenid Persia with the Christian West's adversarial relationship with Islam" (Emma Bridges, Edith Hall, and P. J. Rhodes, eds., *Cultural Responses to the Persian Wars: Antiquity to the Third Millennium* [Oxford: Oxford University Press, 2007], 13). Locating modern conflicts within a framework of ancient historical analogies has been a persistent feature of some later Western writing about the Orient. To quote Hall, Bridges, and Rhodes again, "the facile identification of the entire Islamic world with the caricatured ancient Persians staged by Aeschylus has also been a factor informing the West's crude stereotype of the Eastern tyrant, Muslim despot, and the polemical terminology of Freedom and Democracy that has often played an unhelpful role by fomenting aggression on both local and global scales" (13).

41. For the study of non-elite reception of classics, see Siobhán McElduff, "Fractured Understandings: Towards a History of Classical Reception among Non-elite Groups," in Martindale and Thomas, *Classics and the Uses of Reception*, 180–191.

42. See esp. Daniel, *Islam and the West*.

43. Said, *Orientalism*, 70.

44. Southern, *Western Views of Islam*, 14.

45. Norman Daniel, *Islam, Europe and Empire* (Edinburgh: Edinburgh University Press, 1966), xvi.

46. See Albert Hourani, *Islam in European Thought* (Cambridge: Cambridge University Press, 1991).

47. Catharine Edwards, ed., *Roman Presences: Receptions of Rome in European Culture, 1789–1945* (Cambridge: Cambridge University Press, 1999), 9.

2. The Uses of Classics

1. Richard Jenkyns, "United Kingdom," in *A Companion to the Classical Tradition*, ed. Craig W. Kallendorf (Oxford: Blackwell, 2007), 265–278, 266. On the classical legacy in Britain, see Richard Jenkyns, ed., *The Legacy of Rome: A New Appraisal* (Oxford: Oxford University Press, 1992); Charles Martindale and David Hopkins, eds., *Horace Made New: Horatian Influences on British Writing from the Renaissance to the Twentieth Century* (Cambridge: Cambridge University Press, 1993); Howard Erskine-Hill, *The Augustan Idea in English Literature* (London: Edward Arnold, 1983); Howard D. Weinbrot, *Augustus Caesar in "Augustan" England: The Decline of a Classical Norm* (Princeton, NJ: Princeton University Press, 1978); Frank M. Turner, *The Greek Heritage in Victorian Britain* (New Haven, CT: Yale University Press, 1981); Richard Jenkyns, *The Victorians and Ancient Greece* (Oxford: Blackwell, 1980).

2. On the importance of classics to the English education system, see Christopher Stray, *Classics Transformed: Schools, Universities, and Society in England, 1830–1960* (Oxford: Clarendon Press, 1998).

3. Richard Hingley, *Roman Officers and English Gentlemen: The Imperial Origins of Roman Archaeology* (London: Routledge, 2000), 5.

4. Robert Irwin, *For Lust of Knowing: The Orientalists and Their Enemies* (London: Allen Lane, 2006), 209.

5. Richard Hingley, *The Recovery of Roman Britain, 1586–1906: A Colony So Fertile* (Oxford: Oxford University Press, 2008).

6. Ibid., 10.

7. Ibid.

8. *Another World and yet the Same: Bishop Joseph Hall's* Mundus Alter et Idem, trans. and ed. John Millar Wands (New Haven, CT: Yale University Press), 1981.

9. Carsten Niebuhr, *Travels through Arabia and Other Countries in the East,* trans. Robert Heron, 2 vols. (Dublin: printed for Gilbert, Moore, Archer, and Jones, 1792), 1:138.

10. See Edith Hall, *The Return of Ulysses: A Cultural History of Homer's Odyssey* (London: Tauris, 2008).

11. See Edith Hall, "Putting the Class into Classical Reception," in *A Companion to Classical Receptions,* ed. Lorna Hardwick and Christopher Stray (Oxford: Blackwell, 2008), 386–397, 393.

12. On Herodotus's use of triangulation, see François Hartog, *The Mirror of Herodotus: The Representation of the Other in the Writing of History,* trans. Janet Lloyd (Berkeley: University of California Press, 1988).

13. For an introduction to the subject of quotations, see Ruth Finnegan, *Why Do We Quote? The Culture and History of Quotation* (Cambridge: OpenBook, 2011).

14. Quoted in ibid., 201. Sen. *Suas.* 3.7.

15. Bruce Lincoln, *Discourse and the Construction of Society: Comparative Studies of Myth, Ritual, and Classification* (Oxford: Oxford University Press, 1989).

16. Bruce Lincoln, *Authority: Construction and Corrosion* (Chicago: University of Chicago Press, 1994), 4.

17. Edward Backhouse Eastwick, *Journal of a Diplomate's Three Years' Residence in Persia,* 2 vols. (Smith, Elder and Co., 1864), 1:26–27.

18. Stephen A. Nimis, *Narrative Semiotics in the Epic Tradition: The Simile* (Bloomington: Indiana University Press, 1987). On allusion, see also William Irwin, "What Is an Allusion?," *Journal of Aesthetics and Art Criticism* 59 (2001): 287–297; and Christopher Ricks, *Allusion to the Poets* (Oxford: Oxford University Press, 2002).

3. *Classics and Medieval Images of Islam*

1. Richard W. Southern, *Western Views of Islam in the Middle Ages* (Cambridge, MA: Harvard University Press, 1962), 4–5.

2. See John V. Tolan, *Saracens: Islam in the Medieval European Imagination* (New York: Columbia University Press, 2002), 19. This and Tolan, ed., *Medieval Christian Perceptions of Islam: A Book of Essays* (New York: Garland, 1996), provide the best analysis of early Christian attitudes toward Islam.

3. See Tolan, *Saracens*, 12–13. For Simon Magus, see *Acts of the Apostles*, 8:9–24.

4. Tolan, *Saracens*, xx.

5. *Passio Thiemonis archiepiscopi Monumenta Germaniae Historia Scriptores* 11:51–62; quoted in Tolan, *Saracens*, 108.

6. Eusebius *HE* 6.34, 38, 39; 41.9; 7.10.3; John Chrysostom *PG* 50.541–542; Jerome, *Chronicon et Liber de viris illustris* 54, *qui primus de regibus Romanis Christianus fuit.*

7. See Norman Daniel, *Islam and the West: The Making of an Image* (1960; Oxford: Oneworld, 1993), 84, 369n73.

8. Daniel, *Islam and the West*, 100.

9. For example, Jerome, *Comm in Ezek.*; Soz. *HE* 6.38.

10. *PL* 115: 939–960; see Tolan, *Saracens*, 100–103.

11. See John Block Friedman, *The Monstrous Races in Medieval Art and Thought* (Cambridge, MA: Harvard University Press, 1981), 27–28.

12. Solinus 30; see Friedman, *The Monstrous Races*, 117.

13. See Edward Dudley and Maximillian E. Novak, eds., *The Wild Man Within: An Image in Western Thought from the Renaissance to Romanticism* (Pittsburg: University of Pittsburg Press, 1972).

14. See Friedman, *The Monstrous Races*, 67.

15. Ibid., 61.

16. See Walter Emil Kaegi, *Byzantium and the Decline of Rome* (Princeton, NJ: Princeton University Press, 1968), chaps. 4–6.

17. Quoted in David R. Blanks, ed., "Images of the Other: Europe and the Muslim World before 1700," *Cairo Papers in Social Science* 19, no. 2 (1996): 119–120.

18. Liudprand of Cremona, *The Embassy to Constantinople*, chaps. 47 and 51.

19. *Alexiad* 10.5.

20. Ibid.

21. Ibid., 15.3.

22. Ibid., 11.7.

23. Edith Hall, "Aeschylus' Persians via the Ottoman Empire to Saddam Hussein," in *Cultural Responses to the Persian Wars: Antiquity to the Third Millennium,* ed. Emma Bridges, Edith Hall, and P. J. Rhodes (Oxford: Oxford University Press, 2007), 167–199, 175.

24. As the Greeks had done by substituting foreigners for mythical Amazons after the Persian Wars; see Edith Hall, *Inventing the Barbarian: Greek Self-Definition through Tragedy* (Oxford: Clarendon, 1989), 68.

25. On Guibert, see Paul J. Archambault, *A Monk's Confession: The Memoirs of Guibert of Nogent* (University Park: Pennsylvania State University Press, 1996).

26. Hor. *Ars* 180–181; Guibert de Nogent, *Gesta Dei per Francos,* 4.1. All translations are from Robert Levine's version, *The Deeds of God through the Franks* (Woodbridge: Boydell Press, 1997).

27. Lucan 1.8, 9, 12

28. *Gesta Dei* 1.1. Trogus Pompeius was a contemporary of Livy in the first century BCE who wrote 44 books of history, of which survive only a few fragments and an epitome of Justin.

29. *Gesta Dei* 1.2.

30. Tolan, *Saracens,* 136.

31. Hor. *Od.* 3.30.1–2 *aere perennius . . . vitabit libitiam.* His new version reads (1.4): *Manditur ore suum, qui porcum vixerat, huius/membra beata cluunt, podice fusa suum./ quum talos ori, tum quod sus fudit odori,/digno qui celebrat cultor honore ferat.*

32. *Gesta Dei* 1.3–4.

33. On William, see Peter W. Edbury and John Gordon Rowe, *William of Tyre: Historian of the Latin East* (Cambridge: Cambridge University Press, 1988). For a translation, see William of Tyre, *A History of Deeds Done beyond the Sea,* 2 vols., trans. Emily Atwater Babcock and A. C. Krey (New York: Columbia University Press, 1943). I have used this version as the basis of all the translations quoted.

34. On William's classical influences, see Edbury and Rowe, *William of Tyre,* 32–43.

35. *History of Deeds* 16.21.

36. Ibid. 21.7.

37. Ibid. 21.25; Pers. *Sat.* 5.60.

38. Virg. *Ecl.* 7.22.

39. *History of Deeds* 23 *pr.*; Livy *pref.*

40. David R. Blanks and Michael Frassetto, eds., *Western Views of Islam in Medieval and Early Modern Europe: Perception of Other* (Basingstoke: Macmillan, 1999), 111.

41. On the development of early missionary work, see Benjamin Z. Kedar, *Crusade and Mission: European Approaches toward the Muslims* (Princeton, NJ: Princeton University Press, 1984).

42. Tolan, *Saracens*, 75–76.

43. Katharine Scarfe Beckett, *Anglo-Saxon Perceptions of the Islamic World* (Cambridge: Cambridge University Press, 2003), 200. See 212–217 on the alleged Saracen devotion to Venus and/or stone worship.

44. 2.953–955.

45. *de Principis Instructione* 8.68–71; see Tolan, *Saracens*, 168.

46. 9.132–134.

47. See Alan Lupack, ed., *Three Middle English Charlemagne Romances: The Sultan of Babylon, The Siege of Milan, and The Tale of Ralph the Collier* (Kalamazoo: Western Michigan University, 1990).

48. John Lydgate, *Fall of Princes*, 9.152, 154.

4. *Traders and Travelers*

1. Matthew Dimmock, *New Turkes: Dramatizing Islam and the Ottomans in Early Modern England* (Aldershot: Ashgate, 2005), 9.

2. Gerald M. MacLean, *Looking East: English Writing and the Ottoman Empire before 1800* (Basingstoke: Palgrave Macmillan, 2007), 20.

3. Nabil I. Matar, *Islam in Britain, 1558–1685* (Cambridge: Cambridge University Press, 1998), 73.

4. Samuel C. Chew, *The Crescent and the Rose: Islam and England during the Renaissance* (Oxford: Oxford University Press, 1937), 234.

5. Matar, *Islam in Britain*, 11.

6. See Robert Markley, *The Far East and the English Imagination, 1600–1730* (Cambridge: Cambridge University Press, 2006).

7. Alastair Hamilton, *Arab Culture and Ottoman Magnificence in Antwerp's Golden Age* (Oxford: Oxford University Press, 2001), 1.

8. Theodore of Gaza, *de Origine Turcarum PG* 161.997–1006.

9. Robert Schwoebel, *The Shadow of the Crescent: The Renaissance Image of the Turk*, 1453–1517 (New York: St. Martin's Press, 1967), 188.

10. Felix Fabri, *Evagatorium* 3.236–239; quoted in ibid., 189.

11. See T. Spencer, "Turks and Trojans in the Renaissance," *Modern Language Review* 47 (1952): 330–333.

12. Denys Hay, *Europe: The Emergence of an Idea* (Edinburgh: Edinburgh University Press, 1968), 49.

13. A story first found in the ninth-century *Historia Brittonum*, attributed to Nennius and later fleshed out by Geoffrey of Monmouth in the twelfth century in his *Historia Regum Britanniae*, 1.3–18, 2.1. On the supposed Trojan origins of Britons, see Hugh A. MacDougall, *Racial Myth in English History: Trojans, Teutons, and Anglo-Saxons* (Hanover, NH: University Press of New England, 1982), 7–27.

14. Quoted in Schwoebel, *Shadow of the Crescent*, 1.

15. *Orationes PG* 161.651–653; quoted in Schwoebel, *Shadow of the Crescent*, 158.

16. Quoted in Schwoebel, *Shadow of the Crescent*, 5.

17. Ibid., 152.

18. See ibid., 170.

19. Sir Anthony Sherley, *Relation of Travels into Persia* (1613), 6.

20. Ibid., 16.

21. Ibid., 109.

22. Ibid., 29.

23. William Lithgow, *A Most Delectable, and True Discourse, of an Admired and Painefull Peregrination from Scotland, to the Most Famous Kingdomes in Europe, Asia and Affricke*, 2nd ed. (London: Printed by Nicholas Okes, and are to be sold by Thomas Archer, at his shop in Popes-head Pallace, neere the Royall Exchange, 1614), B2 and E3–4.

24. Ibid., K1.

25. Ibid., G3–H.

26. Ibid., K2.

27. Ibid., N3.

28. Ibid., E3.

29. See Nebahat Avcioglu, "Ahmed I and the Allegories of Tyranny in the Frontispiece to George Sandys's *Relation of a Journey*," in *Muqarnas XVIII: An Annual on the Visual Culture of the Islamic World*, ed. G. Necipoglu (Leiden: E. J. Brill, 2001), 203–226.

30. Jonathan Haynes, *The Humanist as Traveler: George Sandys's Relation of a Journey begun An. Dom. 1610* (Cranbury, NJ: Associated University Presses, 1986), 15.

31. Ibid., 60.

32. Ibid., 40.

33. George Sandys, *The Relation of a Journey Begun An. Dom. 1610. Foure Bookes: Containing a Description of the Turkish Empire, of Ægypt, of the Holy Land, of the Remote Parts of Italy, and Ilands Adioyning* (printed for W. Barrett, 1615), 15.

34. Ibid., 21–22.

35. Ibid., 36.

36. Ibid., 38.

37. Haynes, *The Humanist as Traveler*, 131.

38. Sandys, *The Relation of a Journey*, 17.

39. Ibid., 59.

40. Tib. *Eleg.* 1.3; Sandys, *The Relation of a Journey*, 58.

41. Juv. *Sat.* 1.

42. Mart. 12.50. Sandys, *The Relation of a Journey*, 34.

43. Ibid., 66.

44. Ibid., 69–70; Hor. *Serm.* 1; *Sat.* 2.

45. Sandys, *The Relation of a Journey*, 70; Juv. *Sat.* 6.

46. Sandys, *The Relation of a Journey*, 72.

47. Ibid., 57–58; Lucan 1.

48. Sandys, *The Relation of a Journey*, 103.

49. Ibid., 78–79.

50. Ibid., 77.

51. Richard Knolles, *The Generall Historie of the Turkes . . .* , (Printed by Adam Islip, 1603), 131.

52. Francis Osborne, *Politicall Reflections upon the Government of the Turks . . .* (Printed by J.G. for Thomas Robinson, 1656), 2.

53. Ibid., 114.

54. Paul Rycaut, *The Present State of the Ottoman Empire,* 1668 (repr.; New York: Arno Press, 1971). Page numbers are for this edition.

55. Ibid., Epistle Dedicatory and 1.

56. Ibid., 2; Tac. *Ann.* 3.18 *mihi quanto plura recentium seu veterum revolvo, tanto magis ludibria rerum mortalium cunctis in negotiis observantur.*

57. Rycault, *The Present State,* 82.

58. Ibid., 23–24.

59. Ibid., 24.

60. Ibid., 26.

61. Ibid., 47. Tac. *Ann.* 3.30 *fato potentiae raro sempiternae.*

62. Tac. *Hist.* 2.20 *Insita mortalibus natura recentem aliorum felicitatem aegris oculis introspicere, modumque fortunae a nullis magis exigere, quam quos in aequo vident.*

63. Tac. *Ann.* 13.19 *Nihil rerum mortalium tam instabile ac fluxum est, quam fama potentiae non sua vi nixae.*

64. Rycaut, *The Present State,* 49; Tac. *Ann.* 4.20.

65. Rycaut, *The Present State,* 78.

66. Ibid., 8–9; Tac. *Ann.* 3.65.

67. Rycaut, *The Present State,* 10.

68. Ibid., 169, 166.

69. Ibid., 197.

70. Ibid., 83.

71. Ibid., 87.

72. Ibid., 85.

73. Ibid., 79.

74. Ibid., 67.

75. Virg. *Aen.* 8.728 *Indomitique Dacae et pontem Indignatus Araxes;* Juv. Sat. 6.205 *Dacius et scripto radiat Germanicus antro.*

76. Rycaut, *The Present State,* 60.

77. Ibid., 69.

78. Ibid., 73; Tac. *Ann.* 2.59 *ne fame urgeret Italiam quisquis eam provinciam claustraque terrae ac maris quamvis levi praesidio adversum ingentis exercitus insedisset.*

79. Rycaut, *The Present State,* 77; Livy *ab Urbe Cond.* 5.51 *omnia prospera sequentibus deos, aduersa autem spernentibus.*

80. Rycaut, The *Present State,* 75–76; Tac. *Hist.* 1.66 *diu sordidus, repente dives mutationem fortunae male regit, accensis egestate longa cupidinibus immoderatus.*

81. Richard Pococke, *A Description of the East and Some Other Countries,* 2 vols. (printed for the Author, by W. Bowyer; and sold by J. and P. Knapton [et al.], 1743), 1:177–178.

82. E. M. Wherry, *A Comprehensive Commentary on the Qurán: Comprising Sale's Translation and Preliminary Discourse,* 4 vols. (1882; London: Routledge, 2000), 1:56.

83. Ibid., 1:63.

84. Ibid., 1:189.

85. Ibid., 1:71; Amm. Marc. 14.4.

86. Wherry, *A Comprehensive Commentary,* 1:195.

87. Ibid., 1:202–204.

5. *Gibbon's Islam*

1. Philip Ayres, *Classical Culture and the Idea of Rome in Eighteenth-Century England* (Cambridge: Cambridge University Press, 1997), 61.

2. *Characteristicks of Men, Manners, Opinions, Times,* 3 vols. (1711), 1:346.

3. Ayres, *Classical Culture,* 57.

4. The Roman model did, however, remain important in the British imagination. See Jonathan Sachs, *Romantic Antiquity: Rome in the British Imagination,* 1789–1832 (Oxford: Oxford University Press, 2010).

5. Ayres, *Classical Culture,* 153.

6. Richard Hingley, *Roman Officers and English Gentlemen: The Imperial Origins of Roman Archaeology* (London: Routledge, 2000), 2.

7. Ellen T. Harris, "With Eyes on the East and Ears on the West: Handel's Orientalist Operas," *Journal of Interdisciplinary History* 36 (2006): 419–443.

8. Maria Wyke, *Caesar: A Life in Western Culture* (London: Granta, 2007), 105.

9. Rosalind Ballaster, *Fabulous Orients: Fictions of the East in England, 1662–1785* (Oxford: Oxford University Press, 2005), 131.

10. Samuel Holt Monk, ed., *Five Miscellaneous Essays by Sir William Temple* (Ann Arbor: University of Michigan Press, 1963), 40.

11. Ibid., 47–48.

12. Ibid., 45.

13. Ibid., 40.

14. Ibid., 44.

15. William Wotton, *Reflections upon Ancient and Modern Learning: To which is now added a defence thereof . . .* (printed for Tim. Goodwin, 1705).

16. Ibid., 133.

17. Ibid., 134.

18. Ibid., 154.

19. Ibid., 155–156.

20. Ibid., 156–157.

21. Simon Ockley, *An Account of South West Barbary . . .* (Printed for J. Bowyer and H. Clements, 1713), 34.

22. Ovid *Am.* 3.4.17 *nitimur in vetitum semper cupimusque negatum.*

23. Billie Melman, *Women's Orients: English Women and the Middle East, 1718–1918* (Basingstoke: Macmillan, 1995), 78.

24. Robert Halsband, ed., *The Complete Letters of Lady Mary Wortley Montagu*, 3 vols. (Oxford: Clarendon, 1965–1967), 1:320

25. Ibid., 421; letter dated July 31, 1718.

26. Ibid., 364; letter dated May 29, 1717.

27. Ibid., 316; letter dated April 1, 1717.

28. Ibid., 335; letter dated April 1, 1717.

29. Ibid., 332–333.

30. Ibid., 406; letter dated May 1718. The epithilamium is to be found in Theocritus *Idyll* 18.

31. Bernard Lewis, *Islam and the West* (Oxford: Oxford University Press, 1993), 98.

32. Edward Gibbon, *The History of the Decline and Fall of the Roman Empire*, ed. David Womersley, 3 vols. (London: Allen Lane, Penguin Press, 1994), 3:419.

33. Peter Gay, *Style in History* (London: Jonathan Cape, 1975), 24.

34. Gibbon, *Decline and Fall*, 3:908–909.

35. Ibid., 978.

36. Roy Porter, *Edward Gibbon: Making History* (London: Weidenfeld and Nicolson, 1988), 17–18.

37. Ibid., 92.

38. Gibbon, *Decline and Fall,* 3:303.

39. Ibid., 307–308.

40. Ibid., 309.

41. Xen. *Anabasis* 4.

42. Gibbon, *Decline and Fall,* 3:631 and n37.

43. Ibid., 158–159.

44. Ibid., 159–160.

45. Ibid., 162.

46. Ibid., 161.

47. Ibid., 196.

48. Ibid., 212–213.

49. Ibid., 324.

50. Porter, *Edward Gibbon,* 132.

51. Gibbon, *Decline and Fall,* 3:151.

52. Ibid., 204.

53. Ibid., 206.

54. Ibid., 253–255.

55. Ibid., 360.

56. Ibid., 535–536.

57. Ibid., 536–537 and n34.

58. Ibid., 537–538.

59. Ibid., 538–539.

60. Ibid., 352.

61. Ibid., 284–286.

62. Ibid., 352.

63. Ibid., 353.

64. Ibid., 417.

65. Peter Brown, "Gibbon's Views on Culture and Society in the Fifth and Sixth Centuries," in *Edward Gibbon and the Decline and Fall of the Roman Empire,* ed. G. W. Bowersock, John Clive, and Stephen R. Graubard (Cambridge, MA: Harvard University Press, 1977), 37–52, 39.

66. Porter, *Edward Gibbon*, 94.
67. Gibbon, *Decline and Fall*, 3:421.
68. Porter, *Edward Gibbon*, 104–105.
69. Gibbon, *Decline and Fall*, chap. 48.
70. Ibid., 3:322.
71. Ibid., 237.
72. Ibid., 311.
73. Ibid., 410–411.
74. Ibid., 365–366.
75. François Furet, "Civilization and Barbarism in Gibbon's History," in Bowersock, Clive, and Graubard, *Edward Gibbon*, 159–166, 166.
76. Gibbon, *Decline and Fall*, 3:588.
77. Ibid., 587.
78. Ibid., 589.
79. Ibid., 601.
80. Ibid., 695–697.
81. Ibid., 727.
82. Ibid., 652.
83. Ibid., 910–911.
84. Ibid., 823.
85. Ibid., 950.

6. The Roman Raj

1. Kate Teltscher, *India Inscribed: European and British Writing on India, 1600–1800* (Delhi: Oxford University Press, 1995).
2. Rama Sundari Mantena, "Imperial Ideology and the Uses of Rome in Discourses on Britain's Indian Empire," in *Classics and Imperialism in the British Empire*, ed. Mark Bradley (Oxford: Oxford University Press, 2010), 54–73, 57.
3. J. P. V. D. Balsdon, *Romans and Aliens* (London: Duckworth, 1979), 60.
4. Strabo 2.1.9 Loeb translation; compare 15.1.57–66. On ancient descriptions of India, see also Dio Chrysostom *Or.* 35, 18–24; Arrian *Indica* 1–17; compare Lucian *True History* 2.6–16 for a similar list of the marvels to be encountered in foreign lands.
5. Strabo 15.1.56 and 61.

6. Ibid., 2.1.9.

7. Dio Chrysost. *Or.* 35.18–24.

8. See Grant Parker, *The Making of Roman India* (Cambridge: Cambridge University Press, 2008).

9. Strabo 15.1.53 and 54.

10. Parker, *The Making of Roman India*, 312.

11. Sir William Jones, *The Third Anniversary Discourse, On the Hindus* (Feb. 2, 1786), 34.

12. *The Works of Sir William Jones*, ed. Teignmouth, 13 vols. (Printed for John Stockdale, Piccadilly; and John Walker, Paternoster-Row, 1807), 2:457.

13. Ibid., 467.

14. Ibid., 455.

15. See Tony Ballantyne, *Orientalism and Race: Aryanism in the British Empire* (Basingstoke: Palgrave, 2002).

16. *The Works of Sir William Jones*, 2:483.

17. Ibid., 3, 12.

18. "On the Gods of Greece, Italy, and India," in *Works of Sir William Jones*, 3:391.

19. Ibid., 3:386.

20. See Javed Majeed, *Ungoverned Imaginings: James Mill's* The History of British India *and Orientalism* (Oxford: Clarendon Press, 1992).

21. Ronald Inden, *Imagining India* (Oxford: Basil Blackwell, 1990), 45.

22. Majeed, *Ungoverned Imaginings*, 131.

23. Javed Majeed, "Comparativism and References to Rome in British Imperial Attitudes to India," in *Roman Presences: Receptions of Rome in European Culture, 1789–1945*, ed. Catharine Edwards (Cambridge: Cambridge University Press, 1999), 88–109, 91.

24. See A. Bain, "The Early Life of James Mill," *Mind* 1 (1876): 97–116.

25. See Majeed, "Comparativism and References to Rome," 92–98. See also Phiroze Vasunia, "Greek, Latin and the Indian Civil Service," *Cambridge Classical Journal* 51 (2005): 35–71.

26. James Mill, *The History of British India*, 5th ed., with notes and continuation by Horace Hayman Wilson, 9 vols. (J. Madden, 1858), author's preface, xx.

27. Ibid., xxiii.

28. Ibid., xxi.

29. Ibid., xv.

30. Ibid., 2:145n3.

31. On footnotes, see Anthony Grafton, *The Footnote: A Curious History* (London: Faber and Faber, 1997).

32. Mill, *The History of British India,* 1:107.

33. Ibid., 107n3.

34. Ibid., 116n1.

35. Ibid., 115n1.

36. Ibid., 118.

37. Ibid., 2:153n1; quoting Herodot. 3.30.

38. Ibid., 1:150n3; quoting Homer *Iliad* 18.497.

39. Ibid., 157.

40. Ibid., 167n1; quoting Diodorus Siculus bk 1.

41. Ibid., 173.

42. Ibid., 162n1.

43. Ibid., 173n4.

44. Ibid., 176–177.

45. Ibid., 309.

46. Ibid., 186.

47. Ibid., n2.

48. Ibid., 228.

49. Ibid., 231.

50. Ibid., 236 and n1; quoting Plato *de Rep.* 596.6.

51. Ibid., 238.

52. Ibid., 237.

53. Ibid., 262–265; quoting Bryant's *Analysis of Ancient Mythology.*

54. Ibid., 127.

55. Ibid., 120n1.

56. Ibid., 127n1; quoting Herodot. 2.104–105; Strabo 2.765.

57. Herodot. 1.101.

58. Mill, *The History of British India,* 1:130n6; quoting Caesar *BG* 6.13,14.

59. Ibid., 128n1.

60. Ibid., 132 and n2; quoting Cic. *de Leg.* 1.2.9,16.

61. Ibid., 2:1.
62. Ibid., 2n1.
63. Ibid., 14–15.
64. Ibid., 14n2.
65. Ibid., 13.
66. Ibid., 25.
67. Ibid., 28.
68. Ibid., 9n3.
69. Ibid., 32 and n1.
70. Ibid., 36n1.
71. Ibid., 63–64.
72. Ibid., 53.
73. Ibid., 76n3; quoting Gibbon, *Decline and Fall*, 7.294.
74. Ibid., 84.
75. Ibid., n2.
76. Ibid., 84–85.
77. Ibid., 86n1.
78. Ibid., 105.
79. Ibid., 106.
80. Ibid., 54n3.
81. Ibid., 50 and n2; quoting Gibbon, *Decline and Fall*, chaps. 10 and 51.
82. Ibid., 116n1.
83. Ibid., 340.
84. Ibid., 136.
85. Ibid., 141n1.
86. Ibid., 149.
87. Ibid., n1.
88. See Francis G. Hutchins, *The Illusion of Permanence: British Imperialism in India* (Princeton, NJ: Princeton University Press, 1967).
89. T. Roger Smith, "Architectural Art in India," *Journal of the Society of Arts* 21 (1873): 278–287, quoted in Thomas R. Metcalf, *An Imperial Vision: Indian Architecture and Britain's Raj* (London: Faber and Faber, 1989), 2.
90. Ibid., 3.

91. Ibid., 236.

92. Thomas R. Trautmann, *Aryans and British India* (Berkeley: University of California Press, 1997), 5.

93. Ballantyne, *Orientalism and Race*, 188.

94. See Mantena, "Imperial Ideology and the Uses of Rome," 56–57.

95. See the University Calendars for the University of Calucutta. See also Harish Trivedi, "Western Classics, Indian Classics: Postcolonial Contestations," in *Classics in Post-colonial Worlds*, ed. Lorna Hardwick and Carol Gillespie (Oxford: Oxford University Press, 2007), 286–304.

96. Ballantyne, *Orientalism and Race*, 185.

97. Ibid., 303.

98. Bholanauth Chunder, *The Travels of a Hindoo to Various Parts of Bengal and Upper India*, 2 vols. (N. Trübner, 1869).

99. Ibid., 1:1–2.

100. Ibid., 52.

101. Ibid., 53.

102. Ibid., 145.

103. Ibid., 264.

104. Ibid., 285–286.

105. Ibid., 287

106. Ibid., 2:408–409.

7. *Empires Ancient and Modern*

1. Richard Hingley, *Roman Officers and English Gentlemen: The Imperial Origins of Roman Archaeology* (London: Routledge, 2000), 9.

2. Victoria Tietze Larson, "Classics and the Acquisition and Validation of Power in Britain's 'Imperial Century' (1815–1914)," *International Journal of the Classical Tradition* 6 (1999): 185–225, abstract. On the comparison between the British Empire and the Roman Empire, see Phiroze Vasunia, "Greater Rome and Greater Britain," in *Classics and Colonialism*, ed. Barbara Goff (London: Duckworth, 2005), 38–64; and Mark Bradley, ed., *Classics and Imperialism in the British Empire* (Oxford: Oxford University Press, 2010).

3. See Larson, "Classics"; Javed Majeed, "Comparativism and References to Rome in British Imperial Attitudes to India," in *Roman Presences:*

Receptions of Rome in European Culture, 1789–1945, ed. Catharine Edwards (Cambridge: Cambridge University Press, 1999), 98–109, 92–98; and Phiroze Vasunia, "Greek, Latin and the Indian Civil Service," *Cambridge Classical Journal* 51 (2005): 35–71.

4. Christopher Stray, *Classics Transformed: Schools, Universities, and Society in England, 1830–1960* (Oxford: Clarendon Press, 1998), 46.

5. Richard Koebner and Helmut Dan Schmidt, *Imperialism: The Story and Significance of a Political Word, 1840–1960* (Cambridge: Cambridge University Press, 1964), 80.

6. Martin Bernal, "The Image of Ancient Greece as a Tool for Colonialism and European Hegemony," in *Social Construction of the Past: Representation as Power*, ed. George Clement Bond and Angela Gilliam (London: Routledge, 1994), 119–128, 119.

7. Ibid., 127.

8. Rosalind Ballaster, *Fabulous Orients: Fictions of the East in England, 1662–1785* (Oxford: Oxford University Press, 2005).

9. For a recent account, see Simon Goldhill, *Victorian Culture and Classical Antiquity: Art, Opera, Fiction, and the Proclamation of Modernity* (Princeton, NJ: Princeton University Press).

10. Greek authors did, of course, still play an important role in formulating English ideas. On the influence of Xenophon, see Doohwan Ahn, "Xenophon and the Greek Tradition in British Political Thought," in *Reinventing History: The Enlightenment Origins of Ancient History*, ed. James Moore, Ian Macgregor Morris, and Andrew J. Bayliss (London: Institute of Historical Research, 2008), 33–55. On the use of Greece as an alternative political role model, particularly for those seeking a more tolerant precedent, see Krishan Kumar, "Greece and Rome in the British Empire: Contrasting Role Models," *Journal of British Studies* 51 (2012): 76–101.

11. Larson, "Classics," 221.

12. See Richard Hingley, *Globalizing Roman Culture: Unity, Diversity and Empire* (London: Routledge, 2005).

13. Majeed, "Comparativism," 89.

14. Hingley, *Roman Officers*, 5.

15. Roger Owen, *Lord Cromer: Victorian Imperialist, Edwardian Proconsul* (Oxford: Oxford University Press, 2004), vii. On Cromer and the

classics, see Donald Malcolm Reid, *Whose Pharaohs? Archaeology, Museums, and Egyptian National Identity from Napoleon to World War I* (Berkeley: University of California Press, 2002), chap. 4, "Cromer and the Classics: Ideological Uses of the Greco-Roman Past."

16. Lord Cromer, *Political and Literary Essays: Second Series* (London: Macmillan, 1914), 226.

17. Lord Cromer, *Political and Literary Essays: 1908–1913* (London: Macmillan, 1913), 307–316, 310.

18. Reid, *Whose Pharaohs?*, 155.

19. Lord Cromer, *Political and Literary Essays: Second Series*, 227–228.

20. See R. M. Ogilvie, *Latin and Greek: A History of the Influence of the Classics on English Life from 1600–1918* (London: Routledge and Kegan Paul, 1964), 134–171.

21. Lord Cromer, *Political and Literary Essays: 1908–1913*, 340.

22. Lord Cromer, *Ancient and Modern Imperialism* (London: John Murray, 1910), 14.

23. Hingley, *Roman Officers*, 1.

24. Eur. *Supp.* 321–323.

25. Cromer, *Ancient and Modern Imperialism*, 2–3.

26. Lord Cromer, *Modern Egypt*, 2 vols. (London: Macmillan, 1908), 1:11.

27. Ibid., 13.

28. Cromer, *Ancient and Modern Imperialism*, 114.

29. Ibid., 28–29.

30. Ibid., 34–35.

31. Ibid., 35–36.

32. James Bryce, *The Ancient Roman Empire and the British Empire in India: The Diffusion of Roman and English Law throughout the World; Two Historical Studies* (London: Oxford University Press, 1914), 1.

33. Ibid., 30–31.

34. Ibid., 28.

35. Cromer, *Ancient and Modern Imperialism*, 41–42.

36. Ibid., 43.

37. Ibid., 127.

38. Ibid., 51.

39. Ibid., 112.
40. Ibid., 53.
41. Ibid., 65–66; quoting Juv. *Sat.* 14.177–178.
42. Ibid., 69.
43. Ibid., 108.
44. Ibid., 112.
45. Ibid., 113–114.
46. Ibid., 4–5.
47. Ibid., 22.
48. See Hingley, *Roman Officers*, 158.
49. Edwards, *Roman Presences*, 13:1–18.
50. Sir Charles Prestwood Lucas, *Greater Rome and Greater Britain* (Oxford: Clarendon Press, 1912), 149.
51. Ibid., 149–150.
52. Cromer, *Ancient and Modern Imperialism*, 37–38.
53. Ibid., 85.
54. Ibid., 91.
55. Ibid., 90–91.
56. Ibid., 97.
57. Ibid., 101.
58. Ibid., 111.
59. Ibid., 102–103
60. Ibid., 104–105.
61. Ibid., 106.
62. Lucas, *Greater Rome and Greater Britain*, 97.
63. Ibid., 149.
64. Ibid., 153.
65. Cromer, *Ancient and Modern Imperialism*, 95.
66. Lucas, *Greater Rome and Greater Britain*, 100.
67. Ibid., 97.
68. Ibid., 154.
69. Ibid., 107.
70. George Rawlinson, *The Five Great Monarchies of the Ancient Eastern World*, 4 vols. (London: John Murray, 1862–1867), 3:74.
71. Ibid., 118.

72. Ibid., 4:108, 111–112.
73. Ibid., 3:76.
74. Cromer, *Ancient and Modern Imperialism*, 96–97.
75. Ibid., 138.
76. Cromer, *Political and Literary Essays: Second Series*, 206.
77. Ibid., 210–211; quoting Virg. *Ecl.* 10. 38.
78. Cromer, *Ancient and Modern Imperialism*, 29.
79. Lucas, *Greater Rome and Greater Britain*, 158.
80. Cromer, *Ancient and Modern Imperialism*, 29n3.
81. Lord Cromer, *Political and Literary Essays: Third Series* (London: Macmillan, 1916), 76.
82. Lord Cromer, *Modern Egypt*.
83. Ibid., 1:22
84. Ibid., 17–18.
85. Ibid., 105.
86. Ibid., 108.
87. Ibid., 109.
88. Ibid., 46 and n1.
89. Ibid., 129.
90. Ibid., 330.
91. Ibid., 2:137.
92. Ibid., 196; quoting Virg. *Georg.* 1.250–251.
93. Ibid., 157.
94. Ibid., 159; Claudian *In Eutrop.* 1. 76; *Femina quum senuit, retinet connubia partu, Uxorisque decus matris reverantia pensat.*
95. Lord Cromer, *Modern Egypt*, 160; quoting Herodot. 2.132.
96. Ibid., 192.
97. Ibid., 193.
98. Ibid., 525; quoting a speech in the House of Commons made on July 10, 1833.
99. Ibid., 198.
100. Ibid., 542.
101. Ibid., 563.
102. Juv. *Sat.* 10.365–366.

103. Rutilius *de Reditu suo* 1.91.

104. Cromer, *Ancient and Modern Imperialism*, 127.

105. Lucr. *DRN* 2.77–79.

106. Charles Kingsley, *The Roman and the Teuton: A Series of Lectures Delivered before the University of Cambridge* (London: Macmillan, 1864), 18–27.

107. Hingley, *Roman Officers*, 26.

108. Cromer, *Political and Literary Essays: 1908–1913*, 3.

109. Ibid., 7.

110. Ibid., 8–9.

111. Ibid., 14.

112. Ibid., 19.

113. Ibid., 21.

114. Ibid., 22.

115. Ibid., 22–23.

116. Ibid., 35.

117. Ibid., 36–37.

118. Ibid., 40.

119. Ibid., 52.

120. Ibid., 38, 39.

121. Ibid., 6 and n1; quoting Pub. Syr. *male imperando summum imperium amittitur.*

122. Ibid., 5.

8. Colonial Adventures

1. Rana Kabbani, *Imperial Fictions: Europe's Myths of Orient* (London: Pandora, 1994), 6.

2. Ibid., 7.

3. Charles M. Doughty, *Travels in Arabia Deserta*, 2 vols. (1888; London: Constable, 1979), 2:196–197.

4. Sir Richard F. Burton, *Personal Narrative of a Pilgrimage to Al-Madinah and Meccah*, 2 vols. (1855; London: Darf, 1986), 1:213; quoting Virg. *Aen.* 1.159–161.

5. Ibid., 218–219.

6. Edward William Lane, *An Account of the Manners and Customs of the Modern Egyptians* (1836; London: Darf, 1986), 17.

7. Sir James Frazer, *The Golden Bough: A Study in Magic and Religion. Part IV: Adonis, Attis, Osiris: Studies in the History of Oriental Religion*, 2 vols. (1906; London: Macmillan, 1980), 1:v.

8. Burton, *Personal Narrative*, 1:299n2.

9. Ibid., 2:93n1.

10. Ibid., 191.

11. Lane, *Manners and Customs*, 548.

12. Burton, *Personal Narrative*, 2:165n1.

13. Doughty, *Travels in Arabia Deserta*, 2:149.

14. Ibid., 196, 387.

15. Ibid., 387.

16. Quoted in Kabbani, *Imperial Fictions*, 11.

17. Doughty, *Travels in Arabia Deserta*, 1:79.

18. Edward Clarke, *Travels in Russia, Tartary and Turkey* (Edinburgh: Walker and Co., 1839), 573. I would like to thank Pat Storey for introducing me to this source.

19. Doughty, *Travels in Arabia Deserta*, 1:196.

20. Lane, *Manners and Customs*, 143–144.

21. Ibid., 536.

22. Doughty, *Travels in Arabia Deserta*, 1:130–131.

23. David Roessel, *In Byron's Shadow: Modern Greece in the English and American Imagination* (Oxford: Oxford University Press, 2002), 7.

24. Ibid., 27.

25. Burton, *Personal Narrative*, 1:259n2.

26. Clarke, *Travels*, 580.

27. Lane, *Manners and Customs*, 364.

28. Frazer, *Adonis, Attis, Osiris*, 1:215–216.

29. Burton, *Personal Narrative*, 1:210 and n2.

30. Kathryn Tidrick, *Heart-Beguiling Araby* (London: I. B. Tauris, 1989), 11.

31. Ibid., 13.

32. Burton, *Personal Narrative*, 1:88–89.

33. Tidrick, *Heart-Beguiling Araby*, 31.

34. Lane, *Manners and Customs*, 383–384.

35. Holly Edwards, *Noble Dreams, Wicked Pleasures: Orientalism in America, 1870–1930* (Princeton, NJ: Princeton University Press, 2000), 23.

36. Burton, *Personal Narrative*, 2:19n2, 83n1.

37. Ibid., 90.

38. Ibid., 1:422.

39. Ibid., 372.

40. Ibid., 371 and n1.

41. Kabbani, *Imperial Fictions*, 69.

42. For an introduction to women travelers in the Orient, see Barbara Hodgson, *Dreaming of East: Western Women and the Exotic Allure of the Orient* (Vancouver, BC: Greystone Books, 2005).

43. Lady Duff Gordon, *Letters from Egypt, 1862–1869* (London: Routledge and Kegan Paul, 1969), 62.

44. Gertrude Bell, *The Desert and the Sown* (London: Heinemann, 1907), 3.

45. Duff Gordon, *Letters from Egypt*, 65.

46. Bell, *The Desert and the Sown*, 34.

47. Ibid., 241–242.

48. Ibid., 249–250 in El Bārah.

49. Ibid., 92–93.

50. The Duchess of Cleveland, *The Life and Letters of Lady Hester Stanhope* (London: John Murray, 1914), 159, 199–200.

51. Ibid., 223.

52. See Tidrick, *Heart-Beguiling Araby*.

53. Richard Bevis, "Spiritual Geology: C. M. Doughty and the Land of the Arabs," *Victorian Studies* 16 (1972): 163–181, 176.

54. Ibid., 178.

55. Doughty, *Travels in Arabia Deserta*, 2:429.

56. Burton, *Personal Narrative*, 1:37.

57. Ibid., 40.

58. Ibid., 2:89n1, 1:18–19 and n1.

59. Doughty, *Travels in Arabia Deserta*, 2:544.

60. Frazer, *Adonis, Attis, Osiris*, 1:198, 298–301.

61. See Tidrick, *Heart-Beguiling Araby.*

62. Albert Hourani, *Islam in European Thought* (Cambridge: Cambridge University Press, 1991), 121–122.

63. T. E. Lawrence, *Seven Pillars of Wisdom: A Triumph* (London: Jonathan Cape, 1973), 684.

64. Ibid., 42.

65. Ibid., 117.

66. Ibid., 198.

67. Ibid., 199.

68. Ibid., 200.

69. Ibid., 38–39.

70. Ibid., 364.

71. Ibid., 500.

72. Ibid., 219.

73. Ibid., 326.

74. Ibid., 508.

75. Ibid., 608.

9. *Screen Classics*

1. My comments in this chapter relate to the film version, although most could equally be applied to the book, given that the adaptation follows the text quite closely. For an interesting discussion of the differences between the book and the film, see Alan A. Stone, "Herodotus Goes to Hollywood," *Boston Review*, February/March 1997. For a comparison of the structure of the film and book with that of Herodotus's *Histories*, see Thomas Harrison, "Herodotus and 'The English Patient,'" *Classics Ireland* 5 (1998): 48–63.

2. Maria Wyke, *Caesar: A Life in Western Culture* (London: Granta, 2007), 113.

3. Lucy Hughes-Hallett, *Cleopatra: Histories, Dreams and Distortions* (London: Bloomsbury, 1990), 270, 306.

4. Ibid., 274.

5. Matthew Bernstein and Gaylyn Studlar, eds., *Visions of the East: Orientalism in Film* (London: I. B. Tauris, 1997), 32.

6. Maria Wyke, "Screening Ancient Rome in the New Italy," in *Roman Presences: Receptions of Rome in European Culture, 1789–1945*, ed. Catharine Edwards (Cambridge: Cambridge University Press, 1999), 188–204, 198.

7. Bernstein and Studlar, *Visions of the East*, 5.

8. Sarah Graham-Brown, *Images of Women: The Portrayal of Women in Photography of the Middle East, 1860–1950* (London: Quartet Books, 1988), 134. See also Meyda Yeğenoğlu, *Colonial Fantasies: Towards a Feminised Reading of Orientalism* (Cambridge: Cambridge University Press, 1998).

9. See Thomas Harrison, "Oliver Stone, *Alexander*, and the Unity of Mankind," in *Responses to Oliver Stone's Alexander: Film, History, and Cultural Studies*, ed. Paul Cartledge and Fiona Rose Greenland (Madison: University of Wisconsin Press, 2010), 219–242; and Lloyd Llewellyn-Jones, "'Help me, Aphrodite!': Depicting the Royal Women of Persia in *Alexander*," 243–281.

10. I want to thank Pierre Caquet for his help with this paragraph.

11. Hughes-Hallett, *Cleopatra*, 261.

12. See Nicholas J. Cull, "'Infamy! Infamy! They've All Got It in for Me!': *Carry on Cleo* and the British Camp Comedies of Ancient Rome," in *Imperial Projections: Ancient Rome in Modern Popular Culture*, ed. Sandra R. Joshel, Margaret Malamud, and Donald T. McGuire (Baltimore: Johns Hopkins University Press, 2001), 162–190.

13. Hughes-Hallett, *Cleopatra*, 263, 265.

10. *America Roma Nova*

1. On early American travel literature, see Larzer Ziff, *Return Passages: Great American Travel Writing, 1780–1910* (New Haven, CT: Yale University Press, 2000); Brian Yothers, *The Romance of the Holy Land in American Travel Writing, 1790–1876* (Aldershot: Ashgate, 2007); and Alfred Bendixen and Judith Hamera, eds., *The Cambridge Companion to American Travel Writing* (Cambridge: Cambridge University Press, 2009).

2. On Taylor, see Paul C. Wermuth, *Bayard Taylor* (New York: Twayne, 1973).

3. Bayard Taylor, *Travels in Greece and Russia, with an Excursion to Crete* (New York: Putnam, 1859), 40.

4. Ibid., 216.

5. Bayard Taylor, *The Lands of the Saracen: Or, Pictures of Palestine, Asia Minor, Sicily and Spain* (New York: Putnam, 1859), 166–167.

6. Ibid., 149.

7. Ibid., 154–155.

8. Ibid., 178.

9. Bayard Taylor, *Egypt and Iceland in the Year 1874* (London: S. Low, Marston, Low and Searle, 1875), 90.

10. Taylor, *Lands of the Saracen*, 180.

11. Mark Twain, *The Innocents Abroad* (1869; Oxford: Oxford University Press, 1996).

12. See Yothers, *The Romance of the Holy Land*, 96.

13. Twain, *The Innocents Abroad*, 646–647.

14. Ibid., 339–340.

15. Ibid., 354.

16. Ibid., 341–349.

17. Ibid., 423–424, 447.

18. Ibid., 471.

19. Ibid., 357.

20. Ibid., 476–477.

21. Ibid., 406–407.

22. Ibid., 420–429.

23. Ibid., 430–431.

24. Richard Van Alstyne, *The American Empire: Its Historical Pattern and Evolution* (London: Routledge and Kegan Paul, 1960), 10–11.

25. On the Vietnam Veterans Memorial, see Marita Sturken, *Tangled Memories: The Vietnam War, the AIDS Epidemic, and the Politics of Remembering* (Berkeley: University of California Press, 1997); and Elizabeth Hess, "Vietnam: Memorial of Misfortune," in *Unwinding the Vietnam War: From War into Peace*, ed. Reese Williams (Seattle: Real Comet Press, 1987), 262–280.

26. See Sturken, *Tangled Memories*, 53.

27. Ibid., 50.

28. Quoted in ibid., 61.

29. Interview with Maya Lin in 1983 quoted in Hess, "Vietnam," 271–274.

30. On the debate concerning the memorial at the site of the World Trade Center, see Marita Sturken, "The Aesthetics of Absence: Rebuilding Ground Zero," *American Ethnologist* 31 (2004): 311–325.

31. Cullen Murphy, *The New Rome: The Fall of an Empire and the Fate of America* (Thriplow: Icon, 2007), 5. See also Thomas Harrison, "Ancient and Modern Imperialism," *Greece and Rome* 55 (2008): 1–22.

32. Vaclav Smil, *Why America Is Not a New Rome* (Cambridge, MA: The MIT Press, 2010).

33. Samuel P. Huntington, *The Clash of Civilizations and the Remaking of World Order* (New York: Simon and Schuster, 1996), 42. For a response to this from an Asian perspective, see Salim Rashid, ed., *"The Clash of Civilizations?": Asian Responses* (Dhaka, Bangladesh: University Press, 1997).

34. Daniel J. Sherman and Terry Nardin, eds., *Terror, Culture, Politics: Rethinking 9/11* (Bloomington: Indiana University Press, 2006), 24–25.

35. Max Boot, "The Case for American Empire," *The Weekly Standard* (October 15, 2001).

36. Joseph Nye, "The New Rome Meets the New Barbarians: How America Should Wield Its Power," *The Economist*, March 23, 2002.

37. Quoted in Smil, *Why America Is Not a New Rome*, 23.

38. Murphy, *The New Rome*, 126.

39. Ibid., 174–175.

40. Robert Harris, "Pirates of the Mediterranean," *New York Times*, September 30, 2006.

41. J. Rufus Fears, "The Lessons of the Roman Empire for America Today," 2005, http://www.heritage.org/research/lecture/the-lessons-of-the-roman-empire-for-america-today (accessed 9/7/12).

42. Ibid.

43. Ibid.

44. Murphy, *The New Rome*, 139.

45. Ibid., 145.

46. Ibid., 160.

47. Ibid., 176.

Index

www.ingramcontent.com/pod-product-compliance
Lightning Source LLC
Chambersburg PA
CBHW020930310726
48980CB00007B/709/J

* 9 7 8 0 6 7 4 0 7 3 1 4 2 *